Heinrich Heine

THE ROMANTIC SCHOOL
AND OTHER ESSAYS

The German Library: Volume 33

Volkmar Sander, General Editor

Heinrich Heine

THE ROMANTIC SCHOOL AND OTHER ESSAYS

Edited by Jost Hermand
and Robert C. Holub

CONTINUUM • NEW YORK

1985

The Continuum Publishing Company
370 Lexington Avenue, New York, NY 10017

The German Library
is published in cooperation with Deutsches Haus,
New York University.
This volume has been supported with a grant
from The Marie Baier Foundation, Inc.

Printed in the United States of America

Library of Congress Cataloging in Publication Data

Heine, Heinrich, 1797–1856.
The romantic school and other essays.

(The German library ; v. 33)
Contents: Introduction / Robert C. Holub—The
romantic school—Concerning the history of religion
and philosophy in Germany — [etc.]
I. Hermand, Jost. II. Holub, Robert C. III. Title.
IV. Series.
PT2316.A3H43 1985   832'.7   85-17124
ISBN 0-8264-0290-9
ISBN 0-8264-0291-7 (pbk.)

Contents

Introduction

During the past two centuries there has hardly been a German author who has had a more pervasive impact on future generations than Heinrich Heine. Many German writers, of course, have been acclaimed for their artistic and literary achievements; but Heine, though recognized throughout the world as one of the finest poets Germany has produced, has been influential in several other areas as well. Traces of his thought can be found in almost every major figure in German culture during the latter part of the nineteenth century. Karl Marx, who knew Heine personally when he was in Parisian exile from 1843–45, relies heavily on Heine's views on German philosophy and religion from the 1830s; Friedrich Engels even credits Heine with being the first German to understand the implications of Hegelian philosophy for the Left. It is not surprising then that Heine was the most frequently quoted poet in Marx and Engels's *Neue Rheinische Zeitung* during the revolutionary years 1848–49. Richard Wagner borrowed motifs from Heine's works for two of his operas, *The Flying Dutchman* and *Tannhäuser*. Friedrich Nietzsche called Heine "a European event" and considered him to be one of the greatest German stylists of all times. And Sigmund Freud credits Heine with both psychological insight and "exquisite wit" in his *Wit and Its Relation to the Unconscious*. From politics to psychology, from music to philosophy, Heine has left his mark on systems of thought and works of art whose effects are still very much with us today.

In light of the breadth of this influence it is somewhat dismaying to find that Heine's reputation in the English-speaking world still rests almost exclusively on his early lyric poetry. The reason for this somewhat distorted image is easy enough to understand, of course, since the main vehicles for the transmission of Heine's writings have been the texts for German *Lieder*. But from these early poems we get only one dimension of Heine: the young lover pining away, broken hearted because of yet another unhappy love affair. We see Heine, in other words, in the tradition of Romantic poetry, as a second-generation Romantic whose verse comments on and reacts to the conventions of the "Age of Goethe." By the time Heine was thirty, however, he considered this period of his life to be a completed episode, and he turned eagerly to other pursuits. To continue to view Heine through the narrow perspective of his earliest works perpetuates an incomplete picture, analagous to an evaluation of Goethe without *Wilhelm Meister* or James Joyce without *Ulysses*.

The essays in this volume were selected because they contribute to a correction of this one-sided reception of Heine in the English-speaking world. The wide range of Heine's thought is especially evident here; among the topics he discusses are philosophy, literary history, current affairs, religious thought, and political theory. Heine, of course, was not an expert in all of these areas, at least not in the sense that he possessed a detailed knowledge of every subject he treats. The reader should not expect a scholarly discourse on philosophy, aesthetic theory, or politics in Heine's essays. Nor did Heine intend to supply such textbook information when he wrote these essays, although he undoubtedly had a more profound understanding of intellectual matters than many of his detractors would admit. On the contrary, Heine's manner of writing about these various fields was designed precisely to counter the dry academic style that is usually found in these disciplines. In ridding himself of the obscurity that usually accompanies technical jargon and a scholarly format, Heine was able to make the German tradition as well as significant issues in contemporary thought accessible to a general public. In these essays Heine was concerned, above all, with popularity in the most positive sense of the word; for he popularizes not by pandering to the whims of his audience, but with the ultimately democratic intention of introducing important intellectual and cultural matters into a larger public sphere.

This concern for popularity accounts for a good deal of the originality in these essays as well. Since Heine could not accomplish his task of democratizing knowledge with the usual academic baggage, he was forced to develop novel ways to present his material. He used a number of strategies to this end. First, Heine does not hesitate to introduce a journalistic tone into his critical essays; indeed, he was one of the first to recognize the value of journalism for communicating more "philosophical" issues. Just as important, this apparently casual manner of discussing abstruse concepts has the additional function of demystifying scholarly language. Heine had the knack of translating a highly recondite jargon into a language that was more universally understood, and the idiom of the daily press was one of the most important means he employed to facilitate a general understanding. Second, Heine makes frequent use of anecdotes and details from the private lives of the people he discusses. He takes up these matters, however, to raise public concerns, not to provide gossip or to stir up a literary scandal. The events he mentions are always carefully selected to emphasize a more philosophical or political point. Details from Lessing's personal letters are included to demonstrate again the courage and tenacity of this man in the face of adverse conditions. Impotence is associated with A. W. Schlegel to reinforce the view that Romanticism is not a productive literary path. And Heine refers to his own feelings and thoughts in the Börne *Memorial* to reaffirm in the private realm the importance of the July Revolution, as well as the significance of its ultimate failure. Finally, Heine carefully weaves patterns of rhetoric and imagery into his discursive arguments to bolster his central theses. For Heine, writing expository prose was as serious an artistic undertaking as composing a poem. His essays should thus be considered a continuation of his more "poetic" endeavors, rather than a totally different genre. There is almost no other writer in the German tradition for whom the boundary between the creative and the expository is so difficult to define.

The originality, diversity, and influence of Heine's critical essays give them a unique place in the literature of the nineteenth century. But they are unusual in another respect as well: in a century in which the relations between Germany and France were frequently strained, if not openly bellicose, Heine endeavored to promote increased understanding between the two nations with his writings. From his arrival in Paris in 1831 to his death in 1856, Heine continually expressed his mission as a writer in terms of his role as mediator between the land of his birth and his land of exile. During the thirties and forties he served as a correspondent for the *Augsburger Allgemeine Zeitung* and reported on events in Paris. Despite the difficulties resulting from an often paranoid censorship, Heine was able to show his German readers that there were alternatives to the oppressive state of affairs on their side of the Rhine. These articles played an important role in the formation of an oppositional consciousness during the two decades preceding the 1848 Revolution. Heine's essays on German affairs, on the other hand, were supposed to serve as both a corrective and an admonition for the French. Originally written for a French public that Heine felt misunderstood the developments and tradition of German letters, they attempt to rectify false notions of Germany that had become current in French intellectual circles and to warn the French against following certain wayward German fashions. In examining the social and political dimensions of German intellectual history, Heine wants to uncover both the potentially emancipatory, as well as the repressive implications of his native heritage.

The two long essays in this volume, *The Romantic School* and *Concerning the History of Religion and Philosophy in Germany,* represent two of Heine's major attempts to mediate the German tradition to the French public. Written during the first years of Heine's Parisian exile, both attempt to correct the view of German intellectual life found in Madame de Staël's influential book *De l'Allemagne* (1813). It was especially important for Heine to combat de Staël's positive portrayal of German Romanticism, and Heine's first essay, *The Romantic School,* contains a sustained discussion of and attack upon this current in German letters. But Heine's essay is more encompassing than his title would suggest; it includes observations on most of the major figures in German literature during what is commonly called the "Age of Goethe," a period stretching from the middle of the eighteenth century to Goethe's death in 1832. Indeed, the original title for this piece, *Concerning the History of Recent Literature in Germany (Zur Geschichte der neueren schönen Literatur in Deutschland),* is perhaps more appropriate. What emerges from this literary history—which was, incidentally, one of the first of its kind to be written—are two antagonistic tendencies in German letters. The first is identified with the Enlightenment, sensualism, Protestantism, and progressive politics; Lessing, Herder, Schiller, Voss, and the Young Germans are placed in this tradition. Opposing it is a mystical, spiritualist, Catholic, and politically regressive turn to the Middle Ages that Heine associates with the Romantic movement. Towering above both of these strains in Germany, although definitely allied with the Enlightenment heritage, is Goethe. By introducing this typology to deal with German literary history, Heine is attempting to discourage French intellectuals from their admiration of the German Romantics while simultaneously showing them that Germany, too, possesses a critical and forward-looking literature.

The identical set of dichotomies structures Heine's essay on German religious and philosophical thought. Heine sets up an historical narrative according to which the spiritualism of the Catholic Middle Ages is gradually eroded by advances in the domain of German intellectual life. The major stages in this erosion process, which is also the path of political emancipation, are the focal points of the three books. In the first Heine treats Luther's clash with the Roman Catholic Church as a pivotal point in breaking the hegemony of spiritualism. By opposing this foreign, intellectual oppression, Luther managed to assist in the creation of a positive and liberating national identity. Spinoza appears as the hero of the second book because of his doctrine of pantheism, "the clandestine religion of Germany." In this section Heine traces the materialist roots of pantheistic teachings and points to their potentially revolutionary implications. Although the final book deals with German idealist philosophy in general, there is little doubt that Kant is the central figure here. His *Critique of Pure Reason* is compared to the French Revolution; it destroyed the last remnants of deism in German philosophy and made theology in any traditional sense a dead issue. Heine's reading of intellectual life in *Religion and Philosophy in Germany* thus posits a basically emancipatory trajectory, and Heine's exegetical practice elucidates the hidden stations on the enlightened road as well as the intellectual detours.

The shorter pieces in this volume, which Heine wrote over a period of twenty-five years, are arranged chronologically and give important insights into the development of Heine's political and social views. In the Introduction to *Kahldorf Concerning the Nobility* from 1831 Heine mentions for the first time the thesis that political developments in France run parallel to German philosophy. The systems of Kant, Fichte, Schelling, and Hegel correspond in Heine's presentation to the French Revolution, Imperial France, the Restoration, and the July Monarchy respectively. This piece was Heine's last project before leaving Germany in 1831, and it is only fitting that he once again affirms here his hatred of religious obscurantism, political dogmatism, and aristocratic privilege. In "Various Conceptions of History," probably written shortly after Heine's arrival in Paris, but only published posthumously, Heine clearly outlines his reaction to the two dominant historical schemes of his time. Those who propose a circular view of history—here Heine was probably thinking of the so-called "historical school" associated with Karl von Savigny and Leopold von Ranke—are charged with fatalism and quietism. The providential school—a label Heine uses to designate linear schools of history like Hegel's—though more acceptable than the "historical school," is guilty of sacrificing the means to the end. Heine's position, therefore, is that neither conception validates life and Revolution. Anticipating Marx' notorious eleventh thesis on Feuerbach concerning the necessity to change and not merely interpret the world, Heine posits a philosophy of praxis to counter the contemplative stances of speculative historians.

The second book of *Ludwig Börne: A Memorial* (1840) occupies a special place in this volume. It is the only piece that is both excerpted from a longer work and not written in the form of an essay. We have nonetheless decided to include it because it summarizes nicely several of the most important moral, political, and religious themes that preoccupied Heine during the 1830s. Although Heine is apparently printing letters that he wrote just before and after the outbreak of the July Revolution, textual and biographical evidence indicates that these letters were in fact composed around 1839 for inclusion in the *Memorial*. By using this fiction, however, Heine is better able to deal with a revolutionary problematic. His artistic, religious, and political attitudes before he learns of the Revolution highlight the resignation and spiritualism that Heine associates with Restoration Europe. After the Revolution, on the other hand, he begins to celebrate life again, simultaneously declaring the demise of religion ("Pan is dead") and of political indifference. What Heine stresses in these letters and throughout the Börne *Memorial* is the necessity for a revolutionary movement that encompasses all aspects of human existence. A failure to accommodate ethical, aesthetic, and intellectual needs as well as material and political demands means that the Revolution has either been perverted or has not been complete.

The final two pieces bear witness to Heine's continued interest in politics during the last dozen years of his life. The fragmentary "Letters on Germany," probably written in the mid-forties, take up a variety of topics, from Heine's relationship to the Young Germans, a group of liberal writers prominent during the 1830s, to humorous recollections of conversations with Hegel. Heine's politicized interpretation of the German tradition is once again evident: Heine claims to have disclosed the "school secret" of German philosophy, i.e., the activist, this-worldly, emancipatory message hidden beneath an overtly pious and often obscure facade. In the Preface to the French edition of *Lutetia,* one of the last pieces Heine wrote before his death in 1856, he recalls the difficulties surrounding political journalism in the early 1840s. But more important than this discussion of censorship and the tactics adopted to mitigate its effects is Heine's evaluation of the political movements of his era, especially communism. Heine was one of the first to recognize the significance of socialist and communist views, and his articles from the 1840s often contain references to these radical groups. His cautiously affirmative response to what he understood as communism is a tribute to his continued concern for peace and justice. Although the poet in Heine fears that the communists would destroy his "beloved world of art," he nonetheless approves of the movement because of its opposition to petty nationalism and advocacy of economic democracy. The failure of the Revolution in 1848 and a debilitating illness that kept Heine bed-ridden for the last eight years of his life were evidently not enough to shake him in his political resolve.

And if there is any single theme that unites the essays included in this volume, then it is perhaps the consistency with which Heine defends the rights of the people to live in peace and in the absence of material want. Although Heine has often been characterized unjustly as an elusive, fickle, and flighty poet, the writings from the last twenty-five years of his life document a clear continuity in social and political concerns matched by few of his contemporaries. It would be a mistake, of course, to think that Heine never altered his opinions or that he never wavered in his judgments of particular events and persons. He was often compelled to reevaluate his positions; and in retrospect it even appears that whimsy and personal malice occasionally played a part in his stance on more minor issues. But with respect to the overriding concerns of his day Heine was remarkably constant. He always rejected the rabid nationalism that pervaded the German intellectual community during the first half of the nineteenth century; he continuously supported political freedoms and human rights; and he repeatedly advocated a rational system of production and distribution of wealth to insure the satisfaction of basic human needs. For these reasons we should consider him not only one of the foremost German lyricists, but also, as he desired, "a brave soldier in the emancipatory war of humanity." And in this regard his writings live on not only because they had an enormous impact on important figures in subsequent generations, but because Heine's seminal concerns continue to be ours as well.

R. C. H.

The Romantic School

BOOK ONE

M me. de Staël's book *De l'Allemagne*[1] is the only comprehensive information the French have received concerning the intellectual life of Germany. And yet a long time has passed since this book appeared, and meanwhile an entirely new type of literature has developed in Germany. Is it only a literature of transition? Has it already reached its prime? Is it already in a state of decline? Opinions are divided about these questions. Most people think that with Goethe's death[2] a new literary period began in Germany, that the old Germany went to its grave with him, that the aristocratic period of literature came to an end and the democratic period began, or, as a French journalist expressed it recently, "the spirit of man as an individual has ceased to exist, the spirit of collective man has begun."

For my part, I cannot pass judgment in such a categorical fashion on the future evolutions of the German mind. Many years ago, however, I predicted the end of the "Goethean Period of Art," the term I first used to designate this period. It was easy enough to prophesy. I was very familiar with the ways and means of those malcontents who wanted to put an end to the Goethean realm of art, and some even claim to have seen me myself taking part in the mutinies of those days against Goethe. Now that Goethe is dead, a strange sadness overwhelms me.

1. *Concerning Germany.* Since the author was *persona non grata* in France, the work appeared first in London in 1813, but it was published in France the following year.
2. 1832.

1

In announcing these pages as a kind of continuation of Mme. de Staël's *De l'Allemagne*, and while praising the information that can be derived from this work, I must nevertheless recommend a certain caution in using it and characterize it as altogether a coterie book. Mme. de Staël, of glorious memory, established here, in the form of a book, a kind of salon, in which she received German writers and gave them an opportunity to make themselves known to the French civilized world, but in the din of voices of every sort which cry out from the pages of this book, the most distinctly audible is always the clear falsetto of Mr. A. W. Schlegel.[3] In the passages where she is completely herself, where this woman of great sensitivity speaks out directly with all her glowing heart, with the full pyrotechnical display of her intellectual rockets and brilliant eccentricities, the book is good and admirable. The instant she obeys suggestions from without; the instant she does homage to a school whose character is completely alien and incomprehensible to her; the instant she encourages, by praising this school, certain ultramontane tendencies which are in direct contradiction to her Protestant enlightenment, her book is wretched and unbearable. Besides, she exhibits conscious as well as unconscious biases, and in eulogizing intellectual life and idealism in German, her real intention is to criticize the realism of the French at that time, the material splendor of the period of the Empire. In this respect her book *De l'Allemagne* resembles Tacitus' *Germania*,[4] for in his apologia of the Germans he also perhaps intended to write an indirect satire on his own countrymen.

When I mentioned above a school to which Mme. de Staël did homage and whose tendencies she encouraged, I meant the Romantic School. In the following pages it will become clear that in Germany this was something entirely different from what is designated by this name in France and that its tendencies were quite different from those of the French Romanticists.

---

3. August Wilhelm Schlegel (1767–1845) and his brother Friedrich were the leading theoretical writers in German literary Romanticism. Both were critics and interpreters rather than poets. In 1804 Madame de Staël engaged A. W. Schlegel as traveling companion and tutor to her son. He later acted as her adviser in writing *De l'Allemagne*.

4. In *Germania*, written at the end of the first century, Tactius praised the virtue of the Germanic tribes in contrast to the effeminate luxury and moral degeneration apparent among the Romans.

But what was the Romantic School in Germany?

It was nothing other than the revival of the poetry of the Middle Ages as manifested in the songs, sculpture, and architecture, in the art and life of that time. This poetry, however, had had its origin in Christianity; it was a passion flower rising from the blood of Christ. I do not know whether the melancholy flower that we call passion flower in Germany also bears this name in France and whether that mystical origin is likewise attributed to it by folk legend. It is a strange flower of unpleasing color, in whose chalice can be seen depicted the instruments of torture used at the Crucifixion of Christ, namely, hammer, tongs, nails, etc., a flower that is by no means ugly, only eery, indeed, the sight of which even arouses in us an uncanny pleasure like the convulsively sweet sensations which result even from suffering itself. In this respect the flower would be the most fitting symbol for Christianity, whose most gruesome attraction consists in this very ecstasy of suffering.

Although in France the name Christianity means only Roman Catholicism, I must nonetheless emphasize as preface to my remarks that I am speaking only of Roman Catholicism. I am speaking of the religion whose earliest dogmas contain a condemnation of the flesh, and which not merely grants the spirit superiority over the flesh but also deliberately mortifies the flesh in order to glorify the spirit. I am speaking of the religion whose unnatural mission actually introduced sin and hypocrisy into the world, since just because of the condemnation of the flesh the most innocent pleasures of the senses became a sin and just because of the impossibility of our being wholly spirit hypocrisy inevitably developed. I am speaking of the religion which also, due to the doctrine of the evil of earthly possessions and the doctrine that imposed a dog-like humility and an angelic patience, became the most reliable support of despotism. People have now recognized the nature of this religion, they will no longer let themselves be fooled by promissory notes on Heaven, they know that material things also have their good side and are not totally evil, and they now vindicate the pleasures of the earth, of this beautiful garden of God, our inalienable heritage. Just because we now comprehend so completely all the consequences of that absolute spiritualism, we can also believe that the Catholic Christian philosophy of life is doomed. For every epoch is a sphinx that plunges into the abyss as soon as its riddle has been solved.

We by no means deny, however, the good brought about in Europe by the Catholic Christian philosophy of life. It was necessary as a wholesome reaction against the dreadful and colossal materialism which had developed in the Roman Empire and was threatening to destroy all the spiritual grandeur of mankind. As the licentious memoirs of the century just past constitute, so to speak, the *pièces justificatives*[5] of the French Revolution, as the terrorism of a *Comité du salut public*[6] seems to us necessary medicine after reading the confessions of the fashionable world in France since the Regency, so we also recognize the salutariness of ascetic spiritualism if we have read, say, Petronius[7] or Apuleius,[8] books which can be considered *pièces justificatives* of Christianity. The flesh had become so insolent in this Roman world that it needed the Christian discipline to mortify it. After the banquet of a Trimalchio a fasting cure like Christianity was needed.

Or is it possible that just as grey-haired libertines inflame their flagging flesh with whippings to renewed capacity for enjoyment, aging Rome wanted to let itself be scourged in monkish fashion in order to discover subtle pleasures in the torture itself and ecstasy in suffering?

Disastrous overstimulation! It robbed the Roman body politic of its last energies. Rome did not perish because of the division into two kingdoms. On the Bosporus as well as on the Tiber, Rome was swallowed up by the same Jewish spiritualism, and here as well as there, Roman history became a slow ebbing away, an agony that lasted for centuries. Can it be that assassinated Judea, in presenting the Romans its spiritualism as a gift, meant to take revenge on the victorious enemy as did once the dying centaur who so craftily succeeded in passing on to Jupiter's son the fatal garment

5. Supporting documents.
6. Committee of Public Safety, established in 1793, whose members exercised dictatorial power.
7. Roman satirist who died c. 66 A.D. His best-known work, or rather, fragment, *Trimalchio's Dinner,* is the description of a freedman's vulgar display of his newly acquired wealth.
8. A Latin writer of the second century, whose *Golden Ass* is one of the few surviving examples of the Latin novel. Among other things, it deals with the bizarre effects of sensual indulgence.

poisoned with his own blood?[9] It is a fact that Rome, the Hercules of nations, was so effectively devoured by the Jewish poison that helmet and armor dropped from its withering limbs, and its imperial battle cry sank to the praying whimper of priests and the trilling of eunuchs.

But what debilitates an old man strengthens a young one. This spiritualism had a salutary effect on the superhealthy peoples of the north; their all too full-blooded barbaric bodies were spiritualized by Christianity. European civilization began. This is a praiseworthy, venerable aspect of Christianity. In this regard the Catholic Church earned its greatest claims to our respect and admiration. By means of great and ingenious institutions she was able to tame the bestiality of the northern barbarians and to overpower brute matter.

The art works of the Middle Ages show the mastery of matter by the spirit, and often this is actually their whole mission. The epics of this period could easily be classified according to the degree of such mastery.

One cannot speak here of lyric or dramatic works, for the latter did not exist, and the former are pretty much alike in any age, like the songs of the nightingales every spring.

The epic poetry of the Middle Ages was divided into sacred and profane, but both categories were completely Christian in character, for though the sacred poetry celebrated exclusively the Jewish people, who were considered the only sacred people, and their history, recognized as the only sacred history, the heroes of the Old Testament and the New, the legends of saints, in short, the Church, yet in the profane poetry the whole life of the times was reflected with all its Christian views and aspirations. The flower of sacred poetry in the German Middle Ages is perhaps *Barlaam and*

---

9. When the centaur Nessus tried to rape Hercules' wife, Deianira, Hercules killed him. As he lay dying, Nessus advised Deianira to make from his blood a magic salve which would keep Hercules true to her. Soon after, upon Hercules' return from a successful campaign, he ordered his wife to provide him with a white garment in which he could offer the gods a sacrifice as tribute for the victory. Deianira, seeing the beautiful prisoner, Iola, brought back by her husband, rubbed the garment with the magic salve, to discover only too late that it was a fatal poison which would have killed Hercules if the gods had not rescued him from the funeral pyre and taken him to Olympus.

Josaphat,[10] a work in which the doctrine of denial, of temperance, of renunciation, of contempt for all worldly glory was consistently expressed. After it I would consider the Eulogy of St. Anno[11] the best of the sacred literature. But this latter work extends far into the secular realm. In general it differs from the former as, let us say, a Byzantine picture of a saint differs from an ancient German picture. We also see in Barlaam and Josaphat, as in those Byzantine paintings, the utmost simplicity with no accessories such as perspective, and the tall, thin, statuesque bodies with their solemn, idealized faces stand out in sharp outline as if against a soft gold background. In the Eulogy of St. Anno the accessories almost become the main point, and despite the grandiose design every detail is most minutely executed, and one doesn't know whether to admire in the work the conception of a giant or the patience of a dwarf. Otfried's poem on the Gospels,[12] usually praised as the chief work of the sacred literature, is not nearly so good as the two works mentioned.

In the profane literature we find, as I indicated above, first the epic cycle of the Nibelungen[13] and the Book of Heroes;[14] in these the whole pre-Christian way of thinking and feeling still prevails; crude energy has not yet been refined into chivalry; the unyielding warriors of the north still stand like statues of stone, and the gentle light and moral spirit of Christianity have not yet penetrated their

10. Written c. 1220–1230 by Rudolf von Ems. It is one of the many versions found in western literature of an old Buddhistic legend which tells how the Indian prince, Josaphat, becomes a convert to the Christian asceticism of the hermit Barlaam.

11. A biography of Anno II, Archbishop of Cologne, written by a monastic poet at the end of the eleventh century or early in the twelfth. It begins with the Creation, continues with the Fall, the Redemption, the spread of Christianity, and at last arrives at the founding of Cologne and the celebration of Anno's life and work.

12. The so-called Harmony of the Gospels (Evangelienharmonie), written c. 865. It alternates between narrative and exegesis.

13. The Nibelungenlied was the work of an unknown poet, probably during the first decade of the thirteenth century. It is an heroic epic in which Siegfried's courtship of Kriemhild at the court of Worms, his marriage to her, and his early death at the hands of the treacherous Hagen occupy the first part. In the second part, located chiefly in Austria, Kriemhild, who has married Etzel (the historical Attila), plots, and carries out a bloody and successful revenge on Hagen. The narrative, background, and tone are relatively untouched by Christian chivalry.

14. A collection of epic poems dealing with various Germanic heroic legends printed toward the close of the fifteenth century. In many of them Dietrich of Bern (Theodoric the Great) plays a role, as he does at the close of the Nibelungenlied.

iron armor. But dawn is gradually breaking over the ancient Germanic forests, the old sacred oaks are felled, and thus a clear arena is formed, where the Christian battles with the heathen. This we find in the cycle of sagas about Charlemagne, in which it is the crusades with their religious tendencies that are actually portrayed.[15] Now, however, from the vitality spiritualized by Christianity developed the most characteristic phenomenon of the Middle Ages, chivalry, which was ultimately refined into a religious chivalry. The former, secular chivalry, we find most charmingly idealized in the cycle of legends about King Arthur, which are full of the sweetest gallantry, the most refined courtesy, and the most adventuresome knight-errantry. From the delightfully extravagant arabesques and fantastic, flowery tapestries of these works we are greeted by excellent Iwain,[16] peerless Lanzelot of the Lake,[17] and brave, gallant, honest, but somewhat boring Wigalois.[18] In addition to this cycle of legends and closely related to it and interwoven with it, we find the cycle about the Holy Grail, in which religious chivalry is idealized, and here we encounter three of the most magnificent works of the Middle Ages, *Titurel*, *Parcival*, and *Lohengrin*.[19] Here we stand personally face to face with Romantic poetry, as it were, we look deep into its eyes, full of suffering, and before we know it, it entangles us in its scholastic web and draws us down into the mad depths of medieval mysticism. Lastly, however, we also meet with works from that time which do not necessarily pay homage to Christian spiritualism, indeed, works in which this spiritualism is even criticized, in which the poet casts off the fetters of abstract Christian virtues and plunges joyously

15. The legends about Charlemagne are more important for French literature than for Germans. The *Song of Roland (Chanson de Roland)* is well known. There is also a German *Song of Roland* by a priest Konrad, written c. 1140. The French epic was Konrad's source, but the German version emphasizes Christianity and Christian ideals rather than *la douce France*.

16. Heine's spelling. Iwein is the hero of an epic, written c. 1200, by Hartman von Aue, one of the most important Middle High German poets.

17. *Lanzelot* was written by Ulrich von Zazikhoven toward the end of the twelfth century.

18. Written by Wirnt von Gravenberg c. 1205.

19. Wolfram von Eschenbach wrote *Parcival* in the first decade of the thirteenth century. *Titurel*, Wolfram's last work, c. 1219, was not completed, and only two short fragments have been preserved. Both *Parcival* and *Titurel* belong to Arthurian romance. *Lohengrin* is a much later work, whose author is unknown. It is a continuation of Wolfram's *Parcival*, dealing with the adventures of Parsifal's son.

into the epicurean world of glorified sensuality. And it is not exactly
the worst poet who has bequeathed to us the most important work
with this tendency, *Tristan and Isolde*. Yes, I must confess that
Gottfried von Strassburg,[20] the author of this most beautiful work
of the Middle Ages, is perhaps also its greatest poet, even surpassing
all the excellence of Wolfram von Eschilbach,[21] whom we admire
so much in *Parcival* and in the fragments of *Titurel*. Perhaps it is
now permissible to praise and acclaim Master Gottfried unreservedly. At his time the work was certainly considered irreligious,
and similar writings, including even *Lanzelot,* were thought dangerous. And perilous incidents actually did occur. Francesca da
Polenta and her handsome friend had to pay dearly for having one
day read together from such a book. To be sure, the greater danger
lay in the fact that they suddenly stopped reading.[22]

The poetry in all these medieval works possesses a definite
character which distinguishes it from the poetry of the Greeks and
Romans. To mark this difference we call the former romantic and
the latter classical literature. These terms are, however, only vague
labels, and up to now have led to the most unedifying confusion,
which was worse confounded when ancient poetry was called
"plastic" instead of "classical." This was above all the origin of
such misconceptions as that artists should always treat their
material, whether Christian or pagan, in plastic fashion, should
present it in clear outlines—in short, that plastic organization
should be the chief concern in modern Romantic art, as it was in
ancient art. And in fact, are not the figures in Dante's *Divine
Comedy* or in Raphael's paintings just as plastic as the figures in
Virgil or those on the walls of Herculaneum? The difference is that
the plastic figures in ancient art are completely identical with what
is to be represented, with the idea which the artist intended to
present. For example, the wanderings of Ulysses mean nothing
other than the wanderings of a man who was the son of Laertes
and husband of Penelope and whose name was Ulysses. Further,

20. By far the best version of this famous romance, though Gottfried left it
unfinished. It dates from about 1210.
21. Heine's spelling.
22. An allusion to the famous passage at the end of the fifth canto of Dante's
Inferno, where Francesca da Rimini, wife of Guido da Polenta, tells the poet about
the day when she and her lover, Paolo, on reading a certain passage in the romance
of Lancelot and Guinevere, confessed their love for the first time and read no more
that day.

Bacchus, whom we see in the Louvre, is nothing but the charming son of Semele with bold sadness in his eyes and a holy voluptuousness in his soft, arched lips. In romantic art it is different; the wanderings of a knight have an added esoteric meaning; they indicate perhaps the wanderings of life in general; the vanquished dragon is sin; the almond tree that from afar wafts it fragrance so comfortingly toward the hero is the Trinity, God-Father and God-Son, and God-Holy Ghost, who at the same time constitute a unity, just as shell, husk, and kernel are one and the same almond. When Homer describes a hero's armor, it is simply an excellent suit of armor and nothing more, worth so and so many oxen; but when a medieval monk describes in his poem the Madonna's skirts, you can be sure that with these skirts he means a like number of different virtues, that a special significance is concealed beneath the holy coverings of Mary's immaculate virginity, for, quite logically, she is also celebrated in poetry as the almond blossom, since her son is the almond kernel. Such is the nature of medieval poetry, which we call romantic.

Classical art had only to represent the finite, and its figures could be identical with the idea of the artist. Romantic art had to represent, or rather, suggest, the infinite and purely spiritual relationships and had recourse to a system of traditional symbols, or rather, to parables, just as Christ himself tried to make clear his ideas about things of the spirit by using all kinds of nice parables. Hence the mystical, enigmatic, marvelous, and extravagant elements in the art works of the Middle Ages. Fantasy makes her most atrocious efforts to represent pure spirit by means of sense images and invents the most colossal extravaganzas, piling Pelion on Ossa, *Parcival* on *Titurel*, in order to reach Heaven.

Among the peoples whose literature likewise strove to represent the infinite and consequently produced monstrous abortions of imagination, for example, in Scandinavia and India,[23] we find works that we also consider romantic and are accustomed to call romantic.

We cannot say much about medieval music. The documents are lacking. Only very late, in the sixteenth century, did the masterworks of Catholic church music originate, which, as representative of their style, cannot be esteemed highly enough, since they are the purest expression of Christian spirituality. The vocal arts, spiritual

23. Heine is thinking of the *Edda*, the *Ramayana*, the *Mahabharata*, etc.

by their very nature, were able to thrive fairly well under Christianity, but this religion was less advantageous for the plastic arts. Since the latter were also supposed to represent the victory of spirit over matter and yet had to use this very material as their means of representation, they were forced to solve, so to speak, an unnatural problem. Hence those repulsive subjects in sculpture and painting: pictures of martyrs, crucifixions, dying saints, destruction of the flesh. Such tasks were themselves a martyrdom of sculpture, and whenever I look at these distorted works, in which Christian abstinence and passionless spirituality are supposed to be represented by means of crooked, pious heads, long, thin arms, skinny legs, and uneasily awkward garments, I am seized with an inexpressible pity for the artists of that time. The painters probably had it somewhat better, since the medium of their representation, color, in its intangibility, in its many-hued shadings, was not in such crass opposition to spirituality as the sculptors' material; nevertheless, the painters also had to load their groaning canvas with the most repulsive suffering figures. Indeed, if one looks at many collections of paintings and sees nothing pictured but gory scenes, floggings, and executions, one would think the old masters had painted these pictures for an executioners' gallery.

But human genius can transfigure even unnaturalness, many painters succeeded in solving the unnatural problem beautifully and sublimely, and particularly the Italians were able to pay homage to beauty somewhat at the expense of spirituality and to rise to that purity of conception which reached its peak in so many portrayals of the Madonna. In any case, with regard to the Madonna, the Catholic clergy always made some concessions to sensualism. This image of unsullied beauty, transfigured by maternal love and suffering, enjoyed the privilege of being celebrated by poets and painters and adorned with every sensuous charm. For this image was a magnet able to attract the great masses to the bosom of Christianity. Madonna Mary was, as it were, the lovely *dame du comptoir*[24] of the Catholic Church, who attracted its customers, especially the barbarians of the north, with her heavenly smile and held them fast.

24. According to the edition by O. Walzel, Heine means a *Büfettdame*, i.e., a waitress or barmaid.

Architecture in the Middle Ages bore the same character as the other arts; as a rule all manifestations of life harmonized marvelously with each other in those times. In architecture there is the same parabolic tendency as in literature. When we enter an ancient cathedral today, we scarcely sense the esoteric meaning of its symbolism in stone. Only the total impression directly penetrates our minds. We feel here the elevation of the spirit and the trampling of the flesh. The interior of the cathedral itself is a hollow cross, and we stroll there within the very instrument of martyrdom; the stained glass windows cast their red and green lights upon us like drops of blood and pus; funeral dirges moan all about us; beneath our feet tombstones and putrefaction, and like the colossal pillars our spirit strives upward, painfully tearing itself from the body, which sinks to the earth like a weary garment. If you look at them from outside, these Gothic cathedrals, these enormous edifices, fashioned so airily, so finely, so delicately, so transparently that they might be taken for carvings, or Brabant lace made of marble, you feel more than ever the power of that age, which could master even stone so that it seems to be almost uncannily permeated with spirit, so that even this hardest of all substances expresses Christian spirituality.

But the arts are merely the mirror of life, and as Catholicism was extinguished in life, it also faded and died away in the arts. At the time of the Reformation Catholic literature gradually disappeared in Europe, and in its place we find Greek literature, long since dead, coming to life again. To be sure, it was only an artificial spring, a product of the gardener and not of the sun, and the trees and flowers stood in small pots, and a glass sky protected them from cold and the north wind.

Not every event in world history is the direct consequence of another, but all events are mutually interconnected. Love of Hellenism and the mania for imitating it did not become common with us merely because of the Greek scholars who emigrated to Germany after the conquest of Constantinople; in art as in life there arose a simultaneous "Protestantism." Leo X, the splendid Medici, was as zealous a Protestant as Luther;[25] just as in Wittenberg

---

25. Pope Leo X (1475–1521) was Giovanni de Medici, son of Lorenzo de Medici, well-known patron of the arts and sciences.

they protested in Latin prose, so in Rome they protested in stone, in color, and in ottava rima. Michelangelo's powerful marble figures, the laughing faces of Giulio Romano's[26] nymphs, and the exuberant gaiety in the verses of Master Ludovico[27]—aren't these a protesting antithesis to traditionally dismal, languishing Catholicism? The painters in Italy perhaps carried on a much more effective polemic against clericalism than the Saxon theologians. The voluptuous flesh in Titian's paintings—all of this is Protestantism. The loins of his Venus are much more fundamental theses than those the German monk posted on the church door in Wittenberg.—The men of that time seemed to feel themselves suddenly liberated from the constraint of a thousand years; especially the artists breathed freely again when relieved of the nightmare of Christianity; they plunged enthusiastically into the sea of Grecian gaiety, and from its foam the goddesses of beauty rose up to meet them. Once more painters painted the ambrosian joys of Olympus; once more sculptors, with the same ecstasy as of old, chiseled the ancient heroes out of the block of marble; once more poets celebrated in song the house of Atreus and of Laius; the period of neoclassical poetry began.

Just as modern life developed to its greatest perfection in France under Louis XIV, so neoclassical poetry likewise achieved here in France a consummate perfection, indeed, a kind of independent originality. Through the political influence of the great monarch this neoclassical literature spread through the rest of Europe. In Italy, where it had already established itself,[28] it took on a French complexion; with the Angevins the heroes of French tragedy also went to Spain;[29] they went to England with Madame Henriette;[30] and we Germans, of course, built our clumsy temples to the powdered Olympus of Versailles. Their most famous highpriest

26. Romano (c. 1492–1546) was a painter and architect, a pupil of Raphael's.
27. Lodovico Ariosto (1474–1533), Italian epic and lyric poet.
28. Actually the literature of the Renaissance began in Italy and from there spread to the other European countries. Heine seldom hesitated to sacrifice historical accuracy to his desire to pay a compliment.
29. Philip V (1701–1746), the first Bourbon on the Spanish throne, was the grandson of Louis XIV. He had previously held the title of a Duke of Anjou.
30. Henriette Marie (1609–1669), the daughter of Henry IV of France and the sister of Louis XIII, was married in 1625 to Charles Stuart, later King Charles I.

was Gottsched,[31] that big periwig whom our beloved Goethe described so perfectly in his memoirs.[32]

Lessing was the literary Arminius[33] who liberated our theater from this foreign domination. He showed us the vacuity, the absurdity, the bad taste of those imitations of the French theater, which itself seemed to be an imitation of the Greek. He became the founder of modern German national literature, not simply through his criticism, but also through his own creative writings. This man pursued every branch of knowledge, every aspect of life, with enthusiasm and impartiality. Art, theology, the study of antiquity, literature, dramatic criticism, history—he pursued all these with the same zeal and for the same purpose. All his works are animated by that great social idea, that progressive humanism, that religion of reason whose John the Baptist he was and whose Messiah we are still awaiting. He never ceased to preach this religion, though unfortunately often completely alone and in the wilderness. And besides he lacked the art of turning stones into bread; he spent the greatest part of his life in poverty and hardship; this is a curse that weighs upon nearly all great minds in Germany and will perhaps be eliminated only by political liberation. Lessing was also more politically motivated than anyone suspected, a characteristic that we do not find at all among his contemporaries. Only now do we see what he meant by the description of petty despotism in *Emilia Galotti*.[34] In his own time he was regarded merely as a champion of intellectual freedom and an opponent of clerical intolerance, for his theological writings were better understood. The fragments *Concerning the Education of the Human Race,* translated into French by Eugène Rodrigue, may possibly give the French some idea of the comprehensive scope of Lessing's

31. Johann Christoph Gottsched (1700–1766) attempted to reform German poetry and drama by imitation of French models.

32. In *Poetry and Truth (Dichtung und Wahrheit),* Book VII.

33. Arminius, a German national hero because he was the leader of the armies that vanquished the Romans under Varus in the crucial battle of the Teutoburger Wald in 9 A.D.

34. The action takes place in Italy, but the unscrupulous immorality and tyranny of the court could apply as well to some courts in the Germany of Lessing's time. The Prince's attempt to seduce the virtuous heroine Emilia was unsuccessful, but was pursued with such persistence that in the course of the play Emilia's fiancé is killed, she herself is taken prisoner by the Prince's villainous confidant, and finally feels forced to goad her father into killing her in order to preserve her virtue.

mind. The two critical writings that had the greatest influence on art are his *Hamburg Dramaturgy* and his *Laocoön, or An Essay on the Limits of Painting and Poetry*. His best plays are *Emilia Galotti, Minna von Barnhelm,* and *Nathan the Wise*.

Gotthold Ephraim Lessing was born in Kamenz in Lausitz on January 22, 1729, and died in Brunswick February 15, 1781. He was no one-sided man who, while fighting with his polemic to destroy outworn traditions, was himself creating at the same time something new and better. "He resembled," says a German writer, "those devout Jews who, during the second building of the temple, being often disturbed by attacks from their enemies, then fought against them with one hand and continued building the house of God with the other hand." This is not the place for me to say more about Lessing, but I cannot refrain from remarking that in the whole history of literature he is the writer I love best. I want to mention here another writer whose efforts were made in the same spirit and for the same purpose and who may be called Lessing's immediate successor. To be sure, an evaluation of him does not belong here either. Actually he occupies a very solitary place in literary history, and his relationship to his time and his contemporaries cannot yet be judged definitively. He is Johann Gottfried Herder, who was born in Morungen in East Prussia in 1744 and died in Weimar in Saxony in the year 1803.

The history of literature is the great morgue where everyone looks for the dead whom he loves or to whom he is related. When among so many insignificant corpses I catch sight of Lessing or Herder, with their noble human faces, my heart pounds. How could I pass by without lightly kissing your pale lips!

Yet though Lessing resolutely put an end to the imitation of French pseudo-Hellenism, nonetheless, merely by calling attention to the real art works of Greek antiquity, he himself to some extent furthered a new kind of silly imitation. By fighting against religious superstition he even encouraged the pedantic mania for Rationalism that flaunted itself in Berlin and possessed in the late Nicolai its main mouthpiece and in the *Allgemeine deutsche Bibliothek*[35] its arsenal. During those years the most wretched mediocrity began

35. Christoph Friedrich Nicolai (1733–1811), an active and influential champion of Rationalism, was the editor of the journal mentioned here, published from 1765 to 1800.

to play havoc more disgustingly than ever, and triviality and insanity swelled up like the frog in the fable.

It is a great mistake to think that Goethe, who at that time had already appeared on the scene, was then generally recognized. His *Götz von Berlichingen* and his *Werther*[36] had been received with enthusiasm, but so had the works of the most commonplace dabblers, and Goethe was given only a tiny niche in the temple of literature. As I said, the public had received only *Götz* and *Werther* with enthusiasm, more on account of the subject matter than because of their artistic merits, which almost no one was capable of appreciating in these masterpieces. *Götz* was a dramatized novel of chivalry, a genre very popular at that time. In *Werther* people saw only the adaptation of a true story, that of young Jerusalem, a young man who shot himself for love and thus created a tremendous sensation in that time of dead calm; they read his touching letters with tears in their eyes; they noted discerningly that the manner in which Werther was removed from a social gathering of the aristocracy increased his disgust with life;[37] the question of suicide caused more discussion of the book; some idiots hit on the idea of likewise shooting themselves at this opportune moment; thanks to its contents the book was a striking sensation. But August Lafontaine's[38] novels were read just as enthusiastically, and since he never stopped writing, he was more famous than Wolfgang Goethe. Wieland[39] was the great poet then, with whom perhaps only Mr. Ode-Writer Ramler[40] in Berlin could compete in the realm of poetry. Wieland was worshipped idolatrously, more than Goethe ever was. The theater was dominated by Iffland[41] with

36. The first play and the first novel of Goethe's to attract attention.
37. On this occasion Werther, who belonged to the middle class, forgetting the class distinctions with which he was quite familiar, stayed on after an afternoon call at the home of a friend, a Count, and finally had to be asked to leave as the party of aristocrats gathered for an evening of sociability.
38. A writer of sentimental novels, once popular, now completely forgotten.
39. Christoph Martin Wieland (1733–1813), poet and novelist. He also translated seventeen of Shakespeare's plays.
40. Karl Wilhelm Ramler (1725–1788) was a poet and translator, devoid of originality, but much read in his day.
41. August Wilhelm Iffland (1759–1814), dramatist, very popular actor, and from 1811 to 1814 director of the royal theater in Berlin.

his sentimental middle-class plays and Kotzebue[42] with his tritely witty farces.

Such was the literature against which a school arose in Germany during the last years of the past century. We call it the Romantic School, and Messers August Wilhelm and Friedrich Schlegel presented themselves to us as its directors. Jena, where the two brothers and many other kindred spirits sometimes resided, was the center from which the new doctrine of esthetics spread.[43] I say "doctrine" because this school began with a critical examination of the art works of the past and with a recipe for the art works of the future. In both these pursuits the Schlegel school did great service to esthetic criticism. In evaluating art works already in existence, either their defects and weaknesses were demonstrated or their merits and beauties analyzed. In their polemic, in the exposure of artistic defects and weaknesses, the Schlegels were faithful imitators of old Lessing; they seized possession of his great battle sword; but Mr. August Wilhelm Schlegel's arm was much too delicate and feeble and his brother Friedrich's eyes much too beclouded with mysticism for the former to be able to hit the mark as powerfully and the latter as accurately as Lessing. In appreciative criticism, however, where the beauties of a work of art are illustrated, where the important thing was a fine sensitivity for the characteristics of a work, and where these had to be made comprehensible, the Schlegels were far superior to old Lessing. But what shall I say about their prescriptions for producing masterpieces! Here the Schlegels displayed an impotence that we also find in Lessing. Vigorous though he was in negative criticism, even he was weak in affirmative criticism; rarely was he able to establish a basic principle, still more rarely a correct one. He lacked the firm grounding of a philosophy, of a philosophical system. The same is true of the Schlegels to a far more hopeless degree. A lot of nonsense is talked about the influence of Fichte's idealistic philosophy and Schelling's nature philosophy on the Romantic School, even to the

42. August von Kotzebue (1761–1819), prolific writer of shallow plays that were very popular on the stage.
43. A. W. Schlegel lived in Jena from 1796 to 1801 and became a professor at the University of Jena in 1798. His brother was a *Privatdozent* at the university from 1799 to 1801. Ludwig Tieck, Novalis, and Clemens Brentano were also there during part of these years, as well as the philosophers Fichte and Schelling.

extent of maintaining that it had its origin in these philosophies. But I find, at most, the influence of a few fragments of Fichte's and Schelling's ideas, and no influence whatsover of a philosophy. Mr. Schelling, who was then teaching in Jena, did, however, exercise a strong personal influence on the Romantic School; he is a bit of a poet—a fact not known in France—and they say he is still uncertain as to whether he should publish his collected philosophical doctrines in poetic or even metrical form. This uncertainty is characteristic of the man.

Though the Schlegels could specify no fixed theory for the masterpieces that they commissioned from the poets of their school, they compensated for this lack by strongly recommending the best art works of the past as models and by making them accessible to their pupils. These were principally the Catholic-Christian works of the Middle Ages. The translation of Shakespeare, who stands on the border-line of this art and already smiles upon our modern age with Protestant clarity, was intended solely for polemical purposes, a discussion of which would occupy too much space here.[44] Besides, this translation was undertaken by Mr. A. W. Schlegel at a time when enthusiasm had not yet transported him and his followers completely back to the Middle Ages. Later, when this occurred, Calderón was translated[45] and praised far more highly than Shakespeare, for in Calderón the literature of the Middle Ages was found in its purest form, certainly in the two main components, chivalry and monasticism. The pious comedies of the Castilian priest and poet, whose poetic blossoms are sprinkled with holy water and perfumed with churchly incense, were now imitated with all their sacred solemnity, with all their sacerdotal pomp, with all their sanctified absurdity. And in Germany there sprang up those confusedly devout, crazily profound writings in which the characters fell mystically in love, as in *Devotion to the Cross,* or fought in honor of the Blessed Virgin, as in *The Steadfast Prince;*[46] and Zacharias Werner[47] went as far as anyone could

44. In an essay on Shakespeare's female characters Heine presented his theory that the translation of Shakespeare was meant to depreciate Schiller as a dramatist.
45. Schlegel translated five of Calderón's plays. They appeared in Berlin, 1803–1809, under the title of *Spanish Theater.*
46. Calderón's *La devoción de la Cruz* and *El príncipe constante.*
47. A talented, but unbalanced person whose life ranged from the extreme of

without being locked up in an insane asylum by order of the authorities.

Our literature, said the Schlegels, is old, our Muse is an old woman with a spinning wheel, our Cupid is not a fair-haired boy, but a shriveled-up dwarf with grey locks, our emotions have withered, our imagination has dried up, and we must renew our strength, we must seek again the choked-up springs of simple, artless, medieval poetry, and the fountain of youth will gush forth. The arid, parched nation did not need to be told this twice; especially the poor thirsty souls who lived on the sands of Brandenburg wanted to become verdant and youthful once more, and they rushed to the miraculous springs to swill and lap and gulp with extravagant greediness. But they fared as did the elderly lady's-maid about whom the following story is told. She had noticed that her mistress possessed a magic elixir that restored youth; when her mistress was absent, she took from her dressing table the little flask containing the elixir, but instead of drinking only a few drops, she took such a big, long swallow that, due to the greatly intensified magic power of the rejuvenation potion, she became not merely young again, but turned into a tiny little child. And this is exactly what happened to our admirable Mr. Tieck,[48] one of the best poets of the School. He had gulped down so many of the medieval chapbooks and poems that he became almost a child again and retrogressed to that babbling simplicity which Mme. de Staël found so very difficult to admire. She admitted herself that it seemed strange to her for a character in a play to make his first appearance with a monologue that begins, "I am valiant Boniface, and have come to tell you," etc.[49]

In his novel *Sternbald's Travels*[50] and in *Heartfelt Sentiments of an Art-Loving Friar*, edited by him and written by a certain

---

debauchery to the devout Catholicism of his later years. Most of his plays dealt with religious subjects, and his dramatic technique was often bizarre and crudely melodramatic.

48. Ludwig Tieck (1773–1853), poet, dramatist, novelist, writer of novellas, critic, and translator.

49. A very free, in fact, inaccurate, rendering of the opening words of Tieck's dramatic fairy tale *The Life and Death of Saint Genevieve*. St. Boniface speaks a prologue and an epilogue to the play.

50. *Franz Sternbald's Travels*, published in 1798.

Wackenroder,[51] Mr. Ludwig Tieck had presented the naive, crude beginnings of art as models even for sculptors and painters. The piety and the childlike quality of these works, which are revealed by the very awkwardness of their technique, were recommended for imitation. Raphael was completely ignored, and little was heard even about his teacher, Perugino,[52] who, to be sure, was ranked higher and in whom were discovered vestiges of the virtues so devoutly admired in all their abundance in the immortal masterpieces of Fra Giovanni Angelico da Fiesole. If you want to get an idea of the taste of these art enthusiasts, you must go to the Louvre, where the best paintings of those masters, then unreservedly revered, still hang; and if you want to get an idea of the great multitude of poets who were then imitating in every conceivable kind of verse the writings of the Middle Ages, you have to go to the insane asylum at Charenton.[53]

But in my opinion the pictures in the first hall of the Louvre are much too charming to give a true notion of the taste of the day. One must, in addition, imagine these old Italian pictures translated into old German. For the works of the old German painters were considered far more simple and childlike than those of the old Italians, and therefore more worthy of imitation. The Germans are able, so it was said, by virtue of their temperament (a word for which the French language has no equivalent),[54] to comprehend Christianity more profoundly than other nations, and Friedrich Schlegel and his friend Mr. Joseph Görres[55] rummaged through

51. Wilhelm Heinrich Wackenroder, 1773–1798. His principal writings are the essays Heine mentions here, one of the earliest of Romantic writings in Germany, with the characteristic emotional approach to art and the passionate seriousness with which art, here particularly painting and music, became a religion. Heine exaggerates in what follows. Wackenroder admired Raphael greatly.

52. Pietro Vannucci, called Perugino (c. 1445–c.1523), head of the Umbrian school of painters.

53. Near Paris.

54. Nor does the English. The word *Gemüt* means many things. One word connoting "mind, soul, heart, spirit" would be needed to convey the total meaning of the German word.

55. German author (1776–1848), interested in medieval literature and active as a journalist and political writer. He was a devout Catholic. In this work and in the *History of Religion and Philosophy* Heine uses the title "Mr." in referring to certain persons but omits it when writing of others. Here, for instance, the title is used with Görres' name, but not with Friedrich Schlegel's. I have retained in my translation Heine's use of the title because I believe it was deliberate. He uses the

the old towns on the Rhine for remains of old German paintings and sculpture, which were worshipped in blind faith like holy relics.

I have just compared the German Parnassus of that time with Charenton, but I think that here, too, I have said much too little. French madness is far from being so mad as German madness, for in the latter, as Polonius would say,[56] there is method. The Germans cultivated that madness with unequalled pedantry, with horrifying conscientiousness, with a thoroughness which a superficial French madman cannot even conceive of.

Political conditions in Germany were still especially favorable for the old German Christian movement. "Misery teaches us to pray," runs the proverb, and indeed, never was the misery greater in Germany, hence the nation was never more susceptible to prayer, religion, and Christianity than then. No people retains more devotion for its rulers than the Germans, and it was the pitiful sight of their conquered sovereigns, whom they saw groveling at Napoleon's feet, that distressed the Germans beyond endurance, far more than the sorry state to which the country had been reduced by war and foreign domination. The whole nation resembled those faithful old servants of great families who feel all the humiliations which their gracious masters must endure even more deeply than the latter themselves and who shed in private their most sorrowful tears when, for example, the family silver has to be sold and who even secretly use their pitiful savings so that no middle-class tallow lights will be placed on the master's table instead of aristocratic wax candles, scenes we view with suitable emotion in old plays. The general distress found consolation in religion, and there arose a pietistic resignation to the will of God, from whom alone help was expected. And in fact, against Napoleon no one else *could* help but the good Lord Himself. People could no longer count on the secular forces and had to turn their eyes trustfully toward Heaven.

We would have endured Napoleon with equanimity. But our rulers, while hoping to be liberated from him by God, at the same

---

title when referring to men he disliked, for example, A. W. Schlegel and Joseph Schelling, but usually omitted it when discussing writers whom he liked or toward whom he felt no antipathy; hence the title seems to add a note of sarcasm or disdain, or at the least, a touch of irony.

56. *Hamlet*, II, 2. "Though this be madness, there is method in it."

time indulged in the idea that the collective forces of their peoples might also be of great help. With this intention an attempt was made to arouse public spirit among the Germans, and even the most exalted personages began to talk of German nationality, of a common German fatherland, of the unification of the Christian Germanic tribes, of the unity of Germany. We were ordered to be patriotic, and we became patriots, for we do everything our rulers order us to. One must not think of this patriotism, however, as the same emotion which bears this name here in France. A Frenchman's patriotism means that his heart is warmed, and with this warmth it stretches and expands so that his love no longer embraces merely his closest relative, but all of France, the whole of the civilized world. A German's patriotism means that his heart contracts and shrinks like leather in the cold, and a German then hates everything foreign, no longer wants to become a citizen of the world, a European, but only a provincial German. So now we saw the perfect boorishness which Mr. Jahn[57] developed into a system; there began the mean, coarse, uncultured opposition to the most magnificent and venerable convictions that Germany has produced, namely, to the humanism, to the universal brotherhood of man, to the cosmopolitanism which our great minds, Lessing, Herder, Schiller, Goethe, Jean Paul,[58] which all educated Germans have always believed in.

What happened soon afterward in Germany is all too familiar to you. When God, the snow, and the Cossacks had destroyed Napoleon's best forces, we Germans received the royal command to free ourselves from the foreign yoke, and we flared up in manly indignation at the servitude endured all too long, and we were inspired by the good melodies and bad verse of Körner's[59] songs, and we fought and won our freedom, for we do everything we are ordered to do by our rulers.

57. Ludwig Jahn, one of the founders of the student union known as the *Burschenschaft* in 1815. It was open to all students, regardless of class distinctions, and attempted to combine ethics and patriotism in its goal of personal and political reform. This was the beginning of other, widespread student movements throughout Germany.
58. Pseudonym for Johann Paul Richter (1763–1825), a German novelist.
59. Theodor Körner, a poet who died in battle in 1813 at the age of twenty-two. His patriotic poems written during the Wars of Liberation were very popular, and his early death on the battlefield helped to keep his memory alive.

The period of preparation for this struggle was naturally the most favorable soil for a school that was hostile to the French spirit and extolled everything characteristically German in art and life. At that time the Romantic School went hand in hand with the aims of the governments and the secret societies, and Mr. A. W. Schlegel conspired against Racine with the same objective as that of Prime Minister Stein when he conspired against Napoleon. The School swam with the current of the time, the current that was flowing back to its source. When at last German patriotism and German nationality were completely victorious, the national-Germanic-Christian-Romantic School, the "neo-German-religious-patriotic art"[60] also triumphed conclusively. Napoleon, the great Classicist, as classic as Alexander and Caesar, fell, and Messers August Wilhelm and Friedrich Schlegel, the inconsequential Romanticists, just as romantic as Tom Thumb and Puss in Boots,[61] rose up as conquerors.

But here too the reaction which follows in the wake of every exaggeration was not slow to appear. As spiritual Christianity was a reaction against the brutal domination of imperial Roman materialism; as the renewed love for the serene joyousness of Greek art and science should be viewed as a reaction against the degeneration of Christian spirituality into idiotic asceticism; as the revival of medieval romanticism can also be regarded as a reaction against the pedantic imitation of ancient classical art, so we now see a reaction against the reintroduction of that Catholic, feudalistic turn of mind, that chivalry and clericalism, which had been preached in paintings and in words, and under the strangest circumstances. For when the old artists of the Middle Ages, the recommended models, were so highly praised and admired, their merit could be explained only by the fact that these men believed in the subject that they represented; that in their artless simplicity they could achieve greater things than the later masters who were vastly superior in technique, but lacked faith; that faith had worked

60. Under this title Goethe's friend Heinrich Meyer published an essay in 1817 in Goethe's journal *Über Kunst und Altertum.* Meyer, and implicitly Goethe also, here rejected the Romantic movement in Germany.
61. A reference to two "fairy-tale" plays by Ludwig Tieck. Heine chose these two plays because the subject matter was familiar to the French from Charles Perrault's fairy tales.

miracles in them. And indeed, how could one explain the splendors of a Fra Angelico da Fiesole or Brother Otfried's poem[62] otherwise? Hence the artists who took art seriously and wished to imitate the magnificent distortion of these miraculous paintings and the godly awkwardness of these miraculous poems, in short, the inexplicable mystical quality of the ancient works, decided to go to the very same Hippocrene from which the old masters had drawn their miraculous inspiration; they pilgrimaged to Rome, where, with the milk of his jenny ass, the representative of Christ would restore to health tubercular German art; in a word, they betook themselves to the bosom of the Roman Catholic Apostolic Church, the only true faith. For several members of the Romantic School there was no need of any formal conversion, they being Catholic by birth, for example, Mr. Görres and Mr. Clemens Brentano, and they merely renounced the freethinking views they had previously held. Others, however, had been born and reared within the bosom of the Protestant Church, for example, Friedrich Schlegel, Mr. Ludwig Tieck, Novalis, Werner, Schütz, Carové, Adam Müller,[63] etc., and their conversion to Catholicism required a public record. I have mentioned here only writers; the number of painters who renounced the Protestant faith and reason in droves was far larger.

When these young people were seen standing in line, so to speak, in front of the Roman Catholic Church and crowding back into the old prison of the mind from which their forefathers had freed themselves so vigorously, people in Germany shook their heads very doubtfully. But when it was discovered that the propaganda of priests and *Junkers,* who had formed a conspiracy against the religious and political freedom of Europe, had a hand in the matter, and that it was really Jesuitism that succeeded in luring German youth to their destruction with the sweet tones of Romanticism as the mythical pied piper had once lured the children of Hamlin, great indignation and flaming wrath broke out among the friends of freedom of thought and of Protestantism in Germany.

I have mentioned freedom of thought and Protantism together, but I hope that no one will accuse me of bias in favor of the latter, even though I belong to the Protestant Church in Germany. I have

62. See above, p. 6, note 12.
63. Neither Tieck nor Novalis ever became a Catholic. Carové attempted in his writings to introduce a uniform religion including both Catholics and Protestants.

mentioned freedom of thought and Protestantism together without any bias whatsoever; it is a fact that in Germany a friendly relationship exists between the two. In any case they are related to each other like mother and daughter. Although the Protestant Church is accused of much disastrous bigotry, one claim to immortal fame must be granted it: by permitting freedom of inquiry in the Christian faith and by liberating the minds of men from the yoke of authority, it enabled freedom of inquiry in general to take root in Germany and made it possible for science to develop independently. German philosophy, though it now puts itself on an equal basis with the Protestant Church or even above it, is nonetheless only its daughter; as such it always owes the mother a forbearing reverence, and affinity of interests required them to become allies when both were threatened by the common enemy, Jesuitism. All friends of freedom of thought and of the Protestant Church, the sceptics as well as the orthodox, rose up simultaneously against the restorers of Catholicism; and of course the liberals, who were not really concerned about the interests of philosophy or of the Protestant Church, but about the interests of middle-class freedom, likewise joined this opposition group. In Germany, however, the liberals had also always been, up to this time, academic philosophers and theologians, and it was always the same idea of freedom for which they fought, whether they were treating a purely political or a philosophical or a theological subject. This is shown very clearly in the life of the man who was undermining the Romantic School in Germany from its very beginning and contributed the most to overthrowing it. He is Johann Heinrich Voss.

He is completely unknown in France, and yet there are few men to whom the German people are more indebted for their intellectual development. After Lessing he is perhaps the greatest middle-class writer in German literature. At any rate, he was a great man and deserves a discussion that is not all too scanty.

The biography of the man is almost that of nearly every German writer of the old school. He was born in Mecklenburg in 1751 of poor parents, studied theology, neglected it after becoming acquainted with literature and the Greeks, applied himself seriously to both subjects, tutored to keep from starving, became a schoolteacher in Otterndorf in the district of Hadeln, translated the classics, and lived poor, frugal, and industrious to the age of seventy-five. He had a distinguished reputation among poets of the old school, but the modern Romantic poets constantly plucked at his laurel wreath and sneered profusely at decent, old-fashioned Voss, who, in unsophisticated language, even in Low German, had celebrated in verse the petty-bourgeois life on the Lower Elbe, who did not select medieval knights and madonnas as heroes of his works, but a simple, Protestant pastor and his virtuous family, and who was so thoroughly wholesome and middle-class and natural, whereas they, the modern troubadours, were so somnambulistically sickly, so chivalrously refined, and so brilliantly unnatural. How odious he must have been to Friedrich Schlegel, the ecstatic bard of the lasciviously romantic *Lucinde*,[64] this pedantic Voss with his chaste Luise and his venerable old Pastor of Grünau![65] Mr. August Wilhelm Schlegel, who never had such honorable intentions about lasciviousness and Catholicism as his brother, was able to get along much better with old Voss, and there existed between them merely a rivalry as translators, which, incidentally, was of great benefit to the German language. Even before the rise of the new school Voss had translated Homer; now he also translated, with incredible industry, the other pagan poets of antiquity, while Mr. A. W. Schlegel translated the Christian poets of the Romantic-Catholic age. The works of both were occasioned by an indirectly polemic purpose; Voss wanted to promote classical literature and ideas with his translations, whereas Mr. A. W. Schlegel wanted to make the Christian, Romantic poets accessible to the public in good translations for imitation and edification. Indeed, the antagonism even manifested itself in the linguistic forms of the two translators. While Mr. Schlegel polished his words ever more sweetly and fastidiously, Voss became ever more austere and blunt in his translations; his later efforts are almost unpronounceable because of the roughness filed into them; the result was that while the reader easily slips on the bright and smoothly polished mahogany parquet of Schlegel's verse, he stumbles just as easily over the versified marble blocks of old Voss. At last Voss, not to be outdone, decided that he too would translate Shakespeare, whom Mr. Schlegel had translated into German so excellently during his first period,

64. An erotic novel published in 1799 in which Schlegel earnestly, but inartistically, crusades against the "double standard."
65. Main characters in *Luise,* a popular epic idyll by Voss.

but old Voss suffered for this and his publisher even more, since the translation was an utter failure. Where Mr. Schlegel perhaps translates too smoothly and his verses are sometimes like whipped cream, so that you don't know, when you take them into your mouth, whether to eat them or drink them, Voss is hard as stone, and you risk breaking your jaw by reading his verses aloud. But precisely what distinguished Voss so sharply was the energy with which he struggled against all difficulties, and he struggled not only with the German language, but also with that Jesuitical, aristocratic monster which was then rearing its misshapen head from the forest-like darkness of German literature, and Voss dealt it a mighty wound.

Mr. Wolfgang Menzel,[66] a German writer who is known as one of the most bitter opponents of Voss, calls him a Low Saxon peasant. Despite the abusive intention, this designation is very suitable. Voss was, in fact, a Low Saxon peasant, just as Luther was; he was completely lacking in chivalry, knightly courtesy, and grace; he was a true descendant of that sturdily vigorous, strongly masculine German stock to whom Christianity had to be preached with fire and sword, who submitted to this religion only after losing three battles, who have still retained much of the Nordic pagan obstinacy in their customs and manners, and in their material and spiritual struggles show themselves to be as courageous and unyielding as their old gods. Indeed, when I look at Johann Heinrich Voss, his polemics and his whole character, I feel as if I were seeing old one-eyed Odin himself, who left his Asenburg to become a schoolteacher in Otterndorf in the district of Hadeln and who drilled Latin declensions and Christian catechism into the blond Holsteiners and in his free time translated the Greek poets into German, borrowing Thor's hammer to pound the verses into shape, and who, finally, disgusted with this tiresome business, hit poor Fritz Stolberg over the head with his hammer.

That was quite a well-known story. Count Friedrich von Stolberg was a poet of the old school and exceptionally famous in Germany,

---

66. Menzel, journalist and writer, was an extreme nationalist and an opponent of political liberalism. It was his attacks against the young writers who came to be known as "Young Germany" that were the chief occasion for the decree of 1835 prohibiting the publication of politically suspect writers and works. Heine himself suffered from the restrictions and in turn attacked Menzel more than once.

perhaps less because of his poetic talent than because of his aristocratic title, which at that time was worth more in German letters than it is today. But Fritz Stolberg was a liberal man, of noble heart, and he was a friend of those middle-class youths who founded a poetic school in Göttingen. I recommend that French literati read the preface to the poems of Hölty; here Johann Heinrich Voss portrays the idyllic community of the literary circle to which both he and Fritz Stolberg belonged. These two were finally the last remaining members from the original youthful throng of poets. When with an *éclat* Fritz Stolberg converted to Catholicism, abjuring reason and the love of liberty; when he became a propagator of obscurantism and even enticed many weak-willed fellows to follow his noble example; it was then that Johann Heinrich Voss, the seventy-year-old man, openly opposed his old friend by writing the pamphlet *How Did Fritz Stolberg Become Unfree?*. In it he analyzed Stolberg's entire life and showed how the aristocratic nature had always lay lurking and hidden in the amiable Count; how it gradually became more evident after the events of the French Revolution; how Stolberg furtively joined the so-called "Chain of Nobility," which endeavored to work against the French principles of freedom; how these nobles united with the Jesuits; how they thought to promote further the interests of the nobility by restoring Catholicism; and in general how they pursued the restoration of the Christian-Catholic, feudal Middle Ages as well as the demise of Protestant freedom of thought and the political middle-class. German democracy and German aristocracy, which before the revolution had fraternized in youthful ingenuousness—since the former had nothing to hope for and the latter had nothing to fear—now stood opposed as old men and fought to the death.

The part of the German public that did not understand the significance and the utter necessity of this struggle reprimanded poor Voss for his merciless disclosure of domestic circumstances, of minute occurrences that, after they were brought together, formed an incriminating whole. There were also the so-called refined souls, who, in all their sublimity, decried his narrow-minded punctiliousness and chastised poor Voss for idle prattle. Others—philistines who were concerned that someone could tear the veil off their own miserable existences as well—got their dander up about the injury to the literary convention, according to which all personal matters, all disclosures from the private life, are strictly prohibited. When at about this time Fritz Stolberg died and his death was attributed to grief from this affair; when after his death the *Pamphlet of Love* was published and in it he spoke of his poor blinded friend in a piously Christian, forgiving, genuinely Jesuit tone; then the tears of German sympathy flowed, then the German Hans sobbed his thickest tears. Much tender-hearted fury began to collect itself against poor Voss, and most invectives came from people for whose spiritual and material well-being Voss had entered the fray.

Generally in Germany you can count on the pity and the tearglands of the great multitude if you are soundly thrashed in a polemic. The Germans are like old women who never miss witnessing an execution, who push themselves forward as the most curious onlookers, but who yammer most bitterly at the sight of the poor sinner and his suffering, and even defend him. These female mourners who behave so compassionately at literary executions would be extremely annoyed, however, if the poor sinner whose flogging they await would be suddenly pardoned, and they would have to trudge home without having seen anything. Then an even greater wrath would fall upon those who disappointed their expectations.

Meantime the Voss polemic had a powerful impact on the public and turned public opinion against the increasing partiality for the Middle Ages. This polemic had aroused Germany; a large portion of the public declared itself unreservedly for Voss; a larger portion declared itself only for his cause. A war of pamphlets ensued, and the old man's last days were not a little embittered by these quarrels. He was dealing with the worst of opponents, with the clergy, who attacked him under all disguises. Not only the crypto-Catholics, but also the Pietists, the Quietists, the Lutheran mystics, in short, all the supernatural sects of the Protestant Church, which hold such very different opinions, nonetheless united with equally intense hatred for the Rationalist, Johann Heinrich Voss. In Germany one designates with this name those who recognize the rights of reason even in religion, in contrast to the supernaturalists, who in religious matters more or less renounced any recognition of reason. The latter, in their hatred of the poor rationalists, are like the insane in an insane asylum, who, though seized by the most antithetical lunacies, still get along fairly well with one another but are full of the most violent bitterness toward the person whom they regard as their common enemy, none other than the psychiatrist who is trying to restore their reason.

If the Romantic School was wrecked by the revelation to the general public of Catholic intrigues, it suffered at the same time a catastrophic protest within its own temple, and that from the lips of one of the gods whom they themselves had enshrined there. It was Wolfgang Goethe who stepped down from his pedestal and pronounced judgment on the Messers Schlegel, the very high priests who had enveloped him in such thick clouds of incense. His voice destroyed the entire phantasma; the ghosts of the Middle Ages fled; the owls crept back into the dark castle ruins; the ravens fluttered back to their old church towers; Friedrich Schlegel went to Vienna, where he attended mass every day and ate roast chicken; Mr. August Wilhelm Schlegel withdrew into Brahma's pagoda.[67]

Frankly speaking, Goethe played at that time a very ambiguous role, and it is impossible to praise him unreservedly. To be sure, the Schlegels never acted quite honestly with him. It may only have been because, in their polemic against the old school, they felt bound to set up a living poet as model and found no one more suitable than Goethe, also because they expected some literary assistance from him, that they built him an altar, burned incense to him, and bade the people to kneel before him. Then, too, he was their near neighbor. An avenue of lovely trees, with plums growing on them, connects Jena with Weimar; these plums taste very good when you are thirsty from the summer heat. The Schlegels traveled this road very often, and in Weimar they had many a conversation with Privy Councillor von Goethe, who was always a consummate diplomat and listened quietly to the Schlegels, smiled approvingly, sometimes gave them something to eat, did them other favors as well, and so on. They had also approached Schiller, but he was an honest man and would have nothing to do with them. The correspondence between him and Goethe, published three years ago,[68] throws considerable light on the relations of both poets to the Schlegels. Goethe dismissed them with a superior smile;

---

67. From 1818 on, when he became professor at the University of Bonn, A. W. Schlegel pursued his studies of Sanskrit.
68. 1828–29.

Schiller was annoyed at their impertinent scandal-mongering, at their habit of attracting attention by means of scandals, and he called them "show-offs."[69]

No matter how superior Goethe acted, he nonetheless owed the greatest part of his fame to the Schlegels. They introduced and promoted the study of his works. The disdainful, insulting manner in which he finally rejected these two men smacks very much of ingratitude. Perhaps Goethe, perceptive as he was, was angered because the Schlegels tried to use him only as a means to achieve their aims; perhaps these aims threatened to compromise him, the minister of state of a Protestant government; perhaps it was the ancient pagan divine wrath that awoke in him when he saw the covert Catholic machinations:—for just as Voss resembled the inflexible, one-eyed Odin, so Goethe resembled the mighty Jupiter in his figure and in his thinking. To be sure, Voss had to bang hard with Thor's hammer; Goethe had only to shake his head with its ambrosian locks indignantly, and the Schlegels trembled and slunk away. A public document of this protest by Goethe appeared in the second number of a journal edited by him, *Kunst und Altertum,* and it bore the title "Concerning Christian Patriotic Modern German Art." This article was, as it were, Goethe's 18th Brumaire[70] in German literature, for by so rudely driving the Schlegels out of the temple, by attracting many of their most enthusiastic disciples to himself, and receiving the acclamations of the public, to which the Schlegels' Directory had long since been an abomination, he established his absolute monarchy in German literature. From this moment on nothing more was heard of the Messers Schlegel; only now and then were they mentioned, as one now speaks occasionally of Barras or Gohier;[71] people no longer talked about Romanticism and classical literature, but about Goethe, and then Goethe all over again. Meanwhile, to be sure, several poets appeared on the scene who were not greatly inferior to Goethe in power and imagination, but out of courtesy they

69. Schiller used the word *Laffen* only in reference to Friedrich Schlegel.

70. On November 9 (18th Brumaire) Napoleon, with the help of some members of the Directory, carried out a *coup d'état* against the government of the Directory and established the government of the Consulate.

71. Paul Jean François Nicolas, Count of Barras (1755–1829), and Louis Jérôme Gohier (1746–1830), members of the French Directory.

recognized him as their sovereign, surrounded him admiringly, kissed his hand, and knelt before him. These grandees of Parnassus were distinguished from the great masses, however, by being allowed to keep their laurel wreaths on their heads even in Goethe's presence. Occasionally they opposed him, but they became angry when any lesser person considered himself justified in criticizing Goethe. However angry aristocrats are at their sovereign, they still become annoyed if the rabble also revolts against him. And during the last two decades the intellectual aristocrats in Germany had very just grounds for being angry at Goethe. As I myself stated publicly at that time, with plenty of bitterness, Goethe resembles the Louis XI who oppressed the nobility and exalted the *tiers état*.[72]

It was disgusting that Goethe was afraid of any writer with originality and praised and eulogized all the insignificant nobodies. He carried such praise so far that at last it was considered a testimonial of mediocrity to have been praised by Goethe.

I shall discuss later the new poets who appeared during Goethe's reign as Emperor. They are still saplings whose trunks are only now showing their size since the fall of the centennial oak whose branches towered far above them and overshadowed them.

As I have already said, there was no lack of an opposition declaiming bitterly against Goethe, that mighty tree. People of the most conflicting opinions united in this opposition. The traditionalists, the orthodox party, were annoyed at finding in the trunk of the great tree no niche with a saint's image and at discovering that the naked dryads of paganism were actually carrying on their witchery in it, and, like Saint Boniface, they would have liked to take the consecrated axe and fell this ancient magic oak. The moderns, the followers of liberalism, on the other hand, were annoyed that this tree could not be used as a liberty tree, least of all as a barricade. Indeed the tree was too tall; you couldn't hang a red cap on its top and dance the carmagnole beneath it.[73] The general public, however, revered the tree just because it was so magnificent in its independence, because it filled the whole world so sweetly with its fragrance, because its branches towered so

72. Third Estate.
73. A popular song and dance at the time of the first French Revolution.

splendidly right up into the heavens that the stars seemed to be merely the golden fruits of the grand and wondrous tree.

The opposition to Goethe really began with the appearance of the so-called spurious *Wanderjahre,* which were published by the firm of Gottfried Basse in Quedlinburg in 1821, hence shortly after the decline of the Schlegels, under the title *Wilhelm Meisters Wanderjahre.*[74] Goethe had already announced, under this very title, a sequel to *Wilhelm Meister's Apprenticeship,* and oddly enough this sequel appeared at the same time as its literary double, in which not only Goethe's style was imitated, but also the hero of Goethe's original novel figured as one of the characters. This parody gave evidence not so much of great intellectual powers as of great discretion, and since the author managed for some time to preserve his anonymity, and people tried in vain to guess his identity, the interest of the public was artfully heightened still more. It came out at last that the author was a hitherto unknown country parson by the name of "Pustkuchen,"[75] which in French means *omelette soufflée,* a name which also characterized his entire person. The book was nothing but the old Pietistic sourdough, puffed out with the help of esthetic techniques. Goethe was reproached by the writer for having no moral purpose in his writings, for not being able to create noble characters, but only vulgar ones, whereas Schiller had represented characters most noble in their ideals and was thus a greater poet.

This last statement, that Schiller was greater than Goethe, was the particular controversial point the book raised. A mania developed for comparing the works of the two poets, and opinions were divided. The Schiller faction boasted of the moral grandeur of a Max Piccolomini, of a Thekla,[76] of a Marquis Posa,[77] and of others among Schiller's dramatic heroes, whereas they declared Goethe's characters, a Philine,[78] a Käthchen,[79] a Klärchen,[80] and other such

74. The translation of *Wanderjahre* as *Years of Travel* is a distortion of the meaning, hence the retention of the German title.
75. Johann Friedrich Wilhelm Pustkuchen-Glanzow (1793–1834), a Lutheran minister and writer, produced several parodistic sequels to Goethe's first novel about Wilhelm Meister.
76. Characters in Schiller's tetralogy *Wallenstein.*
77. A character in *Don Carlos.*
78. A character in *Wilhelm Meister's Apprenticeship.*

lovely creatures to be immoral hussies. The Goethe faction remarked with a smile that these heroines could hardly be defended as moral, nor Goethe's heroes either, but that the promotion of morality, which was being demanded of Goethe's works, was by no means the purpose of art; in art there were no purposes, just as in the universe itself, where only man had read into it the concepts of ends and means; art, like the world, existed for its own sake, and just as the world forever remains the same, despite the constant change of man's views in his judgment of it, so art too must remain independent of the transient opinions of mankind; hence art must remain particularly independent of morality, which is constantly changing on earth as often as a new religion arises and supplants the old religion. In fact, since a new religion always appears in the world in the course of a few centuries and, passing over into life and manners, establishes itself as a new morality, every age would charge the art works of the past with moral heresy if these were judged by the standard of current morality. As we have seen in real life, good Christians, who damn the flesh as the realm of the devil, always take offense at the sight of the statues of Greek deities; chaste monks tied an apron around ancient Venus; even in recent times a ridiculous fig leaf has been pasted on naked statues; a pious Quaker sacrificed his entire fortune to buy up and burn the most beautiful paintings by Giulio Romano—for this he truly deserves to go to heaven where he should be beaten daily with a switch. A religion, for instance, that found God only in matter, and hence regarded only the flesh as divine, would perforce, in passing over into life and manners, produce a code of morals according to which only those art works were praiseworthy which glorify the flesh, and the Christian art works, which represent only the vanity of the flesh, would be rejected as immoral. Indeed, art works that in one country can be regarded as moral, can be considered immoral in another country where a different religion has merged into the national manners and customs; for example, our plastic arts arouse disgust in a strictly orthodox Moslem, while many arts which are considered completely innocent in the harems of the Orient are an abomination to a Christian. Since in India the

---

79. Heine must mean Gretchen in Goethe's *Faust.*
80. In Goethe's *Egmont.*

position of a Bajadere is not condemned by the moral code, *Vasantaséná*,[81] a play whose heroine is a prostitute, is not considered immoral at all, but if one ventured to produce this play in the *Théâtre Français*, the whole orchestra floor would howl about immorality, the same audience that watches every day with pleasure the plays of intrigue, whose heroines are young widows who marry happily in the end instead of burning with their deceased husbands, as Indian morality requires.

By proceeding from such a point of view the Goetheans regard art as an independent second world which they rank so highly that all activities of human beings—their religion, and their morality—course along below it, changing and changeable. I cannot, however, subscribe unconditionally to this point of view; because of it the Goetheans allowed themselves to be misled into proclaiming the supremacy of art and turning away from the demands of that original real world which, after all, must take precedence.

Schiller attached himself to this original world much more firmly than Goethe, and we must praise him for this. The spirit of his age took strong hold of him, Friedrich Schiller, he wrestled with it, was conquered by it, followed it to battle, bore its banner, and it was the same banner under which those on the other side of the Rhine fought so enthusiastically and for which we are still ready to shed our best blood. Schiller wrote for the great ideas of the Revolution; he destroyed the Bastilles of the intellectual and spiritual world; he helped to build the temple of liberty, that very great temple which is to embrace all nations like a single community of brothers; he was a cosmopolitan. He began with the hatred for the past which we see in *The Robbers*,[82] where he resembles a young Titan who has run away from school, gotten drunk, and smashes Jupiter's windows. He ended with that love for the future which bursts into blossom like a forest of flowers as early as *Don Carlos*, and he himself is the Marquis Posa who is both prophet and soldier, who also fights for what he prophesies and under his Spanish cloak bears the noblest heart that ever loved and suffered in Germany.

A poet, the small imitator of the Creator, also resembles the good Lord in that he creates his characters after his own image.

81. Not the title of the play, but an important character in an Indian play entitled *Mricchakatika (The Clay Cart)* by Sudrakā.
82. Schiller's first play.

Hence if Karl Moor[83] and Marquis Posa are Schiller to the life, Goethe resembles his Werther, his Wilhelm Meister, and his Faust, and in them one can study the various phases of his genius. Schiller threw himself heart and soul into history, became enthusiastic about the social progress of mankind, and wrote about world history; Goethe tended to become absorbed in the emotions of the individual, or in art, or in nature. It was inevitable that in the end Goethe, the pantheist, occupied himself with natural history as his chief study and gave us the results of his investigations not merely in literary, but also in scientific works. His indifferentism was likewise the result of his pantheistic philosophy of life.

Unfortunately it is true—we must admit it—that pantheism has not rarely turned people into indifferentists. They thought if everything is God, it does not matter what we concern ourselves with, whether with clouds or with antique gems, whether with folksongs or with the bones of apes, whether with human beings or with actors. But herein lies the fallacy; everything is not God, but God is everything. God does not manifest Himself in like manner in all things; on the contrary, He manifests Himself in various degrees in the various things, and each bears within it the urge to attain a higher degree of divinity; and this is the great law of progress in nature. The recognition of this law, most profoundly revealed by the Saint-Simonists, transforms pantheism into a philosophy of life which certainly does not lead to indifferentism but to forging ahead by means of the most passionate self-sacrifice. No, God does not manifest Himself equally in all things as Wolfgang Goethe believed, an opinion which made of him an indifferentist occupied only with the toys of art, anatomy, the theory of colors, botany, and observations of clouds, instead of with the loftiest concerns of mankind. God manifests Himself in things to a greater or lesser degree; He exists in this continual manifestation; God is to be found in movement, in action, in time; His sacred breath wafts through the pages of history, and history is the real book of God. Friedrich Schiller sensed this and became a "prophet in retrospect,"[84] and he wrote *The Defection of the Netherlands, The Thirty-Years' War,* and *The Maid of Orleans* and *Tell.*[85]

83. The hero of *The Robbers.*
84. From Friedrich Schlegel's *Atheneum* fragment no. 80: *Der Historiker ist ein rückwärts gekehrter Prophet* (The historian is a prophet in retrospect).
85. Schiller's play *Wilhelm Tell.*

To be sure, Goethe also celebrated some great histories of emancipation, but he celebrated them as an artist. Since he irritatedly rejected Christian fervor, which was odious to him, and did not understand or did not want to understand the philosophical fervor of our time simply for fear of being wrenched away from his placid self-composure, he treated fervor in general as completely historical, as something given, as material to be dealt with; in his hands spirit turned to matter, and he gave it beautiful, pleasing form. Thus he became the greatest artist in our literature, and everything he wrote became a perfectly rounded work of art.

The master's example governed the disciples, and there began in Germany that literary period which I once characterized as the "Age of Art" and whose harmful influence on the political development of the German people I demonstrated. I did not deny, however, in so doing, the intrinsic merit of Goethe's masterpieces. They adorn our dear fatherland as beautiful statues adorn a garden, but they are, after all, statues. You can fall in love with them, but they are sterile; Goethe's works do not beget deeds as do Schiller's. A deed is the child of the word, and Goethe's beautiful words are childless. This is the curse on everything that has originated in art alone. The statue that Pygmalion made was a beautiful woman, even the artist fell in love with her, she came to life from his kisses, but as far as we know she never had children. I believe Mr. Charles Nodier[86] once said something similar in this connection, and I was reminded of it yesterday when, wandering through the lower halls of the Louvre, I looked at the ancient statues of the gods. There they stood with their blank white eyes, a secret melancholy in their marble smiles, perhaps a sad recollection of Egypt, the land of the dead, from which they came, or painful longing for life, from which they have now been crowded out by other deities, or even sorrow at their lifeless immortality:—they seem to await the word that will bring them back to life, that will release them from their cold, rigid immovability. Strange! These antiquities reminded me of Goethe's works, which are just as perfect, just as magnificent, just as serene, and also seem to feel with melancholy that their rigidity and coldness separate them from the stir and warmth of

---

86. A prolific French writer (1780–1844) who imitated Goethe's *Werther* in several novels and even tried his hand at a *Faust*.

modern life, that they cannot suffer and rejoice with us, that they are not human, but unfortunate half-breeds of divinity and stone. These few hints will explain the animosity of the various groups in Germany who have been clamoring against Goethe. The Orthodox were indignant at the great pagan, as Goethe is commonly called in Germany; they feared his influence on the people, whom he imbued with his philosophy of life by pleasant writings, even by the most unpretentious little lyric; they saw in him the most dangerous enemy of the Cross, which, as he said, was as repulsive to him as bedbugs, garlic, and tobacco. For this is the approximate wording of the epigram that Goethe dared to utter right in Germany, in the country where these vermin, garlic, tobacco, and the Cross, rule everywhere in Holy Alliance. It was not this aspect of Goethe, however, which displeased us, the men of the movement.[87] As I have already said, we condemned the sterility of his writing, the sphere of art which he fostered in Germany, which had a quietive effect on German youth, and which frustrated the political regeneration of our fatherland. Thus the indifferent pantheist was attacked from the most opposite quarters. The extreme Right and the extreme Left (to borrow the French phrase) joined forces against him, and while the blackcoated priests attacked him with the Crucifix, the raging sansculottes charged him at the same time with their pikes. Mr. Wolfgang Menzel, who led the battle against Goethe with a display of wit worthy of a better cause, did not exhibit so one-sidedly in his polemic the spiritual Christian or the dissatisfied patriot, but based his attacks in part on the last dicta of Friedrich Schlegel, who after his fall, from the depths of his Catholic cathedral, cried out his lament over Goethe, over the Goethe "whose poetry had no central focus." Mr. Menzel went even further and proved that Goethe was not a genius but merely a man of talent, he eulogized Schiller as contrast, and so on. This happened some time before the July Revolution. Mr. Menzel was then the greatest admirer of the Middle Ages, both of the art works and of the institutions of the period; he reviled Johann Heinrich

87. Heine is not referring to any special political action. He is thinking of the liberals among his, the younger generation, who were not organized into a party but who shared with each other certain liberal ideas.

Voss with unceasing fury and praised Mr. Joseph Görres[88] with incredible enthusiasm. His hatred of Goethe was thus genuine, and he wrote against him from conviction and not, as many thought, in order to gain notoriety. I myself was at that time an opponent of Goethe, but I was displeased by the harshness with which Mr. Menzel criticized him, and I deplored this lack of reverence. My comment was that Goethe was still the king of our literature, and that if the critics knifed him, they should at least not be found wanting in the courtesy like that shown by the executioner who had to behead Charles I and, before performing his office, knelt down before the king and requested his royal pardon.

Among the adversaries of Goethe numbered also the famous Privy Councillor Müllner and his only remaining loyal friend, Professor Schütz, son of the older Schütz. A few others, whose names are less famous, for example, a certain Mr. Spaun, who was imprisoned for a long time because of political crimes, belonged to the public opponents of Goethe. Just between us, it was a rather mixed group. What was propounded I have already indicated in sufficient detail; it is more difficult to divine the particular motives which may have moved each individual to voice publicly his anti-Goethean convictions. I know the motives of only one person exactly, and since I here refer to myself, I shall honestly confess: it was envy. To my credit, however, I should mention that I never attacked the poet in Goethe, only the man. I have never found fault with his works. I have never been able to find defects in them, as have those critics who have even detected moon spots with their finely cut lenses.—These sharp-sighted people! What they took for spots are blossoming forests, sublime peaks, and laughing valleys.

Nothing is sillier than the disparagement of Goethe in favor of Schiller, towards whom the critics' intentions were by no means honorable and whom they praised all along in order to degrade Goethe. Or did people really not know that those much praised, much idealized characters, those altar-pieces of virtue and morality,

88. Joseph von Görres (1776–1848), a Catholic writer and journalist. In the beginning he supported the French Revolution, but later turned against it and became a liberal nationalist with an intense dislike for Napoleon. From 1814–1816 he edited *Der Rheinische Merkur*, the most influential paper in Germany as long as he was editor. In later years he took up the cause of ultramontanism, and his liberal views and activities of the earlier years were neglected or forgotten.

which Schiller undertook, were far easier to create than the sinful, provincial, imperfect beings which Goethe lets us see in his works? Don't they know that mediocre painters usually daub life-sized saints' pictures on the canvas, but that only a great master can paint a Spanish beggar lad delousing himself, a Dutch peasant vomiting or having a tooth pulled, and ugly old women as we see them in small Dutch miniatures, true to life and technically perfect? It is far easier to portray grand and terrible subjects in art than tiny, trivial things. Egyptian magicians were able to imitate many of Moses' feats, for instance, the snakes, the blood, even the frogs, but when he produced seemingly far easier magic things, namely, vermin, they admitted their powerlessness, and they could not copy the tiny vermin, and they said, "This is the finger of God." Go ahead and scold about the vulgarities in *Faust,* about the scenes on the Brocken,[89] in Auerbach's tavern, scold about the dissoluteness in *Meister*[90]—you still can't imitate any of it. This is the finger of Goethe! But you don't want to imitate it anyway and I hear you declare with disgust, "We are not wizards, we are good Christians." That you are not wizards I already know.

Goethe's greatest merit is precisely the perfection of everything he creates. There are no passages that are powerful while others are weak; no portion is portrayed in detail while another was merely sketched; there is no bungling, no conventional padding, no predilection for details. He treats every character in his novels and plays, wherever he appears, as if he were the protagonist. So it is also in Homer and in Shakespeare. There are actually no secondary characters in the works of any great poet; every character is the leading figure in its province. Such poets are like absolute monarchs, who attribute no individual value to human beings but who themselves, at their own discretion, award them their highest value. When a French ambassador once mentioned to Emperor Paul of Russia that an important person in his kingdom was interested in a certain matter, the Emperor interrupted him sternly with the remarkable words, "In this kingdom there is no person of importance except him with whom I am speaking at the moment, and he is important only so long as I speak with him." An absolute

89. A mountain in the Harz, where the Walpurgisnacht scene in *Faust* takes place.
90. The novel *Wilhelm Meister's Apprenticeship.*

poet, who has also received his power by God's grace, likewise regards as the most important that person in his spirit-world whom he allows to speak at the moment, about whom he is just writing, and out of such artistic despotism arises that wonderful perfection of the most minor figures in the works of Homer, Shakespeare, and Goethe.

I may have spoken somewhat harshly about Goethe's opponents, but I could say even harsher things about his apologists. In their zeal most of them have uttered still greater nonsense. In this regard a certain Mr. Eckermann approaches the point of the ridiculous, although he is not completely without intellect. In the struggle against Mr. Pustkuchen, Karl Immermann, now our greatest playwright, earned his critical spurs; he brought out a brilliant piece against him. In the main, people from Berlin have excelled in this activity. The most significant champion of Goethe was at all times Varnhagen von Ense, a man who bears in his heart thoughts which are as great as the world and who expresses them in words that are as precious and elegant as finely cut gems. He is the eminent intellect whose judgment Goethe respects most.—It is perhaps useful to mention here that Mr. Wilhelm von Humboldt had already written an excellent book about Goethe at an earlier date. During the last ten years the Leipzig fair has produced several works about Goethe. Mr. Schubarth's studies of Goethe are curiosities of high criticism. Mr. Häring, who writes under the name Willibald Alexis, has published significant and clever pieces about Goethe in various journals. A professor from Hamburg, Mr. Zimmermann, has pronounced the most superb judgments about Goethe in his lectures, and although they are encountered rather sparingly, they are all the more profoundly strewn throughout his dramaturgical writings. Lectures on Goethe were given at various German universities, and of all his works it was chiefly *Faust* with which the public concerned itself. Sequels and commentaries were often written, and it became the secular Bible of the Germans.

I would not be a German if, at the mention of *Faust,* I did not express some explanatory ideas about it. From the greatest thinker to the most insignificant writer, from the philosopher down to the doctor of philosophy, everyone exercises his ingenuity on this book. But it is actually just as comprehensive as the Bible, and like the Bible it includes Heaven and earth and humanity and human exegesis. The subject matter is the main reason why *Faust* is so popular. It is proof of Goethe's unconscious profundity, of his genius, which was always able to seize on the most familiar theme and the right one, that he sought out this subject matter in folk legends. I can safely assume that the content of *Faust* is well known, for the book has recently become famous even in France. But I do not know whether the old folk tale itself is known here, whether in this country too a dingy volume of blotting-paper, poorly printed, and decorated with crude woodcuts, is sold at the annual fairs, a book in which can be read the full story of how the arch-sorcerer Johannes Faustus, a learned doctor who had studied all branches of knowledge, finally cast aside his books and made a pact with the devil by which he could enjoy all the sensuous pleasures of earth, but then had to surrender his soul to destruction in Hell.[91] In the Middle Ages the common people always attributed any great intellectual power, wherever they saw it, to a pact with the devil, and Albertus Magnus, Raimund Lullus, Theophrastus Paracelsus, Agrippa von Nettesheim, even Roger Bacon in England, were regarded as magicians, necromancers, and exorcists. But far stranger things are told about Doctor Faustus, who demanded of the devil not merely the knowledge of phenomena but also the most substantial pleasures, and this is the very same Faust who invented printing[92] and who lived at the time when people were beginning to preach against the rigid authority of the Church and to do independent research, so that with Faust the medieval age of faith ends and the modern critical age of science begins. It is indeed significant that the Reformation began precisely at the time when, according to popular belief, Faust lived, and that he himself should have invented the art which procured for science the victory over faith, namely, printing, an art which, however, also deprived us of the Catholic peace of mind and plunged us into doubts and revolutions—someone other than myself might say "and finally

91. This type of version of the Faust legend was preceded by earlier versions, the first printed in 1587. Another appeared at the end of the sixteenth century, was re-edited in the following century, and this in turn was re-worked and published early in the eighteenth century and formed the basis for the popular version to which Heine refers.
92. A reference to the assumption, for a time widely accepted as a fact, that Faust and Gutenberg's partner Fust were one and the same person. This theory has long since been disproved.

delivered us into the power of the devil." But no, knowledge, the perception of things by means of reason, science, gives us in the end the pleasures which faith, Catholic Christianity, has for so long cheated us of. We realize that human beings are called to equality, not only in Heaven, but also on earth; political brotherhood, preached to us by philosophy, is more salutary for us than purely spiritual brotherhood, which Christianity has helped us to obtain; and knowledge becomes word, and word becomes deed, and we can still enjoy bliss on earth during our own lifetime. If in addition we then partake of heavenly bliss after death, as Christianity so firmly promises us, we will be very pleased.

In profound contemplation the German people has already suspected this for a long time; for the German people is itself that learned Doctor Faust. It is itself that spiritualist who through the spirit finally understood the insufficiency of the spirit and demanded material pleasures, restoring the rights of the flesh.—Yet still ensnarled in the symbolism of Catholic poetry, where God is considered a representative of the spirit and the devil a representative of the flesh, that rehabilitation of the flesh was designated as a fall from God, as a union with the devil.

But it will still require some time until the fulfillment of what was prophesied in that poem with such profound contemplation occurs for the German people; before it recognizes with its spirit the usurpations of the spirit and vindicates the rights of the flesh. That will be the Revolution, the great daughter of the Reformation.

Less well-known here in France than *Faust* is Goethe's *Westöstlicher Divan,* a later work which Madame de Staël did not know yet[93] and which we must here mention particularly. It contains, in bright lyrics and pithy gnomic poems, the Oriental manner of thought and feeling; and there is a fragrance and a glow in the book like a harem full of amorous odalisks with black, rouged, gazelle-like eyes and passionate white arms. For the reader it seems as vividly sensual as it was for the unfortunate Gaspard Debüreau, when he stood on a ladder in Constantinople and saw *de haut en*

---

93. It was first published in 1819, six years after Mme. de Staël's book on Germany. The chief literary inspiration for this book of poetry was the Persian poet Hafis, whose work Goethe became acquainted with, in translation, in 1813. There is no good English translation of the title; it means a collection of poems combining Occidental and Oriental characteristics.

bas what the ruler of the faithful is only accustomed to seeing *de bas en haut.* Sometimes the reader even seems to be stretched out comfortably on a Persian carpet, smoking the golden tobacco of Turkistan from a long-stemmed water pipe, while a black slave woman cools him with a colorful fan of peacock feathers and a handsome lad reaches him a cup of genuine mocha coffee. Here Goethe put the most intoxicating enjoyment of life into verse so light, so fortunate, so aery, so ethereal that one is amazed that such a thing was possible in the German language. In addition, he also gives in prose the most delightful commentaries on customs and activities in the Orient, on the patriarchal life of the Arabs; and while doing so, Goethe is always smiling serenely and is as innocent as a child and as full of wisdom as an old man. The prose is as transparent as the green sea on a bright summer afternoon with no wind, when one can look down quite clearly into the depths where sunken cities with their forgotten splendors become visible; but sometimes the prose is also as magical, as prescient as the sky at twilight, and Goethe's great thoughts then stand out, pure and golden as the stars. The magic of this book defies description; it is a *salaam* sent by the Occident to the Orient, and there are strange flowers in it: sensuous red roses, hortensias like the naked white bosoms of young girls, droll snapdragons, purple foxgloves like long fingers, twisted crocus noses, and in the center, snugly protected, modest German violets. After he had expressed in *Faust* his discontent with abstract intellectuality and his longing for real pleasures, Goethe threw himself heart and soul, as it were, into the arms of sensualism by writing the *Westöstlicher Divan.*

Hence it is very significant that this work appeared soon after *Faust.*[94] It was Goethe's last phase and his example exercised a great influence on literature. Our lyricists now celebrated the Orient in song.—It may also be worth mentioning that while celebrating Persia and Arabia so joyously, Goethe expressed the most decided repugnance for India. He disliked in this country the grotesque, the disorder, the lack of clarity, and this antipathy may have arisen because he suspected Catholic wile in the Sanskrit studies of the Schlegels and their friends. For these gentlemen regarded Hindustan

---

94. Heine is referring to the publication of *Faust, Part I,* in 1808. *Part II* did not appear in entirety until 1832.

as the cradle of the Catholic world order; they saw there the model for their hierarchy; they found there their trinity, their incarnation, their penance, their atonement, their mortification of the flesh, and all their other beloved manias. Goethe's antipathy toward India irritated these people not a little, and Mr. August Wilhelm Schlegel called him with glassy anger "a pagan converted to Mohammedanism."

Among the writings about Goethe which have appeared this year, a posthumous work by Johannes Falk, *A Portrait of Goethe Drawn from Close Personal Association,*[95] deserves very laudatory mention. Besides a detailed discussion of *Faust* (which could not be omitted!), the author has given us in this book the most excellent accounts of Goethe, showing him to us in all his relationships, completely true to life, completely objective, with all his virtues and defects. Here we see Goethe in relation to his mother, whose temperament is so wonderfully reflected in her son; we see him as natural scientist, observing a caterpillar that has spun itself a cocoon and will burst out as a butterfly; we see him in connection with the great Herder, who was seriously angry at the indifference with which Goethe ignored the emergence of mankind itself from its cocoon; we see him sitting among fair-haired ladies-in-waiting at the court of the Grand Duke of Weimar, improvising merrily like Apollo among King Admetus' sheep; we see him again as, with the haughtiness of a Dalai Lama, he refused to recognize Kotzebue; we see how the latter, in order to disparage Goethe, arranged a public celebration in Schiller's honor;[96]—everywhere, however, we see him wise, handsome, lovable, a charmingly refreshing figure, resembling the immortal gods.

As a matter of fact, one found in Goethe the complete harmony between personality and genius that one expects in extraordinary persons. His outward appearance was just as distinctive as the words that lived in his writings; even his figure was harmonious, clear, joyous, nobly proportioned, and you could study Greek art in him just as in a classical statue. This majestic form was never contorted by groveling Christian humility; the features of this countenance were not disfigured by Christian contrition; these eyes

95. Published in 1832. Heine had translated part of the book for the French reading public.
96. Goethe and Schiller joined forces to prevent this celebration.

were not downcast with a Christian sense of sin, not over-pious and canting, not swimming with emotion:—no, his eyes were as calm as a god's. For it is a universal characteristic of the gods that their gaze is steady and their eyes do not twitch back and forth uncertainly. Therefore, when Agni, Varuna, Yama, and Indra assume the form of Nala at Damayanti's wedding, she recognizes her lover by the wink of his eye, since, as I said, the eyes of gods are always steady. Napoleon's eyes also had this feature. Hence I am convinced that he was a god. Goethe's eyes remained just as godly in his old age as in his youth. To be sure, time could cover his head with snow but could not bend it. He always held it proud and high, and when he spoke he became taller and taller, and when he stretched out his hand it was as if with his finger he could prescribe to the stars in the sky the course they should travel. Some claim to have noticed a cold expression of egoism about his mouth, but even this expression is characteristic of the immortal gods and especially so of the father of the gods, the great Jupiter, to whom I have already compared Goethe. I assure you, when I visited him in Weimar[97] and stood face to face with him, I involuntarily glanced to the side, thinking to see beside him the eagle with lightning in his beak. I was about to address him in Greek, but noticing that he understood German, I told him in German that the plums along the road between Jena and Weimar tasted very good. During so many long winter nights I had thought about how many lofty and profound things I would say to Goethe if I ever saw him. And when at last I saw him, I told him that Saxon plums tasted very good. And Goethe smiled. He smiled with the very lips with which he had once kissed the beautiful Leda, Europa, Danaë, Semele, and so many other princesses or even ordinary nymphs—

Les dieux s'en vont.[98] Goethe is dead. He died on March 22 of last year, the momentous year when our earth lost its greatest names. It is as if in this year Death suddenly became an aristocrat, as if he wanted to distinguish particularly the notables of this earth by sending them to the grave at the same time. It is even possible that he wanted to establish a peerage in the other world, in Hades,

97. Heine saw Goethe only once, in the autumn of 1824 after his tour of the Harz mountains. Needless to say, the account given here bears no resemblance to what actually took place at the meeting.
98. The gods are dying.

and in that case his *fournée*[99] was very well chosen. Or, on the contrary, did Death try last year to favor democracy by destroying with the great names their authority as well and promoting intellectual equality? Was respect or insolence the reason why Death spared the kings in the past year? He had absentmindedly raised his scythe against the King of Spain,[100] but changed his mind in time and let him live. Last year not a single king died. *Les dieux s'en vont;*—but we keep the kings.

BOOK TWO

I

With the conscientiousness which I have strictly prescribed for myself, I must mention here that several Frenchmen have complained that my criticism of the Schlegels, especially Mr. August Wilhelm, has been much too harsh. I believe, however, that such a complaint would not occur if people here were better acquainted with the history of German literature. Many Frenchmen know Mr. A. W. Schlegel only from the book by Madame de Staël, his noble patroness. Most of them know only his name, and this name rings in their memory like something venerably famous, such as, for example, the name Osiris, about whom they also know only that he is a peculiar freak of a god who was worshipped in Egypt. About the other points of similarity between Mr. A. W. Schlegel and Osiris they know absolutely nothing.

Since I was once a student of the elder Schlegel at the university, one might think I owed him a certain forbearance. But did Mr. A. W. Schlegel spare old Bürger,[101] his literary father? No, and he

99. Group of people.
100. King Ferdinand VII became seriously ill in 1832 but did not die until the following year.
101. When Schlegel studied at Göttingen in 1786–88, he was aided and encouraged in his own career by Gottfried August Bürger, then a professor at the university and also a poet of some contemporary renown. He was known chiefly for his ballads, of which "Lenore" became by far the most famous. It was not Schlegel's critique of Bürger's work which gave Bürger the *coup de grâce* as a writer but Schiller's scathing article published in 1791.

acted according to custom and tradition. For in literature, as in the forests of the North American Indians, fathers are killed by their sons as soon as they have become old and feeble.

I have already remarked in the preceding section that Friedrich Schlegel was more important than Mr. August Wilhelm, and indeed the latter lived only on his brother's ideas and understood only the art of developing these ideas. Fr. Schlegel was a man of profound mind. He recognized all the glories of the past, and he felt all the sufferings of the present. But he did not understand the sacredness of these sufferings and the necessity of them for the future salvation of the world. He saw the sun going down and gazed sadly at the spot of its setting and lamented the nocturnal darkness that he saw approaching; and he did not notice that a new dawn was gleaming from the opposite direction. Fr. Schlegel once called the historian "a prophet in retrospect." This expression is the best description of Schlegel himself. He hated the present, the future frightened him, and his inspired, prophetic gaze penetrated only into the past, which he loved.

Poor Fr. Schlegel, he did not see in the sufferings of our time the sufferings of rebirth but the agony of dying, and from fear of death he fled to the tottering ruins of the Catholic Church. After all, it was the most suitable refuge for a man of his temperament. He had enjoyed considerable cheerful abandon in his life, but he considered this sinful, a sin which required subsequent expiation, and the author of *Lucinde* had of necessity to become a Catholic.

Lucinde is a novel, and except for his poems and an adaptation of a Spanish play, *Alarkos*,[102] it is the only original work Fr. Schlegel left behind. In its day there was no lack of eulogists of the novel. The present Right Reverend Mr. Schleiermacher[103] published enthusiastic letters about *Lucinde*. There was not even any lack of critics who praised this work and prophesied confidently that it would one day be considered the best book in German literature. The authorities should have arrested these people, just as in Russia the prophets who prophesy a public catastrophe are locked up until their prophecy has been fulfilled. No, the gods have preserved our literature from such a misfortune. Schlegel's novel was soon

102. *Lucinde* appeared in 1799. *Alarkos* in 1802.
103. Friedrich Schleiermacher (1768–1834), the most important Protestant theologian of German Romanticism.

generally condemned because of its dissolute inanity and is now
forgotten. Lucinde is the name of the heroine, a sensual, witty
woman or, rather, a mixture of sensuality and wit. Her worst fault
is simply that she is not a woman but an unpleasant combination
of two abstractions, wit and sensuality. May the Blessed Virgin
forgive the author for having written this book; the Muses will
never forgive him.

A similar novel called *Florentin* is mistakenly attributed to the
late Schlegel. They say this book is by his wife, a daughter of the
famous Moses Mendelssohn, whom he took away from her first
husband and who went over with him to the Roman Catholic
Church.

I believe that Fr. Schlegel was serious about Catholicism. I do
not believe this of many of his friends. In such matters it is very
difficult to ascertain the truth. Religion and hypocrisy are twin
sisters, and the two look so alike that sometimes they cannot be
distinguished. The same figure, clothing, and speech. Except that
the second of the two sisters drawls out the words somewhat more
melodiously and repeats the little word "love" more often.—I am
speaking of Germany; in France the one sister has died, and we
see the other still in deepest mourning.

After the appearance of Madame de Staël's *De l'Allemagne* Fr.
Schlegel presented the public with two more large works, which
are perhaps his best and in any case deserve very laudatory mention.
They are his *Wisdom and Language of India*[104] and his *Lectures
on the History of Literature.*[105] With the former book he not only
introduced the study of Sanskrit into Germany but also founded
it. He became for Germany what William Jones[106] was for England.
He had learned Sanskrit with great ingenuity, and the few fragments
which he gives in this book are skillfully translated. With his
profound powers of intuition he recognized perfectly the significance
of the Indian epic meter, the *sloka,*[107] which flows along as broad

104. *Concerning the Language and Wisdom of India,* published in 1808.
105. Published in 1815. Heine does not use the exact title which, translated, was
History of Ancient and Modern Literature. The content consists of lectures given
in Vienna in 1812.
106. Sir William Jones (1746–1794) was the actual founder of Sanskrit studies,
beginning with a translation of *Sakuntala* in 1789.
107. This meter consists of two lines with sixteen syllables in each and a caesura
in the middle of each line.

as the clear and sacred river, the Ganges. In contrast how petty Mr. A. W. Schlegel shows himself to be when he translates a few fragments from Sanskrit into hexameters and does not know how to praise himself enough for not letting any trochees slip in and for whittling out so many clear little metric art works in alexandrines. Fr. Schlegel's work on India has certainly been translated into French, and I can spare myself further praise. My only criticism is the ulterior motive behind the book. It was written in the interests of Catholicism. These people had rediscovered in the Indian poems not merely the mysteries of Catholicism, but the whole Catholic hierarchy as well and its struggles with secular authority. In the *Mahabharata* and in the *Ramayana* they saw, as it were, an elephantine Middle Ages. As a matter of fact, when in the latter epic King Visvamitra quarrels with the priest Vasistha, this quarrel concerns the same interests about which the Emperor quarreled with the Pope, although here in Europe the point in dispute was called investiture and there in India it was called the cow Sabala.[108]

The same fault can be found with Schlegel's lectures on literature. Friedrich Schlegel surveys the entire literature from an elevated point of view, but this elevated point of view is nonetheless always the belfry of a Catholic church. And with everything Schlegel says you hear these bells ringing; sometimes you even hear the croaking of the church ravens that flutter around him. To me the whole book is redolent of the incense of high mass, and I seem to detect nothing but tonsured ideas peeking out of its most beautiful passages. Yet in spite of these defects I know of no better book in this field. Only by combining Herder's works of a similar kind could one get a better survey of the literature of all peoples. For Herder did not sit in judgment on the various nations like a literary grand inquisitor, condemning or absolving them according to the degree of their faith. No, Herder viewed all mankind as a mighty harp in the hand of the great master, each nation seemed to him one string of this giant harp tuned to its special note, and he understood the universal harmony of the harp's various tones.

Fr. Schlegel died in the summer of 1829, as a result of gastron-

108. Sabala was a sacred cow which could endow its possessor with all the wealth in the world. King Visvamitra tried to obtain the cow from Vasistha, its owner, finally resorting to force when all other efforts failed, but Sabala came to the aid of Vasistha and the king was defeated.

omical intemperance, it was said. He was fifty-seven years old. His death caused one of the most repulsive literary scandals. His friends, the party of the clergy, whose headquarters were in Munich, were annoyed at the discourteous manner in which the liberal press had discussed the death, so they defamed and abused and insulted the German liberals. Yet they could not say of any of them "that he had seduced the wife of an intimate friend and for a long time afterward lived from the alms of the wronged husband."

Now, since it is expected of me, I must speak of the elder brother, Mr. A. W. Schlegel. If I tried to talk about him in Germany, people there would look at me in surprise.

Who in Paris still thinks about giraffes?[109]

Mr. A. W. Schlegel was born in Hanover on September 5, 1767. I do not have this information from him. I was never so ungallant as to ask him about his age. I found this date, if I am not mistaken, in Spindler's *Encyclopedia of German Women Writers*.[110] Hence Mr. A. W. Schlegel is now sixty-four years old. Mr. Alexander v. Humboldt and other natural scientists maintain that he is older. Champollion[111] was also of this opinion. If I am to speak of his literary merits, I must praise him again primarily as translator. In this field his achievements were unquestionably extraordinary. His translation of Shakespeare into German is masterly, incomparable. With the possible exception of Mr. Gries[112] and Count Platen,[113] Mr. A. W. Schlegel is certainly the greatest versifier in Germany. In all his other work he is only second- if not third-rate. In esthetic criticism he lacks, as I have said, the foundation of a philosophy, and other contemporaries far surpass him, particularly Solger.[114] In the study of medieval German Mr. Jakob Grimm towers sublimely

109. Giraffes made their first appearance in Western Europe in 1827, having been sent as presents by Egyptian royalty. In his *Memoirs* Heine mentions them as among his first impressions in Paris.
110. In Heine's text the name of the author and the title of the work are wrong. The book was *German Women Writers of the Nineteenth Century* by K. W. O. A. Schindel, published 1822–1825.
111. Jean François Champollion-Figeac (1791–1832), founder of Egyptian archaeology.
112. Johann Dietrich Gries (1775–1842) translated Tasso's *Jerusalem Delivered*, Calderón's plays, etc.
113. August, Graf von Platen-Hallermünde (1796–1835), a facile writer of verse in the strictest forms.
114. Karl Solger (1780–1819), a noted esthetician.

above him; with his work on German grammar Grimm freed us from the superficiality with which, following the example of the Schlegels, old German literary texts had been edited. Mr. Schlegel could perhaps have achieved something in the study of medieval German if he had not leaped over into Sanskrit. But medieval German had become unfashionable, and with Sanskrit you could create a new sensation. Here too he remained, to a certain extent, a dilettante, the stimulus for his ideas he owed to his brother Friedrich, and the scientific aspects, the actual facts, in his works on Sanskrit were, as everyone knows, the work of Mr. Lassen,[115] his learned collaborator. Mr. Franz Bopp[116] in Berlin is the real Sanskrit scholar in Germany; he is the leader in his specialty. Mr. Schlegel once tried to cling to the reputation of Niebuhr,[117] whom he attacked, but if we compare Schlegel with this great scholar or with a Johannes v. Müller, a Heeren, a Schlosser,[118] and similar historians, we can only shrug our shoulders. But how far has he gotten as a poet? This is difficult to determine.

The violinist Solomons, who gave lessons to the King of England, George III, once said to his illustrious pupil, "Violin players are divided into three classes. To the first class belong those who can't play at all, to the second belong those who play very badly, and to the third class belong those who play well. Your Majesty has already moved up to the second class."

Now does Mr. A. W. Schlegel belong to the first class or to the second class? Some say he isn't a poet at all; others say he is a very bad poet. This much I know, he is no Paganini.

Mr. A. W. Schlegel actually achieved fame only by the unparalleled effrontery with which he attacked the contemporary literary authorities. He tore the laurel wreaths from their old powdered wigs and in so doing raised clouds of dust. His fame is an illegitimate daughter of scandal.

As I have already mentioned several times, the criticism with

115. Christian Lassen (1800–1876), a Norwegian, an important Sanskrit scholar, published with A. W. Schlegel *Hitopadesa,* a collection of fables. This is primarily Lassen's work.

116. A professor in Berlin and the founder of comparative philology.

117. Barthold Georg Niebuhr, a German historian. His chief work was his three-volume history of Rome, published between 1811 and 1832.

118. All three were well-known historians who had published distinguished works.

which Mr. Schlegel attacked the existing authorities was not based on any philosophy.

After recovering from the astonishment aroused in us by every act of insolence, we realize fully the intrinsic barrenness of Schlegel's so-called criticism. For example, when he tried to disparage the poet Bürger, he compared his ballads with the old English ballads that Percy[119] collected, and demonstrated that the latter were written in a much simpler, naiver, more ancient, and consequently more poetic style. Mr. Schlegel understood quite well the spirit of the past, especially of the Middle Ages, and thus he succeeded in pointing out this spirit in the art works of the past and in demonstrating their beauties from this point of view. But he does not understand anything of the present; at most he glimpses only something of the physiognomy, a few external features of the present, and these are usually the less beautiful traits. Not understanding the spirit animating the present, he sees in all our modern life only a prosaic caricature. As a rule, only a great poet can appreciate the poetry of his own age; the poetry of a past time is revealed to us far more easily, and the perception of it is easier to impart. Hence Mr. Schlegel succeeded in exalting, for the great mass of people, the works in which the past lies entombed at the expense of the works in which our modern present lives and breathes. But death is not more poetic than life. The old English poems that Percy collected express the spirit of their age, and Bürger's poems express the spirit of ours. This spirit Mr. Schlegel did not understand; otherwise, in the turbulance with which this spirit occasionally erupts from Bürger's poems, he would not have heard the raucus screeching of an uncultured schoolmaster, but rather the mighty cries of a Titan tortured to death by an aristocracy of Hanoverian Junkers and academic pedants. This was namely the situation of the author of *Lenore* and the situation of so many genial men who hungered as poor lecturers in Göttingen, wasted away, and died in misery. How could the refined, renovated, baronized, decorated knight August Wilhelm von Schlegel, protected by refined patrons, comprehend these verses in which Bürger

---

119. Thomas Percy, Bishop of Dromore, an English man of letters who published *Reliques of Ancient English Poetry* in 1765, thus making available a wealth of ballads and medieval romance and influencing the literary development in both England and Germany.

loudly proclaimed: "An honest man, before he would beg for the favor of the eminent, would rather starve himself to death!"

In Germany the name Bürger is synonymous with the word *citoyen*.

What increased Mr. Schlegel's fame still further was the sensation he later made here in France when he also attacked the literary authorities of the French. With proud joy we saw our pugnacious countryman prove to the French that their entire classical literature was worthless, that Molière was a buffoon and not a poet, that Racine was no good either, whereas we Germans should be regarded as the kings of Parnassus. His refrain was always that the French were the most prosaic people in the world and that no poetry existed in France. The man said this at a time when before his very eyes many a choragus of the Convention, that great tragedy of Titans, was still walking about alive, at a time when Napoleon was improvising a good epic every day, when Paris thronged with heroes, kings, and gods.—Mr. Schlegel, however, saw nothing of all this. When he was here, he constantly saw himself in the mirror, so it is perhaps understandable that he saw no poetry at all in France.

But Mr. Schlegel, as I have said before, could comprehend only the poetry of the past and not of the present. All of modern life inevitably seemed prosaic to him, and the poetry of France, the native soil of modern society, remained inaccessible to him. Racine must have been the first whom he could not understand. For this great poet already stood as herald of the modern age beside the great king with whom the modern age began. Racine was the first modern poet, as Louis XIV was the first modern king. The Middle Ages still breathes in Corneille. In him and the *Fronde* one can still hear the death rattle of the old knighthood. For this reason he is sometimes called romantic. In Racine, however, the medieval way of thinking is entirely eradicated; with him genuinely new feelings are awakened; he is the organ of a new society; the fragrance from the first violets of our modern life welled up in his breast; we can almost see the budding laurels which only later, in more recent times, burgeoned forth so powerfully. Who knows how many deeds blossomed from Racine's tender verses! The French heroes who lie buried at the Pyramids, at Marengo, at Austerlitz, at Moscow, and at Waterloo—they all had once heard Racine's verses, and their

Emperor had heard them from the mouth of Talma. Who knows how many inches of fame on the Column of Vendôme really belong to Racine! I do not know if Euripides was a greater poet than Racine. But I do know that the latter was a living source of love and a sense of honor, and his spirit intoxicated, enraptured, and inspired an entire nation. What more can you ask from a poet? We are all human beings; we sink into the grave and leave only our words behind. And when these have fulfilled their mission, then they return to the bosom of God, the gathering place of poets' words, the home of all harmony.

If Mr. Schlegel had limited himself to asserting that the mission of Racine's words had been accomplished and that this advanced age had need of quite different poets, his attacks would have had some foundation. But they were unfounded when he tried to demonstrate Racine's inferiority by a comparison with poets of earlier times. Not merely did he have no sense for the infinite grace, the sweet jest, the profound charm that derived from Racine's dressing his modern French heroes in ancient costumes and thus adding to the fascination of a modern passion the interesting element of a brilliant masquerade. Mr. Schlegel was even stupid enough to take the masquerade at face value, to judge the Greeks of Versailles by the Greeks of Athens, and to compare Racine's *Phaedra* with the *Phaedra* of Euripides! This habit of measuring the present by the standards of the past was so deeply rooted in Mr. Schlegel that he always used to lash the backs of more modern poets with the laurel-branch of an earlier poet and then, in order to disparage Euripides himself, knew no better recourse than to compare him with the earlier Sophocles or even with Aeschylus.

It would lead too far if I were to explain here what a very great injustice Mr. Schlegel did to Euripides by trying to disparage him in this way, just as Aristophanes had once done. Aristophanes assumed an attitude which shows the greatest similarity to that of the Romantic School; similar feelings and tendencies form the basis for his polemic, and if one called Mr. Tieck a romantic Aristophanes, one might properly call the parodist of Euripides and Socrates[120] a classical Tieck. As Mr. Tieck and the Schlegels, in spite of their own lack of belief, nevertheless regretted the decline of Catholicism;

120. Aristophanes attacked Euripides in *The Frogs* and Socrates in *The Clouds*.

as they wished to restore this faith among the masses; as, with this intention, they attacked with mockery and calumny the Protestant rationalists, the apostles of Enlightenment, the genuine even more than the false; as they cherished the most violent antipathy toward men who were furthering honorable civic virtue in life and in literature; as they ridiculed this civic virtue as philistine triviality and, in contrast, continually praised and celebrated the great heroic life of the feudal Middle Ages—so, too, Aristophanes, who himself made fun of the gods, hated the philosophers who were undermining all Olympus; he hated the rationalist Socrates, who preached a higher morality; he hated the poets who were already expressing, so to speak, a modern life that differed as much from the earlier Greek period of gods, heroes, and kings as our present age differs from medieval feudalism; he hated Euripides, who was no longer intoxicated, like Aeschylus and Sophocles, with the Greek Middle Ages, but was already verging on middle-class tragedy. I doubt whether Mr. Schlegel was aware of the true motives for his disparagement of Euripides in comparison with Aeschylus and Sophocles. I think a subconscious feeling guided him; he smelled in the old tragic poet the modern democratic and Protestant element which was so very repulsive to the chivalric and Olympian-Catholic Aristophanes.

Perhaps, however, I am doing Mr. A. W. Schlegel an undeserved honor by attributing to him definite sympathies and antipathies. It is possible that he had none at all. In his youth he was a Hellenist and only later became a Romantic. He became the choragus of the new school, it was named after him and his brother, and he himself was perhaps the very one who was least serious about the Schlegel School. He supported it with his talents, he worked his way into it with his studies, he took pleasure in it as long as it prospered, but when the School came to a bad end, he again worked his way into a new field with his studies.

Although the School now went to pieces, Mr. Schlegel's efforts still bore good fruit for our literature. In particular, he had shown how to treat scholarly subjects in elegant language. Previously few German scholars had dared to write a scholarly book in a clear and attractive style. The average scholar wrote a confused, pedantic German that reeked of tallow candles and tobacco. Mr. Schlegel was one of the few Germans who do not smoke, a virtue he owed to the society of Madame de Staël. In general, he owes to this lady the outward polish which he was able to show to great advantage in Germany. In this respect the death of the excellent Madame de Staël was a great loss for this German scholar, who found in her salon so much opportunity to become acquainted with the newest fashions and, as her companion in all the main cities of Europe, was able to view the fashionable world and to adopt the most fashionable worldly manners. Such instructive relationships had become for him so very much a necessity for a happy life that after the death of his noble patroness he was not averse to offering the famous Catalani[121] his companionship on her travels.

As I have said, the furtherance of elegance is one of Mr. Schlegel's main merits, and through him more civilization entered the lives of German poets. Goethe had already set the most influential example of how one can be a German poet and still preserve outward dignity. In earlier times German poets despised all conventional forms, and the name "German poet" or even the name "poetic genius" acquired a most unsavory connotation. Formerly a German poet was a man who wore a shabby, tattered coat, fabricated baptismal and wedding poems for a taler apiece, enjoyed in lieu of good society, which rejected him, drinks that were all the better, perhaps even lay drunk in the gutter of an evening, kissed tenderly by Luna's affectionate beams. Grown old, these poets generally plunged still more deeply into their misery; it was, to be sure, a misery without cares, or whose only care consisted in where to get the most liquor for the least money.

This is what I too had imagined a German poet to be. How pleasantly surprised I was, therefore, in 1819 when, as a very young man, I attended the University of Bonn and there had the honor of seeing the poet A. W. Schlegel, the poetic genius, face to face. With the exception of Napoleon he was the first great man I had seen, and I shall never forget this sublime sight. I still feel today the thrill of awe that filled my soul as I stood in front of his rostrum and heard him speak. In those days I wore a rough white coat, a red cap over my long blond hair, and no gloves. Mr. A. W. Schlegel, however, wore kid gloves and still dressed completely in the latest Paris fashion; he was still highly perfumed with good

---

121. Angelica Catalani, a well-known Italian singer.

society and *eau de mille fleurs*.[122] He was grace and elegance personified, and when he spoke about the Lord High Chancellor of England, he added "my friend," and beside him stood his servant in the most baronial Schlegel family livery and trimmed the wax candles that were burning in silver candelabras standing on the desk beside a glass of sugar water in front of the man prodigy. A servant in livery! Wax candles! Silver candelabras! My friend the Lord High Chancellor of England! Kid gloves! Sugar water! What unheard-of things at a German professor's lecture! This splendor dazzled us young people not a little, and especially me, and I wrote three odes to Mr. Schlegel, each beginning with the words "O thou who" etc. But only in poetry would I have dared to address such a distinguished man with "thou." His outward appearance did indeed give him a certain distinction. On his puny little head only a few silver hairs still shone, and his body was so thin, so emaciated, so transparent, that he appeared to be all spirit and looked almost like a symbol of spirituality.

Despite this he got married at that time, and he, the chief of the Romanticists, married the daughter of Parish Councillor Paulus in Heidelberg,[123] the chief of the German Rationalists. It was a symbolic marriage. Romanticism was wedded, so to speak, to Rationalism, but the marriage bore no fruit. On the contrary, because of it the split between Romanticism and Rationalism became even wider, and the very morning after the wedding night Rationalism ran back home and would have nothing more to do with Romanticism. For Rationalism, being always sensible, did not want to be merely symbolically wedded, and as soon as it discovered the wooden worthlessness of Romantic art, it ran away. I know I am speaking obscurely and will try to express myself as clearly as possible:

Typhon, wicked Typhon, hated Osiris (who, as you know, is an Egyptian god), and when he got him in his power, he tore him to pieces. Isis, poor Isis, Osiris' wife, laboriously collected the pieces, patched them together, and succeeded in repairing her mutilated husband completely. Completely? Alas, no, one important piece was missing, which the poor goddess could not find, poor Isis! She

---

122. "Toilet water from a thousand flowers," a fictional scent, of course, used ironically.
123. Heinrich Paulus, professor of theology in Heidelberg.

had to content herself with a replacement made of wood, but wood is only wood, poor Isis! Thus there arose in Egypt a scandalous myth and in Heidelberg a mystical scandal.

After this Mr. A. W. Schlegel disappeared from sight entirely. He was forgotten. Displeasure at being forgotten finally drove him once more, after many years of absence, to Berlin, the former capital of his literary glory, and there he again gave some lectures on esthetics. But meanwhile he had learned nothing new, and he now addressed an audience that had received from Hegel a philosophy of art, a science of esthetics. He was ridiculed and disdained. He fared as does an old actress who, after an absence of twenty years, once more sets foot on the scene of her previous success and wonders why people laugh instead of applauding. The man had changed shockingly, and he delighted Berlin for four whole weeks with his display of absurdities. He had become a vain old fop who let himself be made a fool of everywhere. People tell the most incredible stories about it.

Here in Paris I had the misfortune to see Mr. A. W. Schlegel again in person. I really had no conception as yet of the change until I was convinced of it with my own eyes. It was a year ago, shortly after my arrival in the capital. I was just on my way to visit the house where Molière had lived, for I honor great poets and seek out everywhere with religious piety the traces of their life on earth. This is a form of worship. On my way, not far from that consecrated house, I caught sight of a creature whose features, webbed with wrinkles, showed a similarity with the former A. W. Schlegel. I thought I was seeing his spirit. But it was only his body. His spirit is dead, and his body still walks the earth like a ghost and in the meantime has become quite fat. Flesh had formed again on the thin, spiritual legs; one could even see a belly, and above it hung a great many ribands and orders. The little grey head, formerly so delicate, wore a golden-yellow wig. He was dressed in the latest fashion of the year in which Madame de Staël died. And he was smiling with the old-fashioned sweetness of an aged lady with a lump of sugar in her mouth and tripped along as youthfully as a coquettish child. Truly, a strange rejuvenation had taken place in him; he had experienced, as it were, a facetious second edition of his youth; he seemed to have come into full bloom again, and I even suspect that the redness of his cheeks was not rouge but a healthy irony of nature.

It seemed to me at this moment as if I saw the late Molière standing at the window and smiling down at me, pointing at that apparition both melancholy and gay. Suddenly all its absurdity became completely obvious to me; I understood the whole profundity and fullness of the jest contained it it; I understood completely the comedy-like character of this incredibly ridiculous personage who unfortunately has found no great comic writer to use him suitably for the stage. Molière alone would have been the man to adapt such a figure to the French theater; he alone had the necessary talent. Mr. A. W. Schlegel sensed this very early, and he hated Molière for the same reason that Napoleon hated Tacitus. Just as Napoleon Bonaparte, the French Caesar, probably felt that the republican historian would not have portrayed him in rosy colors, Mr. A. W. Schlegel, the German Osiris, had long sensed that if Molière were still alive, he would never have escaped the great writer of comedy. And Napoleon said of Tacitus that he was the slanderer of Tiberius, and Mr. August Wilhelm Schlegel said of Molière that he was no poet, but only a buffoon.

Mr. A. W. Schlegel left Paris a short time later, after having been decorated with the order of the Legion of Honor by His Majesty Louis Philippe I, King of the French. The *Moniteur* has delayed as yet in reporting properly on this event, but Thalia, the muse of Comedy, hastily jotted it down in her notebook of jests.

II

After the Schlegels, Mr. Ludwig Tieck was one of the most active writers of the Romantic School. He battled and wrote for it. He was a poet, a name that neither of the two Schlegels deserves. He was a true son of Phoebus Apollo, and like his ever-youthful father he carried not only a lyre, but also a bow with a quiver full of ringing arrows. Like the Delphic god, he was drunk with lyric ecstasy and critical brutality. When, like the latter, he had mercilessly flayed some literary Marsyas,[124] he would gaily pluck with bloody fingers the golden strings of his lyre and sing a joyous love song.

The poetic controversy that Mr. Tieck carried on in dramatic form against the opponents of the School[125] is one of the most extraordinary phenomena of our literature. These are satiric dramas usually compared with Aristophanes' comedies. But they differ from the latter almost as a Sophoclean tragedy differs from a Shakespearean. Ancient comedy had the uniform structure, the strict course of action, and the exquisitely polished metrical language of ancient tragedy, of which it may be considered a parody, but Mr. Tieck's dramatic satires are just as daring in structure, as full of English irregularity, as capricious in their prosody, as Shakespeare's tragedies. Was this form an original invention of Mr. Tieck's? No, it already existed among the common folk, particularly in Italy. Anyone who knows Italian can get a fairly accurate idea of these plays of Tieck's if he dreams some German moonlight into Gozzi's motley, bizarre fairy-tale comedies, which are as fantastic as Venice.[126] Tieck even borrowed most of his characters from this merry child of the lagoons. Following Tieck's example many German poets likewise appropriated this form, and we got comedies whose comic effect is produced not by an amusing character or by a funny plot, but by transporting us directly into a comic world, into a world where animals speak and act like human beings and where chance and caprice have taken the place of the natural order of things. We also find this in Aristophanes. Except that the latter chose this form in order to reveal to us his most profound views about the world, as for instance in *The Birds,* where the craziest actions of people are portrayed in the most farcical antics, their passion for building the most magnificent castles in empty air, their defiance of the immortal gods, and their fancied triumphal joy. It is just for this reason that Aristophanes is so great, because his

124. A Phrygian satyr of Greek mythology. He found the flute which Athena had invented but had discarded and became such a skillful player that he challenged Apollo to a contest. Apollo accepted on the condition that the victor might do as he pleased with the loser. The Muses, acting as judges, awarded the victory to Apollo's lyre-playing, and Apollo promptly flayed Marsyas for his presumption.
125. For example, in *Puss in Boots* and *Prince Zerbino.*
126. Carlo Gozzi (1720–1806), Italian dramatist from Venice, who tried to revive the dying *commedia dell'arte* and founded the fable play or fairy-tale play in Italy.

philosophy of life was so great, because it was greater, indeed more tragic, than that of the tragedians themselves, because his comedies were truly "bantering tragedies." For example, Paisteteros[127] is not represented at the end of the work in his ridiculous nullity, as a modern poet would represent him, but, on the contrary, he wins the lovely Basilea, who is gifted with magic powers, ascends to his city in the air with his divine spouse, the gods are compelled to yield to his will, Folly celebrates its marriage with Power, and the play ends with nuptial songs of rejoicing. Is there anything more terribly tragic for a sensible person than this fool's victory and triumph! Our German Aristophaneses, however, have never had such high aspirations; they abstained from any exalted philosophy of life; with great modesty they held their tongues about the two most important conditions of man, the political and the religious; they ventured to treat only the theme that Aristophanes discussed in *The Frogs;* as the main subject of their dramatic satires they chose the theater itself and satirized the defects of our theater more or less entertainingly.

But one must also consider the lack of political freedom in Germany. Our would-be wits have to refrain from any sarcasm in regard to actual rulers and thus want to take substitute revenge for this restriction on the theater kings and stage princes. We Germans, who possessed almost no serious political newspapers, were always doubly blessed with a host of esthetic journals containing nothing but worthless fairy tales and theatrical reviews, so that anyone who saw them was almost compelled to think that the whole German nation consisted simply of babbling nursemaids and theater critics. This would have been unfair to us, however. How little such wretched scribbling satisfied us was demonstrated after the July Revolution when it looked as though a free word could also be uttered in our dear fatherland. Suddenly journals sprang up which reviewed the good or bad acting of real kings, and many of them, who forgot their lines, were booed in their own capitals. Our literary Scheherazades, who used to lull the public, the coarse sultan, to sleep with their little novellas were now forced into silence, and the actors saw with astonishment how empty the

127. In the English translation originally published by The Athenian Society, London, 1912, the name is spelled Pisthetaerus.

orchestra was, no matter how divinely they played, and that even the reserved seat of the formidable town critic very often remained unoccupied. Previously the good stage heroes had always complained that they and only they had to serve as public topic of conversation and that even their domestic virtues were disclosed in the newspapers. How frightened they were when it looked as though there might be no talk about them at all any more!

In point of fact, when the Revolution broke out in Germany, this was the end of the theater and theater criticism, and the alarmed writers of novellas, actors, and theater critics feared quite rightly "that art was dying." But our fatherland was successfully saved from this horrible fate by the wisdom and energy of the Frankfurt Diet of the German Confederation. It is to be hoped that no revolution will break out in Germany; we are protected from the guillotine and all the terrors of freedom of the press; even the chambers of deputies, whose competition had done so much harm to the theaters despite concessions granted these long before, are being abolished, and art has been saved. Everything possible is now being done in Germany for art, especially in Prussia. The museums are ablaze with artful delight in color, the orchestras roar, the danseuses leap their loveliest *entrechats,* the public is enchanted with the Arabian Nights of novellas, and theater criticism flourishes once more.

Justin related the following in his *Histories:* When Cyrus has quelled the revolts of the Lydians, he could only tame their stubborn freedom-loving spirit by ordering them to take up the fine arts and other amusing things. Since that time no one has spoken about Lydian riots; Lydian *restaurateurs,* matchmakers, and *artistes,* however, have become all the more famous.

We now have peace in Germany, theater criticism and the novella are again the main thing, and since Mr. Tieck excels in both, he is shown due admiration by all friends of art. He is in fact the best novella writer in Germany. Not all of his narrative works, however, are of the same genre or of the same value. As with painters, several styles can be perceived in Mr. Tieck. His earliest style still belongs entirely to the old school. At that time he wrote only at the suggestion of or on commission from a book-dealer who was none other than the late Nicolai himself,[128] the most obstinate champion

128. See above, p. 14, and note 35 on that page.

of Enlightenment and humanism, the great enemy of superstition, mysticism, and Romanticism. Nicolai was a bad writer, a prosaic old fogy, and he often made himself extremely ridiculous by his habit of smelling a Jesuit everywhere. But we of the younger generation must admit that old Nicolai was a thoroughly honest man, a genuine friend of the German nation, who, out of love for the sacred cause of truth, did not shrink from even the worst form of martyrdom, becoming ridiculous. As I was told in Berlin, Mr. Tieck at one time lived in his house, one floor above him, and modern times were already trampling over the head of the old.

The works that Mr. Tieck wrote in his earliest style, chiefly stories and big long novels of which *William Lovell*[129] is the best, are very insignificant, with a complete lack of poetic quality. It is as if his rich poetic nature had been miserly in its youth and had saved all its intellectual wealth for a later time. Or did Mr. Tieck himself not know the riches of his own breast, and did the Schlegels first have to discover them with a divining rod? As soon as Mr. Tieck came in contact with the Schlegels, all the treasures of his imagination, his spirit, and his wit were disclosed. Diamonds sparkled there, the clearest pearls welled up, and above all the carbuncle flashed there, the precious stone of fable about which the Romantic poets spoke and sang so much. This rich breast was the real treasure chamber on which the Schlegels drew for the military expenses of their literary campaigns. Mr. Tieck had to write for the School the satiric comedies already mentioned and at the same time prepare according to the new esthetic recipes a quantity of poetic works of every kind. This is Mr. Ludwig Tieck's second style. The dramatic works in this style most worthy of recommendation are *Emperor Octavian, Saint Genevieve,* and *Fortunatus,*[130] three plays adapted from the chapbooks bearing the same titles. The poet clothed these old legends, still preserved by the German people, in luxurious modern garments. But, to be honest, I love them more in their old, naive, and simple form. Beautiful as Tieck's *Genevieve* is, I much prefer the old chapbook very poorly printed in Cologne on the Rhine with its bad woodcuts in which, however, one gets a very moving sight of the poor naked

129. Published 1795–1796.
130. The first, a comedy, appeared in 1804. *The Life and Death of Saint Genevieve,* a tragedy, was written in 1800, and the third, a fairy-tale play, was written in 1815–1816.

Countess Palatinate, with only her long hair to cover her nakedness, holding her babe Schmerzenreich to the teats of a compassionate hind.

The novellas that Mr. Tieck wrote in his second style are far more worthwhile than the plays. They were also usually adapted from old folk legends. *Blond Eckbert* and *The Runic Mountain*[131] are the best. A mysterious inwardness, a strange sympathy with nature, especially with the plant and mineral kingdom, dominate these writings. The reader feels as if he were in an enchanted forest; he hears the subterranean springs murmuring melodiously; at times he fancies he hears his own name in the whispering of the trees; broad-leaved climbers often entangle his feet alarmingly; strange magical flowers gaze at him with their bright, longing eyes; invisible lips kiss his cheeks with teasing tenderness; tall mushrooms like golden bells rise up, chiming, at the base of the trees; great silent birds rock in the branches and nod down at him with their wise, long beaks; everything is breathing, listening, quivering with ex-pectation—then suddenly the mellow French horn sounds, and a beautiful woman, with waving feathers in her cap and her falcon on her fist, gallops past on a white palfrey. And this beautiful lady is as beautiful, as fair-haired, as violet-eyed, as smiling and also as serious, as real and yet as ironic, as chaste and also as passionate, as the imagination of our excellent Ludwig Tieck. Yes, his imagi-nation is a charming lady of noble birth hunting mythical beasts in an enchanted forest, perhaps even the rare unicorn, which permits itself to be captured only by a pure virgin.

But then a remarkable change took place in Mr. Tieck, and this was revealed in his third style. Having been silent for a long time after the fall of the Schlegels, he again made a public appearance, and in a manner one would least have expected from him. The former enthusiast, who out of fanatical ardor had betaken himself into the bosom of the Catholic Church,[132] who had fought so vigorously against Enlightenment and Protestantism, who reveled in the Middle Ages, only the feudal Middle Ages, who loved art only as a naive outpouring of the heart—this man now appeared as an opponent of enthusiasm, as a portrayer of the most modern

---

131. The first was written in 1796, the second in 1802.
132. Tieck did not become a Catholic.

middle-class life, as an artist who demanded the clearest self-awareness in art, in short, as a man of reason. It is thus that we see him in a series of more recent novellas, several of which have also become known in France. The study of Goethe is apparent in them; indeed, Tieck appears in his third style as a true disciple of Goethe. The same artistic clarity, serenity, calm, and irony. If the Schlegel School had earlier been unsuccessful in drawing Goethe over to it, we now see how this School, represented by Mr. Tieck, went over to Goethe. This is reminiscent of a Mohammedan tale. The prophet had said to the mountain, "Mountain, come to me." But the mountain did not go. And behold, the greater miracle occurred; the prophet went to the mountain.

Mr. Tieck was born in Berlin on May 31, 1773. Some years ago he settled in Dresden,[133] where he occupied himself chiefly with the theater, and he, who in his earlier writings had constantly made fun of *Hofräte*[134] as stock figures of absurdity, himself became a royal Saxon *Hofrat*. The good Lord is still a greater ironist than Mr. Tieck.

A strange disparity between this writer's intellect and his imagination now made its appearance. The former, Tieck's intellect, is a respectable, prosaic philistine who subscribes to utilitarianism and will have nothing to do with enthusiasm; the latter, however, Tieck's imagination, is still the noble lady with the waving feathers in her cap and the falcon on her fist. These two lead a curious wedded life, and it is sometimes sad to see how the unfortunate lady of high degree has to help her pedantic middle-class husband in his affairs or even in his cheese store. But sometimes, at night, when her spouse is snoring peacefully with his cotton nightcap on his head, the noble lady arises from the confining conjugal bed, mounts her white steed, and once more gallops as joyously as before in the enchanted forest of romance.

I cannot refrain from remarking that in his latest novellas Tieck's intellect has become even more ungracious, while at the same time his imagination has lost more and more of her romantic character and on cool nights even remains with yawning enjoyment in the nuptial bed and almost lovingly nestles close to her prosy spouse.

133. He lived in Dresden from 1818 to 1841.
134. Plural of *Hofrat*, an honorary title with no English equivalent.

Mr. Tieck, however, is still a great poet. For he can create characters, and from his heart flow words that move our own hearts. But a timorous manner, a certain indefiniteness, uncertainty, and weakness are noticeable in him not only now, but were noticeable from the very beginning. This lack of decisive vigor is all too clearly evident in everything he did and wrote. Certainly no independence is revealed in any of his writings. His first style shows him to be nothing at all; his second shows him to be a faithful squire of the Schlegels; his third style shows him to be an imitator of Goethe. His theater reviews, which he collected under the title *Dramaturgical Notes,* are still the most original work he has produced. But they are theater reviews.

In order to portray Hamlet as a weakling, Shakespeare also lets him appear, in conversation with actors, as a good theater critic.

Mr. Tieck never concerned himself much with serious disciplines. He studied modern languages and older documents of our national literature. Classical studies would always remain foreign to him, as a true Romantic. He never occupied himself with philosophy; it was even repugnant to him. To the fields of scholarship Mr. Tieck brought only flowers and thin riding crops; with the former he treated the noses of his friends; with the latter, the backs of his adversaries. He never spent any time tilling the soil of learning. His works are bouquets and fagots; nowhere a sheath with ears of grain.

Besides Goethe it is Cervantes whom Mr. Tieck imitated most often. The humorous irony—I could also say the ironic humor—of these two modern poets diffuses its fragrance through the novellas in Mr. Tieck's third style. Irony and humor are so closely blended that they seem to be one and the same. We talk a good deal about this humorous irony, the Goethean school of art praises it as a special excellence of their master, and it now plays a large role in German literature. But it is only a sign of our lack of political freedom, and as Cervantes had to take refuge in humorous irony at the time of the Inquisition in order to intimate his ideas without leaving a weak spot exposed for the serfs of the Holy Office to seize upon, so Goethe also used to say in a tone of humorous irony what he, as minister of state and courtier, did not dare to say outright. Goethe never suppressed the truth; when he could not show it naked, he clothed it in humor and irony.

Especially writers who languish under censorship and all kinds of restrictions on freedom of thought and yet can never disavow their heartfelt opinion have to resort to the ironic and humorous manner. It is the only solution left for honesty, and in this disguise such honesty is revealed most movingly. This again reminds me of the strange Prince of Denmark. Hamlet is the most honest soul in the world. His dissimulation only serves as a substitute for external appearances; he is strange because strangeness offends court etiquette less than a blunt, open declaration. In all his humorously ironic jests he intentionally lets one see through his dissimulation; in everything that he does and says his real opinion is quite visible for anyone who knows how to see, and even for the king; he cannot tell him the truth openly (for he is too weak for that), but he does not by any means conceal it from him. Hamlet is thoroughly honest; only the most honest person could say: "We are arrant knaves, all." And by feigning insanity he likewise does not want to deceive us; he is deeply aware that he actually is insane.

In addition, I must praise two other works of Mr. Tieck's by which he has earned the special gratitude of the German public. They are his translation of a number of English plays from the pre-Shakespearean period and his translation of *Don Quixote*. The latter is extraordinarily successful; no one has understood so well and reproduced so faithfully as our excellent Tieck the ridiculous dignity of the ingenuous hidalgo of La Mancha.

It is quite amusing that it was precisely the Romantic School that provided us with the best translation of a book in which its own folly is exposed so very delightfully. For this School was deluded by the same madness that also inspired the noble man of La Mancha to all his follies. It too wished to restore medieval chivalry; it too wanted to revive a dead past. Or did Miguel de Cervantes Saavedra, in his absurd epic, intend to make fun of other knights as well, that is, all human beings who fight and suffer for some idea? Did he really intend to parody in his tall, haggard knight enthusiasm for ideals in general and in the knight's rotund squire realistic common sense? At any rate, the latter plays the more ridiculous role, for realistic common sense, with all its traditional sayings meant to benefit society, must nonetheless trot along on his tranquil donkey behind enthusiasm; despite his better insight he and his donkey must share all the calamities that so often befall the noble knight; in fact, enthusiasm for ideals is so tremendously alluring that realistic common sense, together with its donkeys, is always forced to follow it involuntarily.

Or did the profound Spaniard intend to deride human nature even more astutely? Did he perhaps allegorize the human mind in the figure of Don Quixote and the human body in the figure of Sancho Panza, and the whole work would then be nothing but a great mystery play in which the question of mind and matter is discussed in all its most shocking reality? This much I see in the book: that poor, matter-of-fact Sancho has to suffer greatly for the spiritual Don Quixotisms; that he often gets the most ignoble beatings for the noblest intentions of his master; and that he is always more sensible than his pompous master, for he knows that beatings leave a very bad taste but that the sausages in an olla podrida taste very good. Truly, the body seems to have more judgment than the mind, and a human being often thinks much more accurately with his back or stomach than with his head.

III

Among the lunacies of the Romantic School in Germany the ceaseless praise and eulogy of Jakob Böhme deserve special mention. This name was, so to speak, the shibboleth of these people. Whenever they uttered the name Jakob Böhme, their faces assumed their most profound expression. Was this in earnest or was it a joke?

Jakob Böhme was a shoemaker who first saw the light of this world in 1575 in Görlitz in Oberlausitz and left behind a great many theosophical writings. They are in German and hence were all the more accessible to our Romantics. I cannot judge very exactly whether this strange shoemaker was as distinguished a philosopher as many German mystics maintain, since I have not read him at all. I am convinced, however, that he did not make as good boots as Mr. Sakoski. Shoemakers play quite a role in our literature, and Hans Sachs, a shoemaker who was born in Nürnberg in 1454 and spent his life there,[135] was lauded by the Romantic

135. Hans Sachs (1494–1576) was a very prolific writer known chiefly for his poems and his Shrovetide plays and farces.

School as one of our best poets. I have read him, and I must confess that I doubt whether Mr. Sakoski ever wrote as good verses as our admirable old Hans Sachs.

I have already touched on Mr. Schelling's influence on the Romantic School. Since I shall discuss him separately later, I can spare myself a detailed criticism here. In any case this man deserves our utmost attention. For in his early years, due to him, a great revolution took place in the German intellectual world, and in his later years he changed so much that uninformed people make the greatest mistakes by confusing the early Schelling with the present Schelling. The early Schelling was a bold Protestant who protested against Fichtean idealism. This idealism was a strange system which would necessarily seem especially odd to a Frenchman. For while in France a philosophy was coming into fashion which clothed the spirit in flesh and blood, so to speak, which recognized the spirit only as a modification of matter, in short, while in France materialism had prevailed, there arose in Germany a philosophy which, quite in contrast, admitted only the spirit as reality, declared all matter only a modification of the spirit, and even denied the existence of matter. It seemed almost as if, across the Rhine, the spirit sought revenge for the insult done it on this side. When the spirit was denied existence here in France, it emigrated, as it were, to Germany and there denied the existence of matter. In this respect Fichte could be considered the Duke of Braunschweig of spiritualism, and his idealist philosophy was nothing but a manifesto against French materialism. But this philosophy, which actually forms the highest peak of spiritualism, was just as little able to maintain itself as the crass materialism of the French. Mr. Schelling was the man who came forward with the doctrine that matter or, as he called it, nature, exists not merely in our spirit but also in reality, that our perception of phenomena is identical with the phenomena themselves. This is Schelling's theory of identity or, as it is also called, nature philosophy.

This happened at the beginning of the century. Mr. Schelling was then a great man. Meanwhile, however, Hegel appeared on the philosophical scene; Mr. Schelling, who in later years wrote almost nothing, was eclipsed, indeed forgotten, and retained only a literary-historical significance. Hegelian philosophy became dominant, Hegel became the sovereign in the realm of intellect, and poor Schelling, a fallen, mediatized philosopher, wandered mournfully about among the other mediatized gentlemen in Munich.[136] I once saw him there and could almost have wept tears at the pitiful sight. And what he said was the most pitiful thing of all; it was an envious railing at Hegel, who had supplanted him. As one shoemaker talks about another whom he accuses of having stolen his leather and made boots of it, so I heard Mr. Schelling, when I once saw him by chance, talk about Hegel, about Hegel, who "had taken his ideas"; and "it is my ideas that he took," and again "my ideas"—this was the poor man's constant refrain. I assure you, if the shoemaker Jakob Böhme once talked like a philosopher, the philosopher Schelling now talks like a shoemaker.

Nothing is more absurd than ownership claimed for ideas. Hegel did, to be sure, use many of Schelling's ideas for his philosophy, but Mr. Schelling would never have known what to do with these ideas anyway. He always just philosophized, but was never able to produce a philosophy. And besides, one could certainly maintain that Mr. Schelling borrowed more from Spinoza than Hegel borrowed from Schelling. If Spinoza is some day liberated from his rigid, antiquated Cartesian, mathematical form and made accessible to a large public, we shall perhaps see that he, more than any other, might complain about the theft of ideas. All our present-day philosophers, possibly without knowing it, look through glasses that Baruch Spinoza ground.[137]

Envy and jealousy have caused the fall of angels, and it is unfortunately only too certain that annoyance at Hegel's ever-increasing importance led poor Mr. Schelling to where we find him now, namely in the snares of Catholic propaganda, which has its headquarters in Munich. Mr. Schelling betrayed philosophy to the Catholic religion. All witnesses agree in this; and one could foresee long ago that it was inevitable. From the mouths of several powerful authorities in Munich I had so often heard the words, "Religion and science must be allies." This phrase was as innocent as a flower, and behind it lurked the serpent. Now I know what you wanted. Mr. Schelling must now serve the purpose of justifying the Catholic religion with all his intellectual powers, and everything

136. Schelling lived in Munich from 1808 to 1820, then went to Erlangen, and in 1827 was appointed professor of philosophy at the University of Munich.
137. A reference to the fact that Spinoza earned his living as an optician.

that he now teaches under the name of philosophy is nothing but a justification of Catholicism. The authorities were also gambling on the additional advantage that the celebrated name would lure to Munich young Germans thirsting for wisdom and that the Jesuit lie in the garb of philosophy would fool them all the more easily. These young men kneel down reverently before the man whom they consider the high priest of truth and unsuspectingly receive from his hands the poisoned Host.

Mr. Steffens, who is now professor of philosophy in Berlin, is considered one of Mr. Schelling's most honorable disciples in Germany. He lived in Jena while the Schlegels carried on there, and his name appears frequently in the annals of the Romantic School. Later he wrote several novellas, which contain much acuteness and little poetry. His scholarly works, especially his *Anthropology,* are more significant. They are full of original ideas. In this area he has received less recognition than he deserves. Others have understood the art of working up his ideas and presenting them to the public as their own. Mr. Steffens would be more justified than his mentor in complaining that his ideas have been stolen. Among his ideas, however, there is one that no one has appropriated, and it is his chief idea, his sublime idea: "Henrik Steffens, born May 2, 1773, in Stavangar near Drohntheim in Norway, is the greatest man of the century."

For the past few years this man has fallen into the hands of the pietists, and his philosophy is now nothing but whining, lukewarm, watered-down pietism.

Mr. Joseph Görres, whom I have already mentioned several times and who likewise belongs to the Schelling School, is a kindred spirit. He is known in Germany under the name "the fourth ally." A French journalist had given him this name when, in 1814, under instructions from the Holy Alliance, he preached hatred of France. The man is still living off this compliment to the present day. As a matter of fact, however, no one was able to inflame so violently as he, by means of national memories, the hatred of the Germans toward the French, and the journal that he edited for this purpose, the *Rheinische Merkur,* is full of conjurations which, if it ever came to a war again, might still have some effect. Since then Mr. Görres has almost been forgotten. The sovereigns did not need him any longer and dismissed him. When he began to snarl at this, they even persecuted him. They acted as the Spaniards did on the island of Cuba when during the war with the Indians they trained their large dogs to tear the natives to pieces; but when the war came to an end and the dogs, having acquired a taste for human blood, now occasionally snapped at their masters' calves, they tried to get rid of their bloodhounds through violent means. When, thus persecuted by the sovereigns, Görres had nothing more to eat, he threw himself into the arms of the Jesuits, has been serving them until this very moment, and is a mainstay of Catholic propaganda in Munich. I saw him there some years ago in the flower of his humiliation. He was giving lectures on world history to an audience consisting chiefly of Catholic seminary students and had already gotten as far as the fall of Adam and Eve.[138] What a terrible end the enemies of France come to! The fourth ally is now condemned to relate to Catholic seminary students, the *École polytechnique*[139] of obscurantism, year in, year out, the fall of Adam and Eve! In the man's lectures, as in his books, the greatest confusion prevailed, the greatest disorder in concepts and in language, and he has often been compared, not without reason, with the tower of Babel. He actually resembles an enormous tower in which a hundred thousand thoughts labor and confer with each other and call back and forth and quarrel without any one of them understanding the other. Occasionally the tumult in his head seemed to cease for a moment, and he then spoke at length and slowly and boringly,[140] and from his ill-tempered lips the monotonous words fell like doleful raindrops from a lead gutter.

Sometimes when the old demagogic savagery awoke again in him and contrasted repulsively with his monkishly pious and humble words or when he whimpered with Christian loving kindness while leaping back and forth in blood-thirsty rage, you thought you were seeing a tonsured hyena.

Mr. Görres was born in Koblenz, January 25, 1776.

I beg to be excused from giving further details of his life or those

---

138. Görres was then professor of history at the University of Munich. South Germany was largely Catholic, and the University of Munich was of course a "Catholic" university.

139. Polytechnical School.

140. There is no way to convey in English Heine's pun on the word *lang* in the three adverbs *lang, langsam, langweilig.*

of the lives of most of his companions. In my criticism of his friends, the two Schlegels, I have perhaps overstepped the bounds permissible in the discussion of their lives.

Alas, how gloomy it is, not only when one looks at the dioscura, but also when one examines the remaining stars of our literature from close range. Perhaps the stars in the sky only appear to us to be so beautiful and pure because we are far away from them and do not know their intimate lives. Up above there are certainly a few stars that lie and beg; stars that put on airs; stars that are forced to commit all possible transgressions; stars that kiss and betray each other; stars that flatter their enemies and, what is even more painful, their friends, just as we do here below. Those comets that one sometimes sees up above, like maenads of the heavens, with disheveled hair beams, wandering about—these are perhaps the dissolute stars that wind up crawling into an obscure corner of the firmament in penitence and piety, avoiding the sun.

While on the topic of German philosophers, I cannot refrain from correcting an error concerning German philosophy that I find all too widespread here in France. Ever since several Frenchmen have occupied themselves with Schelling's and Hegel's philosophy, communicated in French the results of their studies, and have also applied these results to conditions in France—since then the friends of clear thought and of liberty complain that the craziest fancies and sophisms are being introduced from Germany with which to confuse the minds and clothe every lie and every act of despotism with the appearance of truth and justice. In a word, these excellent people, concerned for the interests of liberalism, are complaining about the harmful influence of German philosophy in France. But this is unfair to German philosophy. In the first place, what has hitherto been presented to the French under the name of German philosophy, particularly by Mr. Victor Cousin,[141] is not German philosophy. Mr. Cousin has expounded a lot of clever twaddle, but not German philosophy. Secondly, real German philosophy is that which originated directly from Kant's *Critique of Pure Reason* and, preserving the character of its origin, paid little attention to

141. Victor Cousin (1792–1867), founder of the so-called eclectic school of philosophy, was the first to introduce recent German philosophy to the French.

political or religious conditions, but all the more attention to the ultimate grounds of all knowledge.

It is true that the metaphysical systems of most German philosophers bore very close resemblance to mere cobwebs. But what harm did that do? Jesuitism certainly couldn't use these cobwebs for its nets of lies, and despotism was certainly just as unable to use them for braiding its snares to constrain the minds. Only after Schelling did German philosophy lose this flimsy but harmless character. After him our philosophers no longer analyzed the ultimate grounds of knowledge and of being in general; they no longer hovered among idealistic abstractions; instead they sought reasons for justifying the *status quo;* they became vindicators of what exists. While our earlier philosophers squatted, poor and resigned, in wretched little attic rooms and brooded out their systems, our present-day philosophers wear the dazzling livery of power; they became state philosophers, for they invented philosophical justifications for all the interests of the state in which they were employed. Hegel, for example, professor in Protestant Berlin, took into his system the entire Lutheran Protestant dogmatics, and Mr. Schelling, professor in Catholic Munich, now justifies in his lectures even the most extravagant dogmas of the Apostolic Roman Catholic Church.

Yes, just as once the Alexandrian philosophers[142] summoned all their ingenuity to preserve, through allegorical interpretations, the declining religion of Jupiter from total downfall, so our German philosophers are attempting something similar for the religion of Christ. We care little about examining whether these philosophers have a disinterested aim, but when we see them allied with the party of priests whose material interests are connected with the preservation of Catholicism, we call them Jesuits. They should not think, however, that we are confusing them with the earlier Jesuits. They were great and powerful, full of wisdom and strength of will. Alas for the feeble dwarfs who fancy they would overcome the difficulties which were the ruin of even those black giants! Never has the human mind invented grander dialectics than those with which the ancient Jesuits tried to preserve Catholicism. Yet they did not succeed because they were zealous only for the preservation

142. I.e., the Neoplatonists.

of Catholicism and not for Catholicism itself. They really did not care much about the latter for its own sake; hence at times they profaned the Catholic principle itself in order to bring it to power; they came to an understanding with paganism, with the despots of the world, encouraged their lusts, became murderers and merchants, and when necessary, they even became atheists. But in vain did their father confessors grant the friendliest absolutions and their casuists coquette with every vice and crime. They competed in vain with laymen in art and science in order to use both as tools. Here their weakness became quite obvious. They were jealous of all great scholars and artists, yet could not discover or create anything extraordinary. They wrote pious hymns and built cathedrals, but no spirit of freedom flows through their poems, only the sighs of trembling obedience to the superiors in the Order. Even in their buildings one sees only anxious constraint, stony pliancy, sublimity on command. Barrault[143] once said quite rightly, "The Jesuits could not raise the earth up to Heaven, and they dragged Heaven down to earth." All their activities were fruitless. No life can flower from a lie, and God cannot be saved by the devil.

Mr. Schelling was born January 27, 1775, in Würtemberg.

IV

I have been able to give only a few intimations of Mr. Schelling's relationship to the Romantic School. His influence was primarily of a personal nature. In addition, ever since Schelling made nature philosophy the fashion, nature has been interpreted much more thoughtfully by poets. Some plunged into nature with all their human emotions; others had discovered a few magic formulas for evoking from nature a human quality in appearance and language. The former were the real mystics and resembled in many respects the Indian religious, who become a part of nature and finally begin to feel at one with it. The others were more like magicians, summoning from nature at their own will even the hostile spirits; they resembled the Arabian magicians who can at will bring any

---

143. Émile Barrault (1800–1869), a French journalist and an enthusiastic follower of Saint-Simon.

stone to life and turn any life to stone. Novalis[144] belonged, *par excellence*, to the former, Hoffmann[145] to the others. Novalis saw everywhere only marvels, lovely marvels. He listened to the plants conversing with each other, he knew the secret of every young rose, in the end he identified himself with all of nature, and when autumn came and the leaves fell, he died. Hoffmann, on the other hand, saw everywhere only ghosts; they nodded at him from every Chinese teapot and every Berlin wig. He was a magician who transformed humans into beasts and the latter even into royal Prussian *Hofräte;* he could summon the dead from their graves, but life itself rejected him as a dreary phantom. This he felt; he felt that he himself had become a ghost; all of nature now was to him a poorly ground mirror, in which, distorted a thousandfold, he saw only his own death mask, and his works are nothing but a terrible cry of anguish in twenty volumes.

Hoffmann does not belong to the Romantic School. He had no contact with the Schlegels, still less with their views. I mentioned him here only as a contrast to Novalis, who is quite strictly a poet of that School. Novalis is less well-known in France than Hoffmann, who has been introduced to the French public in a most attractive form by Loève-Veimars[146] and thus has acquired a great reputation in France. Hoffmann is now not at all *en vogue* with us in Germany, though he was at one time. In his day he was much read, but only by people whose nerves were too strong or too weak for them to be affected by soft chords. The really gifted and the poetic natures would have nothing to do with him. They much preferred Novalis. But, in all honesty, Hoffmann was much more significant as a poet than Novalis. For the latter, with his idealized figures, always hovered above, his head in the clouds, whereas Hoffmann, with all his bizarre caricatures, still always clung firmly to earthly reality. Just as the giant Antaeus, however, remained invincibly strong when he was touching Mother Earth with his foot and lost his strength as soon as Hercules lifted him up, a poet, too, is strong and vigorous as long as he does not leave the ground of reality,

144. Pseudonym for Friedrich von Hardenberg (1772–1801).
145. E. T. A. Hoffmann (1776–1822).
146. M. Loève-Veimars, French translator who assisted in preparing the French edition of Heine's works.

and becomes feeble the moment he soars about on the wings of fancy and loses himself in the blue.

The great similarity between the two poets probably lies in the fact that their poetry was in reality a disease. It has been said in regard to this that the judgment of their writings is not the business of the critic but of the physician. The rosy light in the works of Novalis is not the color of health but of tuberculosis, and the fiery glow in Hoffmann's *Fantastic Tales* is not the flame of genius but of fever.

But do we have a right to such remarks, we who are not all too blessed with health ourselves? Especially now, when literature looks like a huge hospital? Or is poetry perhaps a disease of mankind, as the pearl is really only the morbid substance from which the poor oyster beast is suffering?

Novalis was born on May 2, 1772. His real name was Hardenberg. He loved a young lady who suffered from tuberculosis and died of it. This sad story pervades everything he wrote, his life was only a dreamy passing away, and he died of tuberculosis in 1801, before completing his twenty-ninth year and his novel. In its present form this novel is only a fragment of a large allegorical work which, like Dante's *Divine Comedy,* was to celebrate all earthly and heavenly things. Heinrich von Ofterdingen, the famous poet,[147] is the hero. We see him as a youth in Eisenach, the pleasant little town that lies at the foot of the ancient Wartburg, where the greatest but also the most stupid things took place, where Luther translated his Bible and some silly Teutomaniacs burned Mr. Kamptz' *Police-Code.*[148] In this fortress that contest of the Minnesingers was also once held,[149] in which, among other poets, Heinrich von Ofterdingen and Klingsohr von Ungerland[150] sang in

147. This is also the title of the novel. As far as is known, he was not an historical figure.

148. Karl von Kamptz, a Prussian statesman. On October 18, 1817, the anniversary of the battle of Leipzig (1813), a national convention of the *Burschenschaften* met at the Wartburg, and as a re-enactment of Luther's burning of the papal bull, old printed paper inscribed with the names of despised reactionary authors was thrown into the fire lit to celebrate the victory of Leipzig over Napoleon.

149. It is not certain that such a contest ever took place. The ultimate source is a thirteenth-century poem about the contest, which was preserved in a fourteenth-century manuscript, but this is of course not a reliable source.

150. I.e., Hungary. Klingsohr appears as an important character in the medieval epic *Parcival* by Wolfram von Eschenbach.

the hazardous competition in poetry which the *Manessische Samm-lung* has preserved for us.[151] The loser's head was to be forfeited to the executioner, and the landgrave of Thuringia was the arbitrator. The Wartburg, scene of his later fame, towers momentously above the hero's cradle, and the beginning of Novalis' novel shows him, as I have said, in his father's house in Eisenach. "His parents were already in bed and asleep, the wall clock beat its monotonous rhythm, and outside the rattling windows roared the wind; intermittently the room was illuminated by the glimmer of the moon.

"The youth lay tossing on the bed, thinking of the stranger and his tales. 'It is not the treasures that have aroused such an inexpressible yearning in me,' he said to himself. 'Avarice is alien to me, but I long to see the blue flower. It is constantly in my mind, and I can think and write of nothing else. I have never felt this way before. It is as if I had been dreaming before or as if I had passed over in my sleep to another world, for in the world in which I used to live who would have cared about flowers? And I certainly never heard there about such a strange passion for a flower.'"

With these words *Heinrich von Ofterdingen* begins, and all through the novel the blue flower shines and exhales its fragrance. It is curious and significant that even the most mythical characters in this book seem as familiar to us as if in earlier times we had lived quite intimately with them. Old memories awake, even Sophia has such familiar features, and we remember whole avenues of beeches where we walked up and down with her in loving communion. But all this lies in the dim past like a half-forgotten dream.

Novalis' muse was a pale, slender girl with serious blue eyes, golden jacinth hair, smiling lips, and a little red birth-mark on the left side of her chin. For I imagine as muse of Novalis' poetry the very same girl who first made me acquainted with him when I saw in her lovely hands the red morocco volume with gilt edges, which contained *Ofterdingen*. She always wore a blue dress, and her

151. A famous manuscript from the fourteenth century containing a collection of medieval poems, among them the poem about the contest in the Wartburg.

name was Sophia. She lived a few stops from Göttingen with her sister, the wife of the postmaster, a cheerful, plump, red-cheeked woman with a high bosom which, with its jagged stiff blond hairs, looked like a fortress. This fortress, however, was impregnable; the woman was a Gibraltar of virtue. She was an active, economical, practical woman, whose only pleasure consisted in reading Hoffmann's novels. In Hoffmann she found a man who knew how to shake her solid nature and set it in pleasant motion. In contrast, the mere sight of one of Hoffmann's books gave her pale delicate sister the most unpleasant sensations, and if she should accidentally touch one of them, she began to tremble. She was as tender as a sensitive plant, and her words were so exquisite, so pure in tone, and when you put them together, they were poetry. I have written down many things she said, and they are strange poems, quite in Novalis' manner, but even more ethereal, dying away to an almost inaudible faintness. I am especially fond of one of these poems which she spoke to me when I took my departure for Italy. In an autumn garden, which had been illuminated for a special occasion, we hear the last lamp, the last rose, and a wild swan conversing together. The morning mists now close in, the last lamp has gone out, the rose is bare of petals, and the swan spreads his white wings and flies southward.

In the area of Hanover there are many wild swans that migrate to the warmer south in autumn and return home to us again in the summer. They probably spend the winter in Africa. For in the breast of a dead swan we once found an arrow that Professor Blumenbach recognized as African. The poor bird with the arrow in his breast had still returned to his northern nest to die. Many swans, however, when pierced with such arrows, may not be able to complete their journey, and they perhaps remain behind without strength on a burning desert or they sit with weary wings on an Egyptian pyramid and gaze longingly toward the north, toward their cool summer nest in the land of Hanover.

When I returned from the south in the late autumn of 1828 (with a burning arrow in my breast as well), my path led me to the neighborhood of Göttingen, and I dismounted at the home of my fat friend, the postmistress, to change horses. I had not seen her for years on end, and the good woman appeared to have changed considerably. Her bosom still resembled a fortress, but a badly damaged one: the bastions were razed; the two watchtowers were merely hanging ruins; a sentinel no longer guarded the entrance; and the heart, the citadel, was broken. As I learned from the postilion Pieper, she had even lost the desire for Hoffmann's novels, and she now drank all the more brandy before bedtime. That is really much simpler; for people always have brandy around the house, while Hoffmann's novels must be acquired from the Deuerlich lending library in Göttingen, which is four hours away. The postilion Pieper was a small and sour-pussed fellow. It seemed as if he had guzzled vinegar and been shriveled up by it. When I asked postilion Pieper about the sister of the postmistress, he answered, "Mademoiselle Sophia will soon die and is already an angel." How admirable a person had to be when even sour-pussed Pieper said she was an angel! And he said this while he frightened away the cackling and fluttering poultry with his knee-high boots. The post office, once a merry white, had changed just like its landlady; it was a sickly yellow, and the walls had buckled like wrinkles. In the courtyard were battered wagons, and next to the dung heap, hanging to dry on a pole, was a thoroughly soaked, scarlet-red postilion's coat. Mademoiselle Sophia was standing upstairs at the window, reading, and when I went up, I found once more in her hands a book bound in red morocco, with gilt-edged leaves, and it was again *Ofterdingen* by Novalis. So she had gone on and on reading this book and had caught tuberculosis from the reading and looked like a transparent shadow. But she was now of a spiritual beauty the sight of which moved me most grievously. I took her two pale, thin hands and looked deep into her blue eyes and finally asked, "Mademoiselle Sophia, how are you?" "I am well," she answered, "and shall soon be even better." And she pointed out the window to the new graveyard, a small hill, not far from the house. On this bare hillside stood a single slender, withered poplar with only a few leaves still hanging on it, and it moved in the autumn wind, not like a living tree, but like the ghost of a tree.

Mademoiselle Sophia now lies beneath this poplar, and the keepsake she bequeathed to me, the book bound in red morocco with gilt-edged leaves, Novalis' *Heinrich von Ofterdingen,* now lies before me on my desk, and I used it in writing this chapter.

BOOK THREE

I

Do you know China, the homeland of winged dragons and porcelain teapots? The whole country is a cabinet of curios surrounded by a tremendous long wall and a hundred thousand Tartar sentinels. But birds and the ideas of European scholars fly over it, and when they have looked around enough there and return home again, they tell us the most delightful things about this strange country and its strange people. There nature, in its glaring colors and ornate forms, fantastic giant flowers, dwarf trees, clipped-off mountains, baroquely voluptuous fruits, crazily adorned birds, is a caricature just as incredible as the men with their pointed queues, polite bows, long nails, their prematurely wise manner, and their childish, monosyllabic language. Man and nature cannot look at each other there without inwardly longing to laugh. They do not laugh aloud, however, because both are much too civilized and polite; and in order to suppress their laughter they make the most seriously droll faces. Neither shading nor perspective exists there. From the houses, which are all colors of the rainbow and are stacked up one above the other, rise a multitude of roofs resembling open umbrellas, their edges hung full of small metal bells, so that even the wind as it passes cannot help making itself ridiculous by a foolish tinkling.

In such a house of bells there once lived a princess whose little feet were even smaller than those of other Chinese women, whose small, slanting eyes blinked even more sweetly and dreamily than those of the other ladies of the Celestial Empire, and in whose small, giggling heart the wildest caprices nested. You see, it was her most supreme delight to rip to pieces costly fabrics of silk and gold brocade. When these rustled and crackled loudly under her lacerating fingers, she rejoiced for joy. But at last, having wasted her entire fortune on this pastime and torn up all her possessions, she was locked up in a round tower, at the advice of all the mandarins, as incurably insane.

This Chinese princess, caprice personified, is also the personified muse of a German poet who must not remain unmentioned in a history of Romantic literature. She is the muse who smiles at us so insanely from the poems of Mr. Clemens Brentano. In them she tears up the smoothest satin trains and the most glittering gold lace, and her destructive amiability and her exuberant madness fill our souls with an uncanny rapture and a voluptuous terror. For fifteen years, however, Mr. Brentano has been living remote from the world, locked up, indeed walled up, in his Catholicism. There was nothing valuable left to tear up. They say he has torn the hearts that loved him, and each of his friends complains of wanton injury. He has exercised his destructiveness most against himself and his poetic talent. I refer in particular to one of his comedies, entitled *Ponce de Leon*.[152] There is nothing that is more dismembered than this work, the ideas as well as the language. But all these tatters are alive and whirl around in confused gaiety. You think you are seeing a masked ball of words and ideas. It is all a bustle of the sweetest disorder, and only the prevailing madness produces a certain unity. The craziest puns run like harlequins through the whole piece, striking out in all directions with their smooth wooden swords. Sometimes a serious expression appears, but it stutters like the Doctor of Bologna.[153] Here a phrase saunters along like a white Pierrot with too broad, trailing sleeves and all too large vest buttons. There humpbacked jokes with short little legs leaped like Pulcinella.[154] Words of love flutter about like teasing Columbines, sorrow in their hearts. And everything dances and hops and whirls and rattles, and above it all sound the trumpets of the Bacchanalian mania for destruction.

A long tragedy by the same poet, *The Founding of Prague*,[155] is also very remarkable. In it are scenes in which the most mysterious terrors of ancient sagas seize you. The gloomy forests of Bohemia rustle there; the angry Slavic gods are still alive; pagan nightingales still warble; but the soft rosy dawn of Christianity is already

152. Written about 1801, published in 1804.
153. The learned *dottore* of Bologna, a pedant, and other characters mentioned here, were stock figures in the Italian *commedia dell'arte*. It was Tartaglia who was the stutterer.
154. One of the servants or men of the lower classes, who were responsible for much of the comic action.
155. Published in 1815.

lighting up the treetops. Mr. Brentano has also written some good stories, especially *The Story of the Just Caspar and Fair Annie*.[156] When fair Annie was still a child and went with her grandmother to the executioner's to buy some healing medicines, as the common people in Germany used to do, all of a sudden something moved in the large cabinet in front of which fair Annie was standing, and the child cried out in fright, "A mouse! A mouse!" But the executioner was even more frightened and became as solemn as death and said to the grandmother, "My dear woman, in this cabinet hangs my executioner's sword, and it moves of its own accord whenever anyone comes near it who shall some day be beheaded with it. My sword is thirsting for this child's blood. Allow me just to graze the child's neck with it. The sword will then be satisfied with a drop of blood and will feel no further longing." But the grandmother paid no attention to this sensible counsel and later regretted it bitterly when fair Annie was actually beheaded with the same sword.

Mr. Clemens Brentano is now about fifty years old and lives in Frankfurt, in hermit-like seclusion, as a corresponding member of the organization for Catholic propaganda. His name has been almost forgotten in recent years, and only when there is discussion of the folksongs that he edited with his late friend Achim von Arnim, is his name occasionally mentioned. In collaboration with Arnim he published under the title *The Boy's Magic Horn*[157] a collection of poems, part of which they found still current among the common people, part in broadsheets and rare publications. I cannot praise this book enough. It contains the fairest flowers of the German spirit, and whoever wishes to know the lovable side of the German people should read these folksongs. The book is lying before me at this very moment, and I feel as if I were smelling the fragrance of German linden trees. For the linden plays a leading role in these songs; in its shade lovers talk in the evenings; it is their favorite tree, perhaps because the linden leaf has the shape of a human heart. This comment was once made by a German poet who is my favorite, namely myself. On the title page of that book is a boy blowing his horn, and if a German in a foreign land

156. Published in 1817.
157. Three volumes published 1806–1808.

looks long at this picture, he fancies he hears the most familiar tones, and homesickness might steal upon him as on that Swiss mercenary who was standing guard on the bastions of Strassburg, heard the call of the Alpine cowherds in the distance, threw away his pike, and swam the Rhine, but was soon caught again and shot as a deserter. *The Boy's Magic Horn* contains this touching song about the incident:

> In Strassburg, at the fort,
> my trouble was to start.
> I heard the alphorn calling from beyond,
> I had to swim back to my fatherland.
> But fate was hard.
>
> They caught me the same night,
> put to an end my flight.
> They dragged me from the river to the shore
> and rushed me to the captain's door.
> I am done for.
>
> Tomorrow morn at ten
> I'll face the captain's men.
> For pardon I'm to plead,
> but it will mean defeat,
> I know indeed.
>
> My friends and company,
> you've seen the last of me.
> O shepherd boy, what did you do?
> The alphorn lured me, that you blew.
> I'm blaming you.

What a beautiful poem! There is a curious magic about these folksongs. Literary poets try to imitate these products of nature in the same way that artificial water is manufactured. But even though they discover the constituents by means of a chemical process, the main thing still escapes them, the indivisible, mysterious force of nature. In these songs you feel the heartbeat of the German people. Here all its gloomy mirth, all its mad sanity are revealed. Here German anger drums, German mockery whistles, German love kisses. Here real German wine and real German tears sparkle, and the tears are sometimes even more precious than the wine; they contain much iron and salt. What naivete in loyalty! In disloyalty, what honorableness! What an honorable fellow the poor tramp is, even though he is a highwayman! Just listen to the stoical, moving story he tells about himself:

> I came upon a village inn,
> they asked me, "What's your line?"
> "I am a ragged vagabond,
> I like good food and wine."
>
> They led me to the common room,
> the drinks began to pass;
> I looked around the company
> and soon put down my glass.
>
> They sat me at the table head,
> gave me a merchant's chair,
> but when I had to pay the bill
> my money bag was bare.
>
> At night I asked where I could sleep,
> they showed me to a shed.
> Not even for a vagabond
> was this a rosy bed.
>
> And when I lay down in the barn,
> I tried to build my nest;
> the hawthorns and the thistles stung
> and did not let me rest.
>
> And when next morning I got up,
> the roof was full of frost.
> I laughed—but for the vagabond
> good luck, I felt, was lost.
>
> So I picked up my trusty sword
> and slung it on my side—
> poor me, I had to go on foot,
> I had no horse to ride.

And so I left and hit the road
for better or for worse;
I met a wealthy merchant's son
and took away his purse.

This poor tramp is the most German character I know. What
composure, what conscious power prevails in this poem! But you
shall also meet our Gretel. She is an honest girl, and I love her
very much. Hans said to Gretel:

"Dress up, dress up, my Gretel,
come with me and be mine,
the grain is safely gathered,
the grapes are off the vine."

She answered happily:

"Ah, Hansel, my dear Hansel,
with you I'll run away;
we'll work the fields on weekdays,
drink wine each holiday."

Now by the hands he took her,
and snow-white was her skin,
then down the road he led her,
until he found an inn.

"O hostess, friendly hostess,
bring wine to drink our fill;
we'll use this dress of Gretel's
to settle up the bill."

Now Gretel started weeping,
Oh, how her anger showed!
And how her tears were shining
as down her cheeks they flowed!

"Ah, Hansel, my dear Hansel,
that's not the way you talked
when you came to my father's
and out the door we walked."

Now by her hands he took her,
and snow-white was her skin,
and when he found a garden
he led his Gretel in.

"Ah, Gretel, my dear Gretel,
don't cry in such distress.
Do you regret your honor?
Repent your wantonness?"

"I care not that I'm wanton,
nor that I'm honorless;
I only fear I'll never
get back my pretty dress."

She is not Goethe's Gretchen, and her remorse would not be a
subject for Scheffer.[158] There is no German moonlight here. There
is just as little sentimentality when a young coxcomb demands that
his girl let him into her room at night and she refuses with the
words:

"Ride on to where you came from,
ride on to yonder heath
whence you have come to me.
There you will find a good-sized rock;
if you will use it as a bed,
there won't be feathers on your head."

But moonlight, moonlight in abundance, flooding the whole soul,
gleams in the lyric:

Were I a little bird,
I'd spread my wings and would
fly to you, dear.
But since this cannot be
I must stay here.

158. Ary Scheffer, Dutch painter in France who painted scenes from the works
of Goethe, Schiller, and Byron.

Though I am far from you,
I'm in my dreams with you,
talking with you.
But when I wake at dawn,
there is but me.

At night I lie awake,
wait for the day to break,
thinking that you,
darling, a thousand times
vowed your love true.

If, charmed, we now inquire about the composers of these songs,
they seem to give the answer themselves in their final words:

Whence came that beautiful song?
Three geese have brought it along,
'cross the river—two gray and one white.

Usually the writers of such songs were wanderers, vagabonds,
soldiers, itinerant scholars, or traveling apprentices, particularly
these last. Very often on my walking tours I joined company with
these people and noticed how, at times, inspired by some unusual
event, they would improvise a snatch of a folksong or whistle it
into the open air. The birds sitting on the tree branches heard this,
and when another lad later came strolling past with knapsack and
walking stick, they would whistle that little snatch of song in his
ear, and he would add the missing lines, and the song was finished.
The words come from out of the blue to the lips of such a lad,
and he needs only to utter them, and they are then even more
poetic than all the fine poetical phrases that we concoct from the
depths of our hearts. The character of these traveling apprentices
lives and moves in such folksongs. They are a strange sort. Without
a penny in their pockets, they travel through all of Germany,
harmless, happy, and free. I usually found that three set out together
on such a journey. Of these three one was always the faultfinder.
He found fault with everything that came along, with every gay-
colored bird flying in the air, with every fine horseman that rode
by, and if they came to a poor quarter with miserable huts and
beggars in rags, he was likely to remark ironically, "The good Lord

created the world in six days, but just look, the result shows it." The second companion interrupted only occasionally with angry comments; he couldn't say anything without cursing; he grumbled furiously about all the masters for whom he had worked; and his continual refrain was how much he regretted not having given his landlady in Halberstadt, who had served him cabbage and turnips every day, a sound thrashing to remember him by. At the word "Halberstadt" the third lad sighed from the depths of his heart. He was the youngest, was setting out into the world for the first time, still thought constantly of his sweetheart's dark brown eyes, always hung his head, and never said a word.

The Boy's Magic Horn is a much too remarkable monument of our literature and had a much too significant influence on the lyricists of the Romantic School, particularly on our excellent Mr. Uhland, for me to leave it undiscussed. This work and the *Nibelungenlied* played an important role during this period. I must also give the latter special mention here. For a long time nothing was talked about in Germany but the *Nibelungenlied,* and classical scholars were not a little annoyed when this epic was compared to the *Iliad* or when people argued about which of the two poems was the better. And the public looked on like a boy who is asked in all seriousness, "Which do you like better, a horse or ginger-bread?" At any rate, the *Nibelungenlied* is possessed of great and mighty vigor. A Frenchman can scarcely get any idea of it. And certainly not of the language in which it is written. It is a language of stone, and the stanzas are like rhymed blocks of stone. Here and there, out of the crevices, red flowers well up like drops of blood, or long sprays of ivy trail down like green tears. Of the gigantic passions stirring in this poem, well-behaved little people like you can get even less of an idea. Imagine a bright summer night, the stars, pale as silver but as large as suns, standing out in the blue sky; and imagine that all the Gothic cathedrals of Europe had arranged a rendezvous on an enormous, broad plain, and that then the Strassburg minster, the Cologne cathedral, the bell tower of Florence, the cathedral of Rouen, etc., strode calmly up and paid court very politely to lovely Notre Dame of Paris. To be sure, their gait is a trifle ungainly, some of them behave very awkwardly, and one might laugh sometimes at their infatuated waddle. But this laughter would end as soon as you saw them fly into a rage and strangle each other and saw Notre Dame of Paris lift both stony arms despairingly toward Heaven and suddenly seize a sword and cut off the head from the rump of the greatest of all cathedrals. But no, even then you cannot get any idea of the main characters of the *Nibelungenlied;* no tower is as tall and no stone as hard as grim Hagen and vengeful Kriemhilde.

Who composed this poem? We do not know the name of the poet who wrote the *Nibelungenlied* any more than we know the composers of the folksongs. Strange! One rarely knows the originator of the best books, poems, buildings, and other monuments of art. What was the name of the architect who planned the Cologne cathedral? Who painted the altarpieces there, in which the lovely Blessed Virgin and the three wise men are so delightfully portrayed? Who wrote the book of Job, which has comforted so many generations of suffering humanity? People forget only too easily the names of their benefactors. The names of the good and noble men who spent themselves for the welfare of their fellow citizens are seldom heard in the mouths of the peoples, and their dull memory preserves only the names of their oppressors and their brutal military heroes. Mankind is a tree that forgets the quiet gardener who cared for it in the cold season, watered it during the drought, and protected it from harmful animals, but it faithfully preserves the names mercilessly carved in its bark with sharp steel and passes them on in ever increasing size to the latest generations.

II

Due to their joint edition of *The Magic Horn* the names of Brentano and Arnim are usually coupled together, and having discussed the former, I must not overlook the other, all the less so as he merits our attention far more. Ludwig Achim von Arnim is a great poet and had one of the most original minds in the Romantic School. Lovers of the fantastic would enjoy him more than any other German writer. In the realm of fantasy he surpasses Hoffmann as well as Novalis. He succeeded in penetrating more intimately into nature than the latter and could conjure up far more uncanny specters than Hoffmann. In fact, sometimes when I watched Hoffmann himself, it seemed to me as if Arnim had invented him.

Arnim has remained completely unknown to the general public; he has a name only among men of letters. These, however, while paying him the most unqualified recognition, have never praised him publicly as he deserves. Indeed, some writers used to speak of him disdainfully, and they were the very ones who imitated his style. One might apply to them Steevens'[159] jibe at Voltaire for belittling Shakespeare after having made use of *Othello* for his *Orosman*: "These people are like the thieves who set fire to the house after robbing it." Why has Mr. Tieck never spoken suitably about Arnim, he who could pay so many brilliant compliments to so many an insignificant piece of trash? The Schlegel brothers also ignored Arnim. Only after his death did he receive a kind of obituary recognition from a member of the School.[160]

In my opinion, it was especially impossible for Arnim's reputation to spread because he always remained too much of a Protestant for his friends, the Catholic party, and also because the Protestant party thought he was a clandestine Catholic. But why did the public reject him, the public to whom his novels and novellas were available in any lending library? Hoffmann, too, was hardly discussed at all in our literary gazettes and esthetic journals, higher criticism observed a genteel silence about him, and yet he was read everywhere. Why, then, did the German public neglect an author whose imagination was of universal scope, whose nature was of the most awesome profundity, and whose powers of description were so unsurpassable? One thing this poet lacked, and it is precisely the one thing that the public looks for in books—life. The public demands that a writer sympathize with their everyday passions, that he excite their emotions, either pleasantly or painfully; the public wants to be moved. This need Arnim could not satisfy. He was not a poet of life, but of death. In everything he wrote the prevailing agitation is not real; the characters bustle about in a hurry, moving their lips as if in speech, but you only see their words, you don't hear them. These figures leap, wrestle, stand on their heads, approach us secretly, and whisper softly in our ears, "We are dead." Such a spectacle would be all too uncanny and

---

159. George Steevens, an English scholar who collaborated with Samuel Johnson in preparing an edition of Shakespeare's plays.

160. Written in 1831 for a Berlin journal by Georg Wilhelm Häring, who wrote historical novels in the manner of Scott under the pseudonym Willibald Alexis.

annoying were it not for Arnim's charm, which pervades each of these works like the smile of a child, but a dead child. Arnim can describe love, sometimes sensuality as well, but even then we cannot feel with him. We see beautiful bodies, heaving bosoms, delicately formed hips, but a cold, moist shroud veils all of it. Sometimes Arnim is witty, and we even have to laugh, but still it seems as if Death were tickling us with his scythe. Usually, however, he is serious, as serious as a dead German. A living German is already a sufficiently serious creature, but a *dead* German! A Frenchman has absolutely no idea how very serious we Germans are when dead; our faces then become much longer still, and the worms that dine off us become melancholy if they look at us while eating. The French think how very dreadfully serious Hoffmann can be, but this is child's play compared with Arnim. When Hoffmann conjures up his dead and they climb out of their graves and dance around them, he himself trembles for terror and dances in their midst, making the wildest, monkey-like grimaces. But when Arnim conjures up his dead, it is as if a general were reviewing his troops, and he sits so calmly on his tall ghost of a white horse and commands the horrible troops to file past him, and they look up at him fearfully and seem to be afraid of him. He, however, nods to them affably.

Ludwig Achim von Arnim was born in Brandenburg in 1784 and died in the winter of 1830.[161] He wrote plays in verse, novels, and novellas. His plays are full of intrinsic poetry, especially one of them, entitled *The Mountain-Cock*.[162] The first scene would not be unworthy even of the very greatest poet. How realistically, how faithfully the most dismal boredom is pictured there! One of the three illegitimate sons of the deceased landgrave is sitting alone in the vast, deserted castle-hall, yawning as he talks to himself and complains that his legs are growing longer and longer beneath the table and that the moaning wind is whistling so icily through his teeth. His brother, good Franz, now comes shuffling in slowly, in the clothes of his late father, which are much too big for him, and he recalls sorrowfully that at this hour he was usually helping his father dress, that the latter often threw him a crust of bread which

161. Heine is in error here. Arnim was born in 1781 in Berlin and died in January, 1831.
162. First published in 1813.

he, with his old teeth, could no longer chew, and that he also sometimes kicked him angrily. This last memory moves good Franz to tears, and he laments that his father is now dead and can no longer kick him.

The titles of Arnim's novels are *The Guardians of the Crown* and *Countess Dolores*.[163] The former also has an excellent beginning. The scene is laid in the upper part of the watch tower in Waiblingen, in a cozy little parlor of the warder and his good, fat wife, who is not, however, so fat as they say down below in the town. As a matter of fact, it is slander when they said she had become so corpulent in the tower rooms that she could no longer descend the narrow tower stairs, and after the death of her first husband, the old warder, had been obliged to marry the new warder. The poor woman up there fretted not a little at such malicious rumors; and the only reason she couldn't go down the tower stairs was that she got dizzy.

Arnim's second novel, *Countess Dolores*, also has a magnificent beginning. The author describes the poetry of poverty, an aristocratic poverty at that, which he, at that time himself living in straitened circumstances, very often chose as his theme. What a master Arnim is here also in the portrayal of ruin! I still feel as though I see young Countess Dolores' desolate castle, looking all the more desolate because the old Count began the building in a gay, Italian style, but did not finish it. Now it is a modern ruin, and in the castle garden everything is dilapidated. The paths of clipped yews have gone shrubby and wild; the trees are growing together; the laurels and oleanders are creeping dismally along the ground; the beautiful tall flowers are smothered by nasty weeds; the statues of the gods have fallen from their pedestals; and a few mischievous beggar boys are crouching beside a poor Venus lying in the tall grass and are lashing her marble bottom with nettles. When the old Count returns to his castle after a long absence, the strange behavior of his household, especially of his wife, astonishes him very much. All sorts of things happen at meals, and this is probably because the poor woman had died of grief, and the other members of the household were also long since dead. Finally the

163. The first was published in 1817; the second had appeared earlier, in 1810. The full title of the latter is *Countess Dolores' Poverty, Wealth, Guilt, and Repentance.*

Count himself seems to suspect that he is living among nothing but ghosts and, without showing that he is aware of this, departs again secretly.

Of Arnim's novellas his *Isabella of Egypt*[164] seems to me the best. Here we see the nomadic life of the gypsies, called in France *Bohémiens,* also *Egyptiens.* This strange fairy-tale people, with their brown faces, friendly soothsayer eyes, and melancholy mysteriousness, comes to life here. The chaotic, deceptive gaiety conceals a great mystic sorrow. For according to the legend, told very charmingly in this novella, the gypsies must wander for a time all over the world as penance for that inhospitable harshness with which their forefathers once turned away the Blessed Virgin with her child when she requested lodging for the night during her flight in Egypt. Thus people felt justified in treating them cruelly. Since they did not yet have any philosophers of the Schelling type in the Middle Ages, literature had to undertake the extenuation of the most shameful and brutal laws. Against no one were these laws more barbaric than against the poor gypsies. In many countries it was permissible to hang any gypsy on suspicion of theft without investigation or judicial sentence. Thus their chief, Michael, called Duke of Egypt, though innocent, was hanged. Arnim's novella begins with this sad event. In the night the gypsies took down their dead Duke from the gallows, placed his royal cloak of red around his shoulders, set the silver crown upon his head, and lowered him into the Scheldt, firmly convinced that the compassionate stream would carry him home to his beloved Egypt. The poor gypsy princess Isabella, his daughter, knew nothing of this sad incident. She lived alone in a dilapidated house on the Scheldt and heard in the night a strange murmuring in the water and suddenly saw her pale father emerge in his crimson death-robes, and the moon cast its sorrowful light upon the silver crown. The heart of the beautiful child almost broke from unutterable grief; in vain she tried to hold fast to her dead father; he floated on toward Egypt, his native wonderland, where people were awaiting his arrival in order to bury him worthily in one of the great pyramids. The funeral feast with which the poor child honored her dead father is touching. She spread her white veil over a fieldstone, and on this she set food

164. Published in 1811.

and drink, which she solemnly consumed. Everything the excellent Arnim tells us about the gypsies is profoundly moving. He had already proffered his sympathy to them in other places, for instance in his epilogue to the *Magic Horn,* where he maintains that we owe the gypsies so many good and beneficial things, in particular most of our medicines, and says we ungratefully rejected and persecuted them. Despite all their love, he laments, they had not been able to secure a home among us. He compares them in this respect with the little dwarfs of whom legend relates that they procured everything their great and powerful enemies desired for banquets but one time were pitifully beaten and chased out of the country for having picked themselves a few peas from the field out of dire need. It was a distressing sight to see the poor little creatures pattering away over the bridge at night like a herd of sheep, and each one having to put down a small coin until they had filled a barrel with them.

A translation of the novella just mentioned, *Isabella of Egypt,* would give the French not merely an idea of Arnim's writings, but would also show that all the terrible, uncanny, gruesome, and ghostly stories that they have toiled so painfully to create in recent years seem to be only the rosy morning dreams of an *opera danseuse* in comparison with Arnim's works. In the whole lot of French thrillers not as much uncanniness has been concentrated as in that coach which Arnim causes to travel from Brake to Brussels[165] and in which the following four persons are seated:

1) An old gypsy woman who is also a witch. She looks like the fairest of the seven deadly sins, lavishly clothed in the most variegated finery of gold tinsel and silk.

2) A dead sluggard who, in order to earn a few ducats, has risen from his grave and contracted to serve as servant for seven years. He is a fat corpse, wears an overcoat of white bearskin, and yet is always cold.

3) A golem, that is, a figure of clay which is shaped like a beautiful woman and behaves like a beautiful woman. On its forehead, concealed under black curls, is written in Hebrew letters the word "truth," and if the word is erased, the whole figure collapses again lifeless, as the mere clay that it is.

---

165. Heine's error. The party drove from Buik to Ghent.

4) Fieldmarshal Cornelius Nepos, who is absolutely not related to the famous historian of this name, who indeed cannot even boast of a middle-class origin, being by birth really a root, a mandrake root, which the French call "mandragora." This root grows under the gallows, on the spot where the most ambiguous tears of a hanged man have flowed. It gave a horrible shriek when beautiful Isabella pulled it out of the ground there at midnight. It looked like a dwarf, except that it had no eyes, mouth, nor ears. The sweet girl planted two black juniper berries and a red rose-hip in its face, from which eyes and mouth developed. After this she strewed a little millet on its head, which grew up as hair, though somewhat shaggy. She rocked the monster in her white arms when it cried like a child; with her sweet rosy lips she kissed its rose-hip-mouth so often that it became all crooked; for sheer love she almost kissed its juniper-eyes out of its head; and the nasty manikin became so spoiled that he finally wanted to become a fieldmarshal and put on a brilliant fieldmarshal's uniform and insisted on being addressed by that title.

These are four very distinguished persons, aren't they? If you plunder the morgue, the graveyard, the Court of Miracles,[166] and all the pest-houses of the Middle Ages, you will still not assemble such a good company as that which rode in a single coach from Brake to Brussels. You French should finally realize that the uncanny is not your forte and that France is not a suitable soil for ghosts of this sort. When you conjure up ghosts, we have to laugh. Yes, we Germans, who can remain perfectly serious at your funniest jokes, we laugh all the more heartily at your ghost stories. For your ghosts are still always Frenchmen. And French ghosts—what a contradiction in terms! In the word "ghost" there is so much that is lonely, morose, German, taciturn; and in the word "French," on the other hand, there is so much that is sociable, polite, French, loquacious! How could a Frenchman be a ghost, or how could ghosts even exist in Paris! In Paris, the foyer of European society! Between twelve and one, the hour that has been allotted to ghosts from time immemorial, the full stream of life is still roaring through the streets of Paris, in the opera the thundering finale is just

---

166. The *cour des miracles* was the sanctuary for Parisian beggars and swindlers, where the blind and the lame could be cured.

sounding, out of the Variétés and the Théâtre-Gymnase[167] come streaming the merriest groups, and the boulevards are thronging with rollicking, laughing, bantering crowds, and everybody goes to the soirées. How unhappy a poor ghost would feel spooking amidst this animated multitude! And how could a Frenchman, even when he is dead, preserve the necessary gravity for haunting when the merriment of the people at their varied pleasures surrounds him on all sides with joyous sound! I myself, though a German, if I were dead and should go haunting at night here in Paris—I could certainly not maintain my ghostly dignity if, let us say, one of those goddesses of frivolity who know how to laugh so delightfully to your face came running to meet me at a street corner. If there were really ghosts in Paris, I am convinced, sociable as the French are, that they would seek each other's friendship, even as ghosts, they would soon form ghost clubs, found a café for the dead, publish a newspaper for the dead, a Paris *Revue for the Dead,* and there would soon be soirées for the dead *ou l'on fera de la musique.*[168] I am convinced that ghosts would have far more fun here in Paris than the living do in Germany. As for me, if I knew that one could exist this way in Paris as a ghost, I would no longer fear death. I would just make arrangements to be buried in Père Lachaise[169] so that I could go haunting in Paris between twelve and one. What an exquisite hour! You German fellow countrymen, if after my death you come to Paris and catch sight of me here at night as a ghost, don't be alarmed. I will not be spooking in the dreadfully unhappy German manner; I will be spooking for pleasure.

In all the ghost stories that I have read the ghost usually has to haunt the places where it buried money. As a precaution, therefore, I am going to bury a few *sous* somewhere on the boulevards. Until now I have only cast my money to the winds in Paris, never buried it under the pavement.

O you poor French writers! You should finally understand that your horror novels and ghost stories are entirely inappropriate for a country where there are no ghosts—or at least where the ghosts behave in as sociably acceptable a manner as we do. It seems to me that you are acting like children who hold masks in front of

167. Theaters for variety shows, comedy, farce, etc.
168. Where music would be played.
169. A cemetery in Paris.

their faces in order to scare each other. They are serious, frightening disguises, but the merry eyes of children peep through the eye slits. We Germans, on the other hand, sometimes wear the most friendly, youthful masks, and out of the eyes peers death itself. You are an elegant, loving, reasonable and lively nation, and only beauty and excellence and humanity belong to the realm of your art. Your older writers have long ago recognized that, and you, the younger generation, will ultimately acquire this insight as well. Leave all these horrors of insanity, hallucination, and the spirit-world to us Germans. Germany is a thriving country for old witches, dead sluggards, golems of every sex, and especially for fieldmarshals like the tiny Cornelius Nepos. Such apparitions could only prosper beyond the Rhine, never in France. When I travelled to France, ghosts accompanied me up to the French border. For the sight of the tricolored flag frightens away ghosts of every sort.—O how I would like to stand on top of the Strassburg cathedral with a tricolored flag in my hands that would stretch to Frankfurt! I believe that if I could wave that sacred flag over my dear fatherland and at the same time recite the proper incantation, then the old witches would fly off on their broom sticks; the cold sluggards would crawl back into their graves; the golems would again disintegrate into mere clay; the fieldmarshal Cornelius Nepos would return to wherever he came from; and this entire spoof would come to an end.

III

The history of literature is as difficult to describe as natural history. In both cases the author must confine himself to the most salient phenomena. But as a small glass of water contains a whole world of curious little creatures which testify just as much to the omnipotence of God as the largest beasts, so the smallest literary journal[170] sometimes contains a great number of poetasters who seem to the tranquil scholar just as interesting as the largest elephants of literature. God is great!

Modern literary historians actually give us a literary history like a well-arranged menagerie and show us, always in separate cages,

170. Literally "Almanac of the Muses," then a favorite title for many journals.

epic mammal poets, lyric aerial poets, dramatic aquatic poets, prose amphibians who write both land and sea novels, humorous mollusks, etc. Others, in contrast, write literary history pragmatically, beginning with the primitive human emotions, following them as they developed in the various epochs and finally assumed artistic form; they begin *ab ovo* like the historian who begins the Trojan War with the story of Leda's egg.[171] And like him, they act foolishly. For I am convinced that if Leda's egg had been used for an omelet, Hector and Achilles would still have met in knightly combat before the Skaian Gate. Great events and great books do not originate from trifles but are inevitable; they are connected with the orbits of the sun, moon, and stars and perhaps originate from their effect on the earth. Events are only the results of ideas.—But how does it happen that at certain times certain ideas make themselves felt so powerfully that they transform in the most miraculous fashion the whole life of man, his desires and aspirations, his thoughts and writings? It is perhaps time to write a literary astrology, explaining from the constellation of the stars the appearance of certain ideas or of certain books in which these ideas are revealed.

Or does the rise of certain ideas merely correspond to certain momentary human needs? Do human beings always look for the ideas with which to justify their wishes of the moment? As a matter of fact, at bottom all men are doctrinaires; they can always find a doctrine to justify all their renunciations or desires. In bad, lean times, when enjoyment has become almost unattainable, they embrace the dogma of abstinence and maintain that earthly grapes are sour. When, however, the times become more affluent and people can reach up for the beautiful fruits of this world, a cheerful doctrine appears, which vindicates all the sweets of life and its full, inalienable right to pleasure.

Are we nearing the end of the Christian Lenten age, and is the rosy age of joy already dawning brightly? How will this cheerful doctrine shape the future?

In the hearts of a nation's writers there already lies the image of its future, and a critic who dissected a modern poet with a knife sharp enough could very easily prophesy, as from the entrails of a

171. Zeus came in the form of a swan as lover to Leda. Helen of Troy was their daughter.

sacrificial animal, how Germany will turn out in the future. With this intention in mind I would be very glad, as a literary Calchas, to slaughter with criticism some of our most recent poets if I were not afraid of seeing in their entrails many things I cannot talk about here. For you cannot discuss our most recent German literature without getting into the depths of politics. In France, where belletristic writers try to withdraw from contemporary political movements, even more than is commendable, you can now pass judgment on the literary figures of the day and leave the day itself undiscussed. On the other side of the Rhine, however, belletristic writers are now plunging ardently into current movements, from which they held themselves remote for so long. For fifty years you Frenchmen have constantly been active, and now you are tired. But we Germans have been sitting at our desks until now, annotating the classics, and would like to get some exercise.

The same reason I indicated above prevents me from discussing with proper appreciation a writer to whom Madame de Staël made only casual reference and of whom, since then, the French public has been made particularly aware through Philarète Chasles'[172] brilliant articles. I am speaking of Jean Paul Friedrich Richter. He has been called unique. An excellent judgment which I only now comprehend fully after having pondered in vain over the proper place to discuss him in a history of literature. He appeared on the scene about the same time as the Romantic School, without participating in it to the slightest degree, and neither did he later have the slightest connection with the Goethean school of art. He stands quite isolated in his age just because, in contrast to both schools, he devoted himself entirely to his own age, and his heart was completely filled with it. His heart and his writings were one and the same. This characteristic, this wholeness, we also find in the writers of present-day Young Germany, who likewise wish to make no distinction between life and writing, who never separate politics from science, art, and religion, and who are simultaneously artists, tribunes, and apostles.

Yes, I repeat the word "apostles," for I know no more expressive word. A new belief animates them with a passion of which writers

172. Philarète Chasles (1798–1873), a French writer. The essay on Jean Paul can be found in his *Études sur l'Allemagne ancienne et moderne.*

of the preceding period had no conception. This is the belief in progress, a belief that originated from science. We have surveyed the lands, weighed the forces of nature, calculated the resources of industry, and behold, we have discovered that this earth is large enough; that it offers sufficient space for everyone to build on it the shelter for his happiness; that this earth can nourish all of us properly if we all work and no one tries to live at another's expense; and that it is not necessary for us to refer the larger and poorer class to Heaven.—To be sure, the number of enlightened persons and believers is still small. But the time has come when the peoples will no longer be counted by heads but by their hearts. And is not the great heart of a single Heinrich Laube[173] worth more than a whole zoo of Raupachs[174] and actors?

I have mentioned the name Heinrich Laube, for how could I speak about Young Germany without mentioning the great, flaming heart that shines forth most brightly from this group. Heinrich Laube, one of the writers who have come to the fore since the July Revolution, has for Germany a social significance, the complete importance of which cannot yet be measured. He has all the good qualities we find in authors of the preceding period, combined with the apostolic zeal of Young Germany. And his intense ardor is softened and transformed by a fine feeling for art. He is just as enthusiastic about beauty as about goodness, he has a sensitive ear and a sharp eye for consummate form, and vulgar natures repel him even when they are useful to the fatherland as champions of noble views. This artistic sense, inherent in him, protected him from the great error of the political rabble which still continues to slander and revile our great master, Goethe.

In this respect another writer of recent times, Mr. Karl Gutzkow,[175] also deserves the highest praise. If I mention him only after Laube, it is not in the least because I do not give him credit for just as much talent and still less because of not being pleased with his tendencies. No, in my opinion Karl Gutzkow is also gifted in

173. A German journalist, author of novels, novellas, and plays, director of the Vienna Burgtheater from 1849 to 1867.
174. Ernst Raupach (1784–1852), German playwright who with his 117 plays rivaled Kotzebue in popularity.
175. German journalist, playwright, and novelist (1811–1878). Soon after the revolution of 1830 he became a leader of progressive thought in Germany.

the highest degree with creative power and a discriminating artistic sense, and his works delight me by their accurate interpretation of our time and its needs. But everything Laube writes is dominated by an all-pervading serenity, a confident grandeur, and a quiet assurance which appeal to me personally more deeply than the picturesque, colorful, stingingly spicy vivacity of Gutzkow's mind.

Like Laube, Mr. Karl Gutzkow, a man of true poetic spirit, had to detach himself in no uncertain terms from those zealots who revile our great master. This is also true of L. Wienbarg[176] and Gustav Schlesier,[177] two very distinguished writers of the recent period whom I must not leave unmentioned here in discussing Young Germany. They certainly deserve to be named among its choir leaders, and their names have won a good repute in Germany. This is not the place to enlarge on their abilities and activities. I have wandered too far from my topic; I shall just say a few more words about Jean Paul.

I have said that Jean Paul Friedrich Richter, in his main tenor, was a predecessor of Young Germany. These writers, however, directed toward the practical, were able to keep away from the abstruse confusion, the baroque manner of description, and the unbearable style of Jean Paul's writings. A clear, logical French mind can never have any idea of this style. Jean Paul's sentence structure consists of nothing but tiny rooms, often so narrow that if one idea meets another there, they bump heads; up above, on the ceilings, are nothing but hooks on which Jean Paul hangs all sorts of thoughts, and in the walls are nothing but secret drawers where he hides emotions. No German author is so rich as he in thoughts and feelings, but he never lets them ripen, and he furnishes us more amazement than pleasure with the riches of his mind and his heart. Thoughts and feelings that would develop into enormous trees if he let them take root properly and spread out with all their branches, blossoms, and leaves—he pulls them out when they have scarcely become small plants or are often even just shoots, and in

176. Ludolf Wienbarg (1802–1872) had presented in his *Esthetic Campaigns* some of the main ideas of these politically and socially minded writers and used here for the first time the term "Young Germany," which soon came into general use.

177. From 1832 to 1834 he worked under Laube in editing the *Zeitung für die elegante Welt,* later published a work on Wilhelm von Humboldt, but is now completely forgotten.

this fashion whole intellectual forests are placed before us in an ordinary dish as vegetables. Now this is strange, unpalatable fare, for not every stomach can digest young oaks, cedars, palm trees, and banyans in such quantities. Jean Paul is a great poet and philosopher, but a more inartistic writer and thinker is hardly conceivable. He gave birth to genuinely poetic figures in his novels, but all these creatures drag an absurdly long umbilical cord around with them and entangle and choke themselves with it. Instead of thoughts he gives us his own process of thinking itself; we see the corporeal activity of his brain; he gives us, so to speak, more brain than thought. And at the same time his jokes are hopping in all directions, the fleas of his impassioned mind. He is the merriest and also the most sentimental of writers. Yes, sentimentality always gets the upper hand, and his laughter suddenly changes to weeping. He often disguises himself as a gross, shabby fellow, but then suddenly, like princes incognito that we see in the theater, he unbuttons his coarse overcoat, and we see the shining star.

In this, Jean Paul is just like the great Irishman with whom he is often compared. The author of *Tristram Shandy,* after losing himself in the crudest trivialities, can also remind us suddenly, by sublime transitions, of his princely dignity, of his equality in rank with Shakespeare. Like Laurence Sterne, Jean Paul, too, exposed his personality in his works and revealed himself in the most human nakedness, but yet with a certain awkward shyness, especially in sexual matters. Laurence Sterne shows himself to the public completely undressed, completely naked; Jean Paul, however, only has holes in his trousers. Some critics wrongly believe that Jean Paul possessed more genuine feeling than Sterne because Sterne, as soon as the subject he is treating reaches a tragic climax, suddenly vaults to the most jesting, laughing tone, whereas Jean Paul, when a joke becomes the least bit serious, gradually begins to blubber and calmly lets his tearglands drip until they're empty. No, Sterne perhaps felt even more deeply than Jean Paul, for he is a greater poet. As I have said before, he is William Shakespeare's equal, and the Muses reared him too, Laurence Sterne, on Parnassus. But in feminine fashion they spoiled him early, especially by their caresses. He was the pet of the pale goddess of tragedy. Once, in a fit of cruel affection, she kissed his young heart so intensely, so passionately, sucking at it so ardently, that the heart began to bleed and suddenly understood all the sorrows of this world and was filled with infinite compassion. Poor young poet's heart! But Mnemosyne's younger daughter, the rosy goddess of jest, quickly sprang toward them and took the suffering boy in her arms and tried to cheer him with laughter and song and gave him the mask of Comedy and the fool's bells as toys and kissed his lips soothingly, kissing onto them all her frivolity, all her defiant gaiety, all her witty raillery.

And after that Sterne's heart and his lips engaged in a curious conflict. Often when his heart was moved by tragedy and he wished to express the deepest feelings of his bleeding heart, then, to his own surprise, there streamed from his lips words of wild laughter and merriment.

IV

In the Middle Ages most people believed that when a building was to be erected, it was necessary to kill some living creature and lay the cornerstone on its blood; in this way the building would stand firm and indestructible. Whether it was the absurd ancient pagan idea that one could win the favor of the gods by blood sacrifices or whether it was a misunderstanding of the Christian doctrine of atonement that produced this notion about the magic power of blood, about healing by blood, about this belief in blood— suffice it to say, the belief was prevalent, and there live on in songs and sagas the gruesome particulars about how to slaughter children or animals in order to strengthen large buildings with their blood. Today mankind is more sensible. We no longer believe in the magic power of blood, neither the blood of an aristocrat nor a god, and the great masses believe only in money. Does present-day religion consist then in God as money incarnate or money as God incarnate? In a word, people believe only in money; they ascribe magic power only to minted metal, to the Host of silver and gold; money is the beginning and the end of all their works; and when they have a building to erect, they take great pains to see that some coins, a capsule with all kinds of coins, is placed under the cornerstone.

Yes, as in the Middle Ages everything, single buildings as well as the whole complex of state and church buildings, rested on the belief in blood, all our present-day institutions rest on the belief in money, in real money. The former was superstition, but the latter is pure egotism. Reason destroyed the former; feeling will destroy the latter. The foundation of human society will some day be a better one, and all noble hearts of Europe are agonizingly engaged in discovering this new and better basis.

Perhaps it was dissatisfaction with the present belief in money and disgust at the egotism they saw sneering out everywhere that had first moved certain poets of the Romantic School in Germany with the best of intentions to flee from the present age to the past and to promote the restoration of medievalism. This may be the case, especially with those who did not form the real coterie. To it belonged the writers I discussed in particular in the second book, after having written in the first book about the Romantic School in general. Only because of their importance for literary history, not because of their intrinsic value, did I speak first and in some detail about those coterie comrades who worked together as a group. Hence I trust I will not be misunderstood for giving a later and scantier report on Zacharias Werner, Baron de la Motte Fouqué, and Mr. Ludwig Uhland. As far as worth is concerned, these three writers would deserve to be discussed and praised far more fully. For Zacharias Werner was the only dramatist of the School whose plays were produced on the stage and applauded by the pit. Baron de la Motte Fouqué was the only narrative poet of the School whose novels appealed to the whole reading public. And Mr. Ludwig Uhland is the only lyric poet of the School whose poems entered into the hearts of the great mass of people and still remain alive on their lips.

In this respect the three poets mentioned deserve preference over Mr. Ludwig Tieck, whom I praised as one of the best writers of the School. For although the theater is his hobby and he has occupied himself with acting and its smallest details from his childhood on, yet Mr. Tieck never succeeded in producing any emotional impact on the public by his use of the stage as Zacharias Werner did. Mr. Tieck was always compelled to keep a drawing-room audience to whom he himself read his plays and whose applause he could safely count on. Whereas Mr. de la Motte Fouqué was read with equal pleasure by the duchess down to the washerwoman and blazed forth as the sun of lending libraries, Mr.

Tieck was merely the astral lamp[178] of teaparties who basked in the light of his poetry and placidly swallowed their tea during the reading of his novellas. The strength of this poetry must have stood out all the more, the more it contrasted with the weakness of the tea, and in Berlin, where one gets the weakest tea, Mr. Tieck must have seemed to be one of the most forceful poets. While the songs of our excellent Uhland resounded in forest and valley and are still bellowed by uproarious students and whispered by tender maidens, not a single lyric by Mr. Tieck has penetrated our hearts; not a one has remained in our ears; the general public does not know a single poem by this great lyricist.

Zacharias Werner was born in Königsberg in Prussia, November 18, 1768. His connection with the Schlegels was not a personal one but only due to kindred interests. From far away he understood their aims and did his best to write in accordance with their ideas. But he could be enthusiastic about only one aspect of the medieval revival, namely, the hierarchic, Catholic aspect; the feudal aspect did not move his spirit as intensely. His fellow countryman T.A. Hoffmann has given us a bit of strange information about this in *The Serapion Brethren.*[179] He says that Werner's mother had a mental disorder and during her pregnancy had fancied that she was the Blessed Virgin and would give birth to the Saviour. Werner's spirit bore the mark of this religious insanity his whole life long. We find the most shocking religious fanaticism in all his works. A single one, *The Twenty-fourth of February,*[180] is free of it and is among the most valuable productions of our dramatic literature. In stage performances it has elicited the greatest enthusiasm, more than Werner's other plays. His other dramatic works had less appeal for the great mass of people because, with all his dynamic vigor, he was almost completely ignorant about the stage.

Hoffmann's biographer, the police detective[181] Hitzig, also wrote a biography of Werner. A conscientious piece of work, just as interesting to the psychologist as to the literary historian. As I was

178. An Argand lamp so constructed that no interruption of light upon the table is made by the flattened ring-shaped reservoir containing the oil.
179. A collection of stories and fairy tales, first published 1819–1821.
180. A tragedy of fate, a very popular type at that time, first published in 1815.
181. Chief of police detectives.

told recently, Werner was for some time here in Paris,[182] where he took particular pleasure in the peripatetic women philosophers[183] who at that time strolled in the evening through the galleries of the Palais Royal in their most dazzling finery. They pursued him and teased him and laughed at his comical suit and his even more comical manners. Those were the good old times! Alas, like the Palais Royal, Zacharias Werner changed greatly later on. The last lamp of joy went out in the troubled man's spirit, he entered the order of the Liguorians[184] in Vienna, and preached there in the church of St. Stephen about the vanity of earthly things. He had discovered that everything on earth was vain. The girdle of Venus, he now maintained, was only an ugly serpent, and majestic Juno wore under her white robe a pair of buckskin coachman's trousers that were not very clean. Father Zacharias now mortified his flesh and fasted and declaimed passionately against our impenitent sensual pleasure. "Cursed is the flesh!" he cried out so loudly and with such a glaring East Prussian accent that the saints' images in St. Stephen's trembled and the Vienna grisettes smiled their sweetest smiles. Besides this important novelty, he constantly told the people that he was a great sinner.

Viewed accurately, the man always remained consistent, only that formerly he merely wrote about what he later actually practiced. The heroes of most of his plays are already monastically abstinent lovers, ascetic libertines, who have discovered in abstinence a heightened ecstasy, who spiritualize their epicureanism by martyrdom of the flesh, who seek the most gruesome delights in the depths of religious mysticism—saintly roués.

Shortly before his death the joy of dramatic creation once more awakened in Werner, and he wrote another tragedy, entitled *The Mother of the Maccabees*.[185] Here, however, it was not a matter of festooning the seriousness of worldly life with romantic jests; for the sacred subject matter he also chose a leisurely, ecclesiastical style, the rhythms are solemnly measured like the pealing of bells, moving as slowly as a procession on Good Friday, and the play is

182. In 1808.
183. The prostitutes.
184. Also known as the Redemptorists, a Roman Catholic order founded in 1732 by Saint Alphonsius Liguori.
185. Published in 1820.

a Palestinian legend in the form of a Greek tragedy. It found little favor among people here below; whether the angels in Heaven liked it better I don't know.

But Father Zacharias died soon after, at the beginning of the year 1823, having walked this sinful earth for more than fifty-four years.

We shall let the deceased rest in peace and turn to the second poet of the Romantic triumvirate. This is the excellent Baron Friedrich de la Motte Fouqué, born in Brandenburg in 1777 and appointed professor at the University of Halle in 1833. Prior to this he was a major in the Royal Prussian army and was one of the bardic heroes or heroic bards whose lyres and swords rang out loudest during the so-called War of Liberation. His laurel wreath is genuine. He is a true poet, and the sanctification of poetry rests upon his head. Few writers have enjoyed as their lot such general admiration as our excellent Fouqué. Now he has his readers only among the patrons of lending libraries. But this public is always large enough, and Mr. Fouqué can boast that he is the only member of the Romantic School whose works even the lower classes relish. While the esthetic tea clubs of Berlin turned up their noses at the knight who had fallen to such depths, I found in a small town in the Harz a very beautiful girl who spoke of Fouqué with charming enthusiasm and blushingly confessed that she would gladly give a year of her life is she could kiss the author of *Undine* just once.— And this girl had the most beautiful lips I have ever seen.

But what a very loveiy poetical work *Undine* is! It is itself a kiss. The spirit of poetry kissed the sleeping Spring, who, smiling, opened her eyes, and all the roses wafted their fragrance, and all the nightingales sang, and what the roses sent forth as fragrance and what the nightingales sang, our excellent Fouqué clothed in words and called *Undine*.

I do not know whether the story has been translated into French. It is the tale of the beautiful nymph who has no soul, and can acquire a soul only by falling in love with a knight—but alas, with this soul she also acquires our human sorrows, her knightly spouse becomes unfaithful, and she kills him with a kiss. For in this work death, like life, is only a kiss.

Undine may be considered the muse of Fouqué's poetry. Though she is beautiful beyond measure, though she suffers just as we do, and the full burden of earthly grief weighs upon her, she is still not a real human being. Our age, however, repudiates all such creatures of air and water, even the most beautiful; it demands real living figures, and the last thing it wants is nymphs who are in love with noble knights. The retrograde tendency, the continual eulogy of the hereditary aristocracy, the unceasing glorification of the old feudal system, the everlasting playing at chivalry—these were the things that displeased the educated middle class among the German reading public, and it deserted the outdated minstrel. As a matter of fact, this constant sing-song about armor, tournament steeds, ladies of the castle, honorable guild masters, dwarfs, squires, castle chapels, love and faith, and whatever else this medieval rubbish is called, finally bored us, and when the ingenious hidalgo Friedrich de la Motte Fouqué became more and more absorbed in his chivalric romances, and in his dream of the past lost the understanding for the present, even his best friends had to turn away from him, shaking their heads.

The works he wrote during this later period are unbearable. The defects of his earlier writings are intensified to an extreme. His knights are all iron and sentiment, without either flesh or common sense. His women are only images, or rather, dolls whose golden locks flow gracefully down over their charming flower-faces. Like Walter Scott's works, Fouqué novels of chivalry are reminiscent of woven Gobelin tapestries, which by their richness of design and magnificent colors, delight our eyes more than our spirits. There are knightly festivals, pastoral games, duels, old costumes, all nicely side by side, romantic without any deeper meaning, showy superficiality. Fouqué's imitators, like Walter Scott's, perfected even more disturbingly this mannerism of portraying only the outward appearance and the costumes of persons and things instead of their inner nature. This superficial style and facile manner are now rampant in Germany as well as in England and France. Even if the works no longer glorify the period of chivalry, but deal with our modern life, it is still always the same old style which grasps only the contingent aspects of the subject matter instead of its essence. Instead of knowledge of human nature our modern novelists manifest only knowledge of dress, perhaps relying on the saying "Clothes make the man." How different the older novelists were, especially the English! Richardson gives us an anatomy of feelings.

Goldsmith treats pragmatically the love affairs of his heroes. The author of *Tristram Shandy* shows us the most secret depths of the soul; he opens a dormer window in the soul, permits us a glance into its abysses, paradises, and dirty corners, and immediately lets the curtain fall again. We have looked from the front into this strange theater, lighting and perspective did not fail to have their effect, and, by seeming to have glimpsed the infinite, we come away with a feeling of infinity, of poetry. As for Fielding, he leads us right behind the scenes, shows us the false rouge on all emotions, the coarsest motives for the most delicate actions, the rosin that will later flare up as enthusiasm, the kettle-drum, and on it, still resting peacefully, the stick that will presently drum out the mightiest thunder of passion—in short, he shows us the entire inner mechanism, the great lie, by which men appear to be other than they really are and by which all the joyous reality of life is lost. Yet why choose the English as examples when our Goethe has provided in his *Wilhelm Meister* the best model for a novel?

The number of Fouqué's novels is legion; he is one of the most prolific writers. *The Magic Circle* and *Thiodolph the Icelander*[186] deserve special praise. His verse plays, which are not meant for the stage, contain great beauties. *Sigurd the Dragon-Killer*, in particular, is a bold work in which the Scandinavian heroic saga is reflected with all its giants and fairy-tale creatures. The main character, Sigurd, is a colossal figure. He is as strong as the cliffs of Norway and as violent as the ocean that surges about them. He has as much courage as a hundred lions and as much intelligence as two donkeys.

Mr. Fouqué also wrote poems. They are charm itself. They are so airy, so colorful, so radiant, flitting along so gaily like sweet lyric hummingbirds.

The real lyric poet, however, is Mr. Ludwig Uhland, who was born in Tübingen in 1787 and now lives as a lawyer in Stuttgart. He has written one volume of poems, two tragedies, and two treatises, one on Walther von der Vogelweide,[187] the other on French troubadours. These are two brief historical investigations

186. The complete title is *The Travels of Thiodolph the Icelander*.
187. One of the best lyric poets in German during the flowering period of medieval German literature at the end of the twelfth century and the beginning of the thirteenth.

and testify to industrious study of the Middle Ages. The titles of the tragedies are *Ludwig the Bavarian* and *Duke Ernst of Swabia*. The former I have not read; I have been told it is not the better of the two. The second, however, contains great beauties and is pleasing because of the nobility of the feelings and the worthiness of its sentiments. A sweet breath of poetry wafts through it such as is no longer found in the plays that now reap so much applause in our theater. German loyalty is the theme of this play, and we see it here, strong as an oak, defying all storms; German love flowers, scarcely noticeable, in the background, but its fragrance of violets penetrates our hearts all the more movingly. This play— it should better be called a poem—contains passages that are among the most beautiful pearls of our literature. But nonetheless the theater public received the play with indifference, or rather, rejected it. I do not want to reproach the good people in the pit all too bitterly. These people have definite needs which they expect the poet to satisfy. The creations of the poet should not merely accord with the inclinations of his own heart but rather with the desire of the public. The public is just like the hungry Bedouin in the desert who, thinking he has found a sack of peas, hastily opens it, but alas, it is only pearls. The public consumes with delight Mr. Raupach's dried peas and Madame Birch-Pfeiffer's broad beans; but Uhland's pearls it cannot stomach.

Since in all probability the French do not know who Madame Birch-Pfeiffer[188] and Mr. Raupach are, I must mention here that this divine pair, standing beside each other like the brother and sister Apollo and Diana, are the most revered figures in the temples of our dramatic art. Yes, Mr. Raupach is just as comparable to Apollo as Madame Birch-Pfeiffer is to Diana. As for their actual positions, Madame Pfeiffer is employed as an imperial Austrian court actress in Vienna and Mr. Raupach as a royal Prussian dramatist in Berlin. The lady has already written a great many plays in which she herself plays a role. I cannot resist mentioning here a fact which to Frenchmen will seem almost incredible. Many of our actors are also dramatic poets and write plays for themselves. They say Mr. Ludwig Tieck brought about this misfortune by an

188. Charlotte Birch-Pfeiffer, German actress and author of popular sentimental plays.

indiscreet remark. In his reviews he noted that actors can always play better in a bad play than in a good one. On the basis of this axiom actors in droves seized their pens, wrote tragedies and comedies by the dozen, and it was sometimes hard for us to decide whether a vain actor intentionally made his play bad in order to play well in it or whether he played badly in such a homemade play in order to make us think the play was good. The actor and the poet, who had previously had a colleague-like relation with each other (approximately like the executioner and the poor sinner), now became openly hostile. The actors tried to push the poets out of the theater altogether with the excuse that they understood nothing of the demands of the stage world and nothing about drastic effects and stage tricks as only the actor learns them in practice and knows how to make use of them in his plays. Therefore the actors or, as they liked best to call themselves, the artists, preferred to act in their own plays or at least in plays written by one of their party, "an artist." These plays did indeed meet their needs completely. Here they found their favorite costumes, their poetry in flesh-colored tights, their exits accompanied by applause, their traditional grimaces, their tinsel phrases, their whole affected Bohemianism of art—a language that is spoken only on the stage, flowers that spring up only from this artificial soil, fruits that have ripened only under the footlights, a kind of nature in which not the breath of God, but of the prompter, blows, a frenzy that shakes the scenery, gentle melancholy with titillating flute accompaniment, rouged innocence with dives into vice, monthly-pay emotions, flourish of the trumpets, etc.

In this way German actors have emancipated themselves from poets and from poetry itself. Only mediocrity did they still permit to practice its art in their sphere. But they watch out carefully that no true poet penetrates their ranks under the cloak of mediocrity. How many tests Mr. Raupach had to endure before he succeeded in gaining a footing on the stage! And even now they keep a sharp eye on him, and if he occasionally writes a play that is not totally bad, he immediately has to produce a dozen more pieces of utter rubbish for fear of being ostracized by the actors. You are surprised at the expression "a dozen"? It is by no means an exaggeration. This man can actually write a dozen plays every year, and people admire his productivity. But "it is not magic," says Jantjen of

Amsterdam, the famous magician, when we are amazed at his tricks, "it is not magic, but simply a matter of speed."

There is another, special reason for Mr. Raupach's success in the German theater. This writer, by birth a German, lived in Russia for a long time, received his education there, and it was the Muscovite muse who initiated him into poetry. This muse, the beauty wrapped in sables, with the charmingly turned-up nose, handed our poet her brimming brandy cup of inspiration, hung around his shoulders her quiver with Kirghiz shafts of wit, and put in his hands her tragic knout. When he first began beating our hearts with it, how he moved us! The strangeness of the whole spectacle astonished us not a little. Civilized Germans certainly did not like the man, but his stormy Sarmatian temperament, a clumsy dexterity, a certain snarling aggressiveness in his behavior, nonplused the public. At any rate it was a queer sight when Mr. Raupach raced along on his Slavic Pegasus, the little nag, over the steppes of poetry, riding his dramatic themes to death beneath the saddle, in genuine Bashkir fashion. This met with approval in Berlin where, as you know, everything Russian is well received. Mr. Raupach succeeded in getting a foothold there; he knew how to get along with the actors, and for some time now, as I have already mentioned, Raupach Apollo has been worshiped next to Diana Birch-Pfeiffer in the temple of dramatic art. He gets thirty taler for every act he writes, and he writes nothing but plays in six acts by giving the first act the title "Prologue." He has already shoved all kinds of subjects under the saddle of his Pegasus and ridden them to death. No hero is safe from this tragic fate. He even got the best of Siegfried, the dragon killer. The muse of German history is in despair. Like a Niobe, she gazes with pale sorrow at her noble children whom Raupach-Apollo has finished off so dreadfully. O Jupiter! he even dared to lay hands on the Hohenstaufens, our beloved old Swabian emperors! It was not enough that Mr. Friedrich Raumer[189] butchered them in history; now comes Mr. Raupach as well and trims them up for the stage. He clothes Raumer's wooden figures in his leather poetry, his Russian hides, and the sight of such caricatures and their foul smell end by spoiling for us the

---

189. A German historian who wrote a history of the Hohenstaufens and their epoch, published 1823–1825.

memory of the finest and noblest emperors of our German fatherland. And the police does nothing to stop such profanation?
Perhaps they themselves even have a hand in it. New, aspiring
royal houses do not like to have their subjects reminded of the
older imperial dynasty whose place it is seeking to take. Neither
Immermann nor Grabbe nor even Mr. Üchtritz—only Mr. Raupach
was commissioned by the Berlin theatrical board to write a
Barbarossa play. But Mr. Raupach is strictly prohibited from riding
roughshod over a Hohenzollern; if he should ever try, he would
be ushered into the jail as his Helicon.

The association of ideas by contrast is responsible for the fact
that, intending to talk about Mr. Uhland, I suddenly got onto Mr.
Raupach and Madame Birch-Pfeiffer. But although this divine pair
does not belong to real literature, our Diana of the theater even
less than our Apollo of the theater, I still felt bound to mention
them because they represent the contemporary world of the stage.
In any case I owed it to our true poets to state in a few words
what sort of people are usurping the control of the theater in
Germany.

V

At this moment I am in a strange dilemma. I must not leave
undiscussed Mr. Ludwig Uhland's collection of poems, and yet I
am not in the right mood for such a discussion. Silence might
appear to be cowardice or even perfidy, and honest, frank words
might be interpreted as lack of charity. In fact, I shall scarcely
satisfy the kith and kin of Uhland's muse and the copyholders of
his fame with the enthusiasm within my reach today. But I beg
you to take into consideration the conditions under which I am
writing, the time and place. Twenty years ago—I was a boy—yes,
then, with what abounding enthusiasm I could have celebrated the
excellent Uhland! Then I felt his excellence perhaps better than
now; he was closer to me in thought and feelings. But since then
so much has happened! What seemed to me so splendid, that
chivalrous, Catholic world, those knights who cut and thrust at
each other in aristocratic tournaments, those gentle squires and
well-bred noble ladies, those Nordic heroes and Minnesingers,

those monks and nuns, those ancestral vaults and awesome shud-
ders, those pallid sentiments of renunciation to the accompaniment
of bell-ringing, and the everlasting melancholy wailing—how bitterly it has been spoiled for me since then! Yes, things were different
then. How often I sat amid the ruins of the old castle at Düsseldorf
on the Rhine and recited to myself the most beautiful of all Uhland's
poems:

> The handsome shepherd wandered by,
> beneath the castle of the king.
> The maiden saw him from up high,
> her heart began to sing.

> She called to him in tender words,
> "Oh, could I but come down to you!
> How white the lambs glow in your herd!
> How red the flowers' hue!"

> In turn, she heard the young man speak,
> "Oh, if you could come down to me!
> How red the glow is on your cheek,
> how white the arms I see!"

> When grievingly each day he led
> his flock past her, he looked above
> till from the turret leaned the head
> of her, his dearest love.

> Then merrily the shepherd cried,
> "Hail, lovely princess fair and fine!"
> She sweetly from above replied,
> "I thank you, shepherd mine!"

> The winter went, back came the spring,
> and flowers bloomed around.
> The shepherd passed the castle's wing,
> his love no more he found.

> The shepherd cried, an anguished moan,
> "Hail, lovely princess fair and fine!"
> Down came a muffled, ghostly tone,
> "Farewell, O shepherd mine!"

Sitting amid the ruins of the old castle and reciting this poem, I sometimes heard the nymphs in the Rhine, which flows by there, imitating my words, and from the waters came a sighing and a moaning with a comical pathos:

> Down came a muffled, ghostly tone,
> "Farewell, O shepherd mine!"

But I ignored the chaffing of the nymphs, even when they giggled ironically at the most beautiful passages in Uhland's poems. At that time I modestly assumed that this giggling was at me, especially toward evening as darkness approached, and I would declaim with voice somewhat raised to overcome the mysterious awe inspired in me by the ancient castle ruins. You see, there was a legend that a headless lady wandered about there at night. Sometimes I thought I heard her long silk train rustling past, and my heart pounded.— This was the time and the place for me to be enthusiastic about the *Poems* by Ludwig Uhland.

I hold this same volume in my hands once more, but twenty years have passed since then, I have heard and seen much in the meantime, a very great deal, I no longer believe there are people without heads, and the old spectral show no longer has any effect on my feelings. The house in which I am sitting and reading is on the Boulevard Montmartre; here the wildest waves of the times break; here screech the loudest voices of the modern age; there is laughing, roaring, and beating of drums; the National Guard marches past in double-quick time; and everyone is speaking French.—Is this the place to read Uhland's poems? I have once more recited to myself three times the last lines of the poem mentioned above, but I no longer feel the inexpressible grief that once seized me when the king's daughter dies and the handsome shepherd called up to her so plaintively, "Hail, lovely princess, fair and fine!"

> Down came a ghostly, muffled tone,
> "Farewell, O shepherd mine!"

Perhaps I have also become somewhat cool toward such poems since I learned that there is a far more painful love than that which never attains possession of the beloved or loses her through death. In reality it is more painful when the beloved lies in our arms day and night but ruins the day and night for us by constant perversity and silly caprices, so that we cast out of our heart what our heart loves most, and we ourselves have to take the cursed, beloved woman to the coach and send her off:

"Farewell, my princess fair and fine!"

Yes, more painful than loss through death is loss through life, for instance, when the beloved turns away from us out of crazy frivolity, when she absolutely insists on going to a ball to which no decent person can accompany her, and when, in quite absurdly garish dress and with hair defiantly curled, she then gives her arm to the first scoundrel she meets and turns her back on us:

"Farewell, O shepherd mine!"

Possibly Mr. Uhland himself did not fare any better than we. His mood, too, must have changed somewhat since then. With few exceptions he has put no new poems on the market for twenty years. I do not believe that this fine poetic temperament was so meagerly endowed by nature that it bore within only a single springtime. No, I explain Uhland's silence by the contradiction between the inclinations of his muse and the demands of his political position. The elegiac poet who was able to celebrate the Catholic feudal past in such beautiful ballads and romances, the Ossian of medievalism, has since become an ardent representative of the rights of the people in the Württemberg Diet, a bold speaker for civic equality and freedom of thought. Mr. Uhland proved that these democratic and Protestant views of his are genuine and pure by the great personal sacrifices that he made for them. Having once won a poet's laurels, he now also won the oak wreath of civic virtue. But precisely because his intentions toward the modern age were so honorable, he could no longer keep on singing the old song about ancient times with his old enthusiasm. And since his Pegasus was only a knight's steed that liked to trot back into the past but immediately became balky when it was supposed to go ahead into modern life, good Uhland dismounted with a smile, and calmly had the intractable beast unsaddled and led to the stable. There he has remained until the present day, and like his colleague, the steed Bayard,[190] he has all kinds of virtues and only a single defect—he is dead.

Sharper eyes than mine claim to have perceived that the tall knightly steed with the gay-colored armorial trappings and proud plumes of feathers never really suited his middle-class rider, who wore on his feet instead of boots with golden spurs only shoes and silk stockings, and on his head, instead of a helmet, only a Tübingen doctoral cap. They claim to have discovered that Mr. Ludwig Uhland never could accord completely with his subject; that he does not really reproduce in idealized veracity the naive, grimly powerful tones of the Middle Ages, but rather dissolves them into a sickly sentimental melancholy; that he soft-boiled, so to speak, in his sentimentality the robust strains of the heroic saga and the folksong to make them palatable to the modern public. And indeed, when observed closely, the women in Uhland's poems are merely lovely phantoms, moonlight personified, with milk in their veins and sweet tears in their eyes, that is, tears without salt. If we compare Uhland's knights with the knights of the ancient songs, they seem to consist of tin armor with nothing but flowers beneath it instead of flesh and bones. Uhland's knights thus have for sensitive noses a fragrance far more suitable for love than the ancient warriors, who wore very thick iron trousers, ate a lot, and swilled even more.

But this is not meant as criticism. Mr. Uhland had no intention of producing a faithful copy of the German past, he perhaps meant to delight us merely by its image, and he created a pleasant reflection of it from the dusky surface of his spirit. This may possibly lend his poems a special charm and win for them the love of many good, gentle souls. Portraits of the past exercise their magic even in the palest evocation. Even men who espouse the modern age always retain a secret fondness for the traditions of olden times; even the weakest echo of these ghostly voices moves us strangely. And we can readily understand that our excellent Uhland's ballads and romances found the greatest favor not simply among the

190. In romances of chivalry a wonderful bay horse, remarkable for his spirit and for his unique ability to fit his size to his rider.

patriots of 1813,[191] among upright youths and lovely maidens, but also among many persons endowed with greater powers and among many modern thinkers.

I have added the year 1813 to the word "patriots" in order to distinguish them from present-day patriots, who no longer live off the memories of the so-called War of Liberation. Those older patriots must derive the sweetest pleasure from Uhland's muse, since most of his poems are completely impregnated with the spirit of their time, a time when they themselves were reveling in youthful emotions and proud hopes. They passed on the preference for Uhland's poems to their disciples, and the boys on the athletic grounds used to be given credit for patriotism if they bought Uhland's poems. They found among them lyrics which even Max von Schenkendorf[192] and Mr. Ernst Moritz Arndt[193] could not have surpassed. And indeed, what descendant of staunch Arminius and blonde Thusnelda is not satisfied with this poem of Uhland's?[194]

"Forward, forward, one and all!
Russia sounds the valiant call:
Forward!

"Prussia hears the noble word,
likes the sound, and joins the chord:
Forward!

"Mighty Austria, arise!
Join your brethren's enterprise!
Forward!

"Forward, ancient Saxon land!
Ever forward, hand in hand!
Forward!

191. The year of the battle of Leipzig, in which Napoleon's forces were roundly defeated.

192. A German poet who wrote many patriotic lyrics.

193. The representative poet of the struggle against Napoleon, combining ardent patriotism with devout Protestantism.

194. This is a poem in honor of Fieldmarshal Blücher, one of the outstanding military leaders against Napoleon. During the War of Liberation he was known as "Fieldmarshal Forward."

"Bavaria, Hesse, Swabia!
To the Rhine, Franconia!
Forward!

"Forward, Holland, Netherland!
High your sword, free in your hand!
Forward!

"Hail, Helvetia's regiment!
Alsace, Burgundy, Lorraine!
Forward!

"Forward, on, Hispania!
Join your kin, Britannia!
Forward!

"Forward! What a gallant sport!
Lucky wind and nearby port!
Forward!

"Forward is a general!
Forward, gallant fighters all!
Forward!"

I repeat—the men of 1813 find the spirit of their time splendidly preserved in Mr. Uhland's poems, and not simply the political, but also the moral and esthetic spirit. Mr. Uhland represents a whole epoch, and he now represents it almost alone, since its other representatives have been forgotten and are actually summed up in Uhland. The dominant tone in his lyrics, ballads, and romances was the tone of all his Romantic contemporaries, and many of them produced just as good things, if not even better. This is the place where I can still praise some members of the Romantic School who, as I have said, in the content and tone of their poems, manifest the most striking similarity to Mr. Uhland, are also not inferior to him in poetic worth, and differ from him perhaps only by less assurance in matters of form. What an excellent poet Baron von Eichendorff is![195] The lyrics that he wove into his novel *Foreshad-*

195. Joseph Freiherr von Eichendorff (1788–1857), a much more gifted poet than Heine's description indicates. He wrote much else besides, but it is for his lyrics that he is remembered.

owing and the Present[196] cannot be distinguished from Uhland's, not even from the best of them. If there is a difference, it lies in the greener forest freshness and the more crystalline genuineness of Eichendorff's poems. Mr. Justinus Kerner,[197] who is almost completely unknown, also deserves honorable mention. He too wrote very fine poems in the same tone and style. He is a fellow countryman of Mr. Uhland, as is Mr. Gustav Schwab,[198] a more famous poet, who likewise burst into bloom in Swabian territory and who still regales us every year with pretty, fragrant lyrics. His forte is the ballad, and in this form he has celebrated native legends most delightfully. Wilhelm Müller, whom death snatched away from us in the very prime of youth, must also be mentioned.[199] In imitating the German folksong he is completely in harmony with Mr. Uhland; I even think he was often more successful in this sphere and excelled him in naturalness. He understood more profoundly the spirit of the old song forms and thus did not need to imitate them in externals; we find in him a freer treatment of nuances and a sensible avoidance of all obsolete idioms and expressions. I must also call to mind here the late Wetzel,[200] now completely forgotten. He too is a kindred spirit of our excellent Uhland, and in some poems of his that I know he surpasses Uhland in sweetness and soulful fervor. These lyrics, half flowers, half butterflies, dissipated their fragrance and fluttered into oblivion in one of the older volumes of Brockhaus' annual *Urania*. It goes without saying that Mr. Clemens Brentano wrote most of his lyrics in the same style and vein as Mr. Uhland; both drew from the same source, the folksong, and offer us the same drink; but in Uhland's poetry the goblet, the form, is more polished. I really must not speak of Adalbert von Chamisso here.[201] Although a contemporary of the Romantic School, in whose activities he took

196. *Ahnung und Gegenwart,* published in 1815.
197. A minor German poet and writer of fiction.
198. A minor German poet and man of letters, a life-long friend of Uhland's and Kerner's.
199. He died in 1827 before his thirty-third birthday. He was a prolific writer of facile verse and, for some reason, was particularly admired by Heine.
200. Karl Friedrich Gottlob Wetzel (1779–1819), author of a collection of poems, also a collection of war-songs, and several tragedies.
201. A Franco-German lyric poet and fiction writer (1781–1838), also a botanist of some repute, serving for many years as keeper of the Royal Botanical Collection in Berlin.

part, yet this man's heart has in recent times been so wonderfully rejuvenated that he modulated to completely different keys, had an influence as one of the most original and most important modern poets, and belongs far more to young Germany than to old Germany. But in the lyrics of his earlier period stirs the same breath that flows toward us from Uhland's poems; the same sound, the same color, the same fragrance, the same melancholy, the same tear— Chamisso's tears are perhaps more moving because, like a spring gushing out of a rock, they well up from a far stouter heart.

The poems that Mr. Uhland wrote in Southern verse forms are also very closely related to the sonnets, assonances, and ottava rima of his schoolmates from the Romantic School and are indistinguishable from them in form or style. But as I have said, most of Uhland's contemporaries together with their poems have fallen into oblivion; they can only be found with great effort in forgotten collections, like *Poetic Woods* and *Minstrel's Journey;* in a few women's magazines and literary almanacs that were published by Mr. Fouqué and Mr. Tieck; in old periodicals, especially in Achim von Arnim's *Lonely Comfort* and in the *Divining Rod* edited by Heinrich Straube and Rudolf Christiani; in older newspapers of the time and God knows where else!

Mr. Uhland is not the father of a school like Schiller or Goethe or some other such writers from whose individuality emerged a particular style that found a definite echo in the works of the contemporaries. He is not the father, but is himself only the child of a School that passed on to him a style which likewise did not originally belong to it but which it had laboriously squeezed out of earlier poetic works. As a substitute for this lack of originality, of individual novelty, Mr. Uhland offers a number of excellent qualities, as splendid as they are rare. He is the pride of fortunate Swabia, and all comrades of the German tongue rejoice in this noble minstrel. He is the epitome in the lyric of most of his comrades from the Romantic School, which the public now loves and honors in the one man. And we honor and love him now perhaps all the more because we are about to part from him forever.

Oh, not from a frivolous whim, but obeying the law of necessity, Germany is stirring.—Pious, peaceful Germany!—It casts a melancholy glance at the past it leaves behind, once more it bends tenderly over the ancient era which gazes at us, so deathly pale,

from Uhland's poems, and it bids farewell with a kiss. And another
kiss, even a tear, for all I care! But let us tarry no longer in idle
compassion.—

> Forward, forward, one and all!
> France now sounds the valiant call:
> Forward!

VI

"When, after many years, Emperor Otto III went to the grave
where Charles' corpse lay buried,[202] he entered the cavern in the
company of two bishops and the Count of Laumel (who related
all this). The corpse was not lying down like others, but sat upright
on a chair like a living person. On his head was a crown of gold,
he held the scepter in his hands, which were covered with gauntlets,
but the fingernails had pierced the leather and grown out. The
arched vault was constructed very durably of marble and plaster.
In order for them to enter, an opening had to be broken; as soon
as they were inside, they smelled a strong odor. All immediately
genuflected and did reverence to the dead. Emperor Otto clothed
him in a white garment, cut his nails, and had all defects repaired.
No part of the limbs was rotted except that a bit of the tip of the
nose was missing; Otto had it replaced with gold. Finally he took
a tooth from Charles' mouth, ordered the vault walled up again,
and departed.—The following night Charles is said to have appeared
to him in a dream and prophesied that Otto would not live to old
age and would leave no heir."

The *German Legends*[203] give us this account, nor is it the only
example of its kind. Your King Francis also had the grave of the
famous Roland opened to see for himself whether the hero had
been of such gigantic stature as the poets say. This took place
shortly before the battle of Pavia.[204] Sebastian of Portugal had the

202. Otto III was Emperor of the Holy Roman Empire from 996 to 1002.
Charles is of course Charlemagne.
203. By Jakob and Wilhelm Grimm, published 1816–1818.
204. Francis I, king of France 1515–1547. He was defeated at Pavia by Emperor
Charles V.

graves of his ancestors opened and viewed the dead kings before going to Africa.[205]

Strange, gruesome curiosity that often impels people to look down into the graves of the past! This happens in unusual times, after the end of an epoch or shortly before a catastrophe. In our modern age we have experienced a similar phenomenon. There was a great sovereign, the French people, who suddenly felt a desire to open the grave of the past and view by the light of day the ages long since buried and forgotten. There was no lack of learned grave-diggers who were right at hand with spades and crow-bars to grub up the ancient rubble and break open the graves. A strong scent could be noticed which, as Gothic *haut-gout*,[206] tickled very pleasantly the noses of those who were blasé about attar of roses. French writers knelt down reverently before the exposed Middle Ages. One clothed it in a new garment, another cut its nails, a third put a fresh nose on it; at last there even came some poets who ripped the teeth out of the Middle Ages—just as Emperor Otto had done.

I do not know whether the ghost of the Middle Ages appeared to these teeth-extractors in a dream and prophesied an early end to their whole romantic rule. In any case, I mention this aspect of French literature only in order to declare categorically that in criticizing rather sharply in this volume a similar occurrence in Germany, I have no intention of attacking the French Romantic School either directly or indirectly. The writers who pulled medievalism out of its grave in Germany had other aims, as can be seen from these pages, and the influence they were able to exercise on the general public endangered the liberty and happiness of my country. The French writers had only artistic interests, and the French public sought only to satisfy its suddenly awakened curiosity. Most of the French looked into the graves of the past merely with the intention of picking out an interesting costume for the carnival. In France the Gothic fad was simply a fad, and it served only to heighten the pleasure of the present. The French let their hair flow down long in medieval fashion, and at a casual remark by the barber that it is not becoming, they have it cut off short together

205. King of Portugal, born 1554, died 1578. He tried to revive the Crusades and died in a crusade against the Moors.
206. Seasoning.

with the rest of their medieval ideas. Alas, in Germany it is different. Perhaps just because in Germany medievalism is not completely dead and putrefied, as it is in France. German medievalism is not lying mouldered in its grave; on the contrary, it is often animated by an evil spirit and steps into our midst in bright, broad daylight and sucks the red life from our hearts.—

Alas, don't you see how sad and wan Germany is? Especially the German youth, who just recently were shouting so joyously and enthusiastically? Don't you see how bloody is the mouth of the fully authorized vampire that resides in Frankfurt and there sucks so horribly slowly and protractedly at the heart of the German people?[207]

What I have indicated in general regarding the Middle Ages has a very special application to its religion. Honesty demands that I distinguish precisely between a group called Catholic in this country and those disgraceful fellows who bear the same name in Germany. In these pages I have spoken only of the latter, and indeed in terms that still seem to me much too lenient. They are the enemies of my country, a fawning rabble, hypocrites, liars, arrant cowards. There's hissing in Berlin, there's a hissing in Munich, and as you are strolling on the Boulevard Montmartre, you suddenly feel the sting in your heel. But we shall crush the old serpent's head under foot. This is the party of lies, the myrmidons of despotism, the restorers of all the misery, horror, and folly of the past. How infinitely different is the party here called Catholic, whose leaders are among the most talented writers of France. Although they are not exactly our comrades-in-arms, we nevertheless fight for the same interests, namely, for the interests of mankind. In our love for mankind we are united; we differ only in our opinions as to what benefits mankind. They believe that mankind needs only spiritual consolation, whereas we are of the opinion that it needs the opposite, material happiness. If they, the Catholic party in France, misjudging their own significance, proclaim themselves the party of the past, the restorers of faith, we must defend them against themselves. The Eighteenth Century so thoroughly crushed Catholicism in France that there is almost no living trace of it left, and anyone

207. Heine is referring to the anti-democratic Confederate Council *(Bundestag)* in Frankfurt.

who tries to restore Catholicism in France is preaching, so to speak, an entirely new religion. By France I mean Paris, not the provinces, for what the provinces think is a matter of as much indifference as what our legs think; the head is the seat of our thoughts. I was told that the French in the provinces are good Catholics; I can neither confirm nor deny it. The people I saw in the provinces all looked like milestones that had written on their foreheads their greater or lesser distance from the capital. The women there may seek consolation in Christianity because they can't live in Paris. In Paris itself Christianity has not existed since the Revolution, and even before that it had lost all real importance. It lay lurking in a remote church corner like a spider and sprang out hastily now and then whenever it could seize a child in the cradle or an old man in his coffin. Yes, only at two times, when he had just come into the world or when he was just leaving it, did a Frenchman get into the power of a Catholic priest. During the whole interval between, he was in his right mind and laughed at holy water and extreme unction. But do you call this the rule of Catholicism? Just because Catholicism had died out completely in France, it was able, under Louis XVIII and Charles X, to win over a few unselfish souls by the charm of novelty. At that time Catholicism was something unheard of, something fresh, something surprising! The religion that was dominant in France shortly before then was classical mythology, and this beautiful religion had been preached to the French people by its writers, poets, and artists with such success that at the end of the last century the French, in action as in thought, were all dressed in pagan costumes. During the French Revolution classical religion flowered in its grandest splendor. This was no Alexandrian mimicking; Paris was a natural continuation of Athens and Rome. During the Empire the classical spirit vanished again, the Greek gods ruled only in the theater, and Roman virtue still had possession only of the battlefield. A new faith had arisen, and it was summed up in the sacred name Napoleon! This faith still prevails among the masses. Thus whoever says that the French are irreligious because they no longer believe in Christ and His saints is wrong. It must rather be said that the irreligion of the French consists in the fact that they now believe in a man instead of in the immortal gods. It must be said that the irreligion of the French consists in the fact that they no longer believe in Jupiter, in Diana, in Minerva, in Venus. This last point is dubious, but so much I know—regarding the Graces, the French women still remain orthodox.

I hope these remarks will not be misunderstood, for they were meant precisely to save the reader of this book from a serious misunderstanding.

Concerning the History of
Religion and Philosophy in
Germany

BOOK ONE

In recent times the French believed they could attain an understanding of Germany if they made themselves acquainted with
the best products of our literature. By so doing they have merely
raised themselves from a state of total ignorance to the level of
superficiality. The best products of our literature will remain for
them only mute blossoms, the whole German mind a dreary puzzle,
so long as they do not know the significance of religion and
philosophy in Germany.

I believe I am undertaking a useful enterprise in trying to provide
some explanatory information about both. This is not an easy task
for me. It is necessary first of all to avoid technical scholarly
language completely unfamiliar to the French. And yet I have not
explored thoroughly enough the subtleties of theology nor those
of metaphysics to be able to formulate them quite simply and
briefly to suit the needs of the French. Therefore I shall deal only
with the large questions which have been discussed in German
theology and philosophy, I shall examine only their social significance, and I shall always bear in mind the limitations of my own
resources as an expositor and the capacity of the French reader for
understanding the subject.

Great German philosophers who may chance to glance at these
pages will shrug their shoulders with a superior air at the inadequate

128

treatment of everything I offer here. But I trust they will be so good as to consider that the little I say is expressed clearly and comprehensibly, while their own works are, to be sure, very thorough, infinitely thorough, very profound, stupendously profound, but equally incomprehensible. Of what help to the people are locked granaries for which they have no key? The people are hungry for knowledge and will thank me for the bit of intellectual bread which I will share fairly with them.

I do not think it is lack of talent which prevents most German scholars from discussing religion and philosophy in a manner suitable for the general public. I think it is fear of the results of their own thinking, results they do not dare to impart to the people. As for me, I do not have this fear, for I am not a scholar; I am one of the people myself. I am not a scholar, I am not among the seven hundred wise men of Germany. I stand with the great multitude before the portals of their wisdom, and if any bit of truth has slipped through, and if this truth has gotten as far as to me, then it has gone far enough;—I write it on paper in pretty lettering and give it to the compositor; he sets it in lead and gives it to the printer; the latter prints it, and then it belongs to the whole world.

The religion we have in Germany is Christianity. My task will therefore be to tell what Christianity is, how it became Roman Catholicism, how from the latter Protestantism developed, and from Protestantism German philosophy.

In beginning now with a discussion of religion, I beg in advance all pious souls for Heaven's sake not to be alarmed. Fear nothing, pious souls. No profane jests shall offend your ears. At most, these are still useful in Germany, where it is important at the moment to neutralize the power of religion. You see, we Germans are in the same situation as you were before the Revolution, when Christianity and the old regime formed an absolutely inseparable alliance. This could not be destroyed so long as Christianity still exerted its influence on the masses. Voltaire had to start up his cutting laughter before Samson[1] could let his axe fall. Yet just as nothing was proved by this axe, neither was anything really proved

---

1. The executioner in Paris who performed the most executions during the French Revolution.

but simply accomplished by that laughter. Voltaire succeeded only in wounding the body of Christianity. All his jokes, derived from ecclesiastical history, all his witticisms about dogma and worship, about the Bible, that holiest book of mankind, about the Virgin Mary, that fairest flower of poetry, the whole dictionary of philosophical arrows that he shot off at the clergy, wounded only the mortal body of Christianity, not its inner essence, not its deeper spirit, not its immortal soul.

For Christianity is an idea, and as such, indestructible and immortal like every idea. But what is this idea?

It is just because this idea has not yet been clearly understood and because externals have been considered the main point that there is still no history of Christianity. Two opposing parties write ecclesiastical history and constantly contradict each other; yet neither the one nor the other will ever state definitely what the idea really is which serves Christianity as a focal point, which strives to reveal itself in the symbolism of Christianity, its dogma as well as its form of worship, and in its entire history, and which has manifested itself in the actual life of Christian people. Neither Baronius,[2] the Catholic cardinal, nor the Protestant Hofrat Schröckh[3] reveals to us what this idea really was. And if you leaf through all the folio volumes of Mansi's collection of the Acts of the Councils,[4] of Assemani's *Code of the Liturgies*,[5] and Sacarelli's *Historia ecclesiastica*,[6] you will still not understand what the idea of Christianity really was. What do you find then in the histories of Oriental and Occidental churches? In the former, Oriental ecclesiastical history, you find nothing but dogmatic subtleties in which ancient Greek sophistry is once more displayed; in the latter, Occidental ecclesiastical history, you find nothing but quarrels about discipline as it concerned ecclesiastical interests, and here

2. Cardinal Caesar Baronius (1538–1607) wrote an important work on ecclesiastical history.
3. Johannes Matthias Schröckh from Vienna, from 1767 on a professor at the University of Wittenberg, wrote a thirty-five-volume history of the Christian Church and a ten-volume history of the Church since the Reformation.
4. Gian Domenico Mansi, archbishop of Lucca, published this collection of thirty-one volumes beginning in 1759.
5. Josephus Aloysius Assemani, professor of Oriental languages in Rome, published this *Codex* in thirteen volumes, 1749–1766.
6. A member of an international order of priests in Rome, he published this history in twenty volumes beginning in 1770.

the legal casuistry and statecraft of ancient Rome again exert their influence in new formulas and constraints. In fact, just as people in Constantinople had quarreled about *logos*, so people in Rome quarreled about the relationship between temporal and spiritual power; and as people in Constantinople had attacked each other about *homousios*,[7] so the Romans attacked each other about investiture. But the Byzantine questions—Whether *logos* is *homousios* with God the Father? Whether Mary should be called Mother of God or Mother of man? Whether Christ suffered hunger for lack of food or was hungry only because he wanted to be hungry?—all these questions had as their background simply court intrigues, and their solution depended on what was whispered and giggled in the private apartments of the *Palatium Sacrum*, whether, for example, Eudoxia or Pulcheria should fall,[8]—for the last-named lady hated Nestorius,[9] the betrayer of her love affairs, and the former hated Cyril,[10] whom Pulcheria protected—everything went back ultimately to nothing but the gossip of women and eunuchs, and in the name of dogma it was actually the man, and in the man a party that was persecuted or supported.[11] It is the same in the Occident. Rome wanted to rule; "when its legions fell, it sent dogmas into the provinces."[12] All disputes about dogma had as their origin Roman usurpations; it was a question of consolidating the supremacy of the Bishop of Rome. The latter was always very indulgent about real articles of faith, but he spit fire and brimstone the minute the rights of the Church were attacked. He did not argue a great deal about the persons in Christ, but he did argue

7. A Greek word meaning "identical." The reference is to the difference of opinion between the Orthodox (Eastern) and Roman Catholic churches as to whether God and Christ are "identical," as Western Christianity believes, or whether they are merely similar in nature.
8. In 395 Eudoxia, daughter of the chieftain of the Franks, became the wife of the East Roman Emperor Arcadius. After the Emperor's death his son Theodosius II succeeded to the throne, but he left most affairs of state in the hands of his sister Pulcheria. Eudoxia opposed her daughter's influence.
9. Patriarch of Constantinople from 428 to 431.
10. Patriarch of Constantinople from 412 to 444.
11. This is not, of course, to be taken at face value as an objective historical account. In dealing with history Heine had no qualms about using only facts that serve his purpose. The facts he gives here are only part of the total picture, as Heine no doubt knew.
12. Heine quotes here from an earlier work of his own, *The North Sea, Part III.*

about the consequence of the Isidorian Decretals.[13] He centralized his power by canonical law, by the investiture of bishops, by reducing the power of the princes, by establishing monastic orders, by celibacy of the priesthood, and so on. But was this Christianity? Is the idea of Christianity revealed to us by reading such histories? What is this idea?

It would probably be possible to discover already in the first centuries after Christ's birth how this idea was shaped historically and how it manifested itself in the physical world by examining, without prejudice, the history of the Manicheans and the Gnostics. Although the former were accused of heresy and the latter were in ill repute, and both groups were condemned by the Church, their influence on the dogma still remained; Catholic art developed out of their symbolism, and their mode of thought permeated the whole life of Christian peoples. In their fundamental principles the Manicheans are not very different from the Gnostics. The doctrine of the two principles, good and evil, opposing each other, is common to both. The one sect, the Manicheans, acquired this doctrine from the ancient Persian religion, in which Ormuzd, light, is opposed to Ahriman, darkness, as his enemy. The other sect, the Gnostics, believed, on the contrary, in the pre-existence of the principle of good and explained the origin of the principle of evil by emanation, by generations of eons which deteriorate all the more, the further they are removed from their origin. According to Cerinthus,[14] the creator of our world was by no means the supreme god, but only an emanation from him, one of those eons, the real Demiurge, who has gradually degenerated and now, as the evil principle, stands hostilely opposed to the *logos*, the good principle, emanating directly from the supreme god. This gnostic cosmogony is of Indian origin and brought with it the doctrine of the incarnation of God, of the mortification of the flesh, and of the contemplative life of the spirit; it gave birth to ascetically contemplative monasticism, the purest flower of the Christian idea.

13. A collection of partly falsified papal decrees and instructions composed by a man who called himself Isidore Mercator. Since they contributed to the increase in papal power, they were used by the popes from the ninth century on in spite of their dubious origin, and for the most part incorporated into the *Corpus juris canonici*.

14. One of the first Christian Gnostics, who lived at the beginning of the second century.

This idea manifested itself only very confusedly in dogma, and only very vaguely in worship. Yet everywhere we see the doctrine of the two principles appear; the evil Satan stands opposed to the good Christ; the world of the spirit is represented by Christ, the material world by Satan; our soul belongs to the former, our body to the latter. The whole world of phenomena, Nature, is therefore evil in its origin, and Satan, Prince of Darkness, tries, by means of it, to lure us to destruction, and it is necessary to renounce all the sensuous pleasures of life, to torture our body, Satan's fief, so that the soul may soar upward all the more gloriously into the bright Heaven, into the radiant kingdom of Christ.

This cosmogony, the real idea of Christianity, had spread over the entire Roman Empire with incredible rapidity, like a contagious disease, at times a raging fever, at times exhaustion, lasted all through the Middle Ages, and we moderns still feel spasms and lassitude in all our limbs. Though many of us have already recovered, we cannot escape the all-pervading hospital atmosphere and feel unhappy in being the only healthy persons among all the diseased. Someday when mankind regains its complete health, when peace is restored between body and soul, and they blend again in their original harmony, we will scarcely be able to comprehend the unnatural discord that Christianity has sown between the two. The happier and finer generations who, begotten in an embrace of free choice, come to flower in a religion of joy, will smile sadly at their poor ancestors, who gloomily refrained from all the pleasures of this beautiful earth and by deadening warm, colorful sensuousness almost faded away into bloodless ghosts! Yes, I say it with conviction—our descendants will be more beautiful and happier than we. For I believe in progress, I believe mankind is destined to happiness, and I therefore cherish a grander conception of the divinity than those pious people who fancy that man was created only to suffer. Even here on earth I would like to establish, through the blessings of free political and industrial institutions, that bliss which, in the opinion of the pious, is to be granted only on the Day of Judgment, in Heaven. The one hope is perhaps as foolish as the other, and there may be no resurrection of humanity either in a political, moral sense, or in an apostolic, Catholic sense.

Perhaps mankind is destined for eternal misery, the peoples are perhaps doomed in perpetuity to be trodden underfoot by despots, exploited by their accomplices, and scorned by their lackeys.

Alas, in this case we would have to try to preserve Christianity even if we know it is a mistake; we would have to journey through Europe barefoot and in monk's cowl, preaching renunciation and the vanity of all earthly possessions, holding up the comforting crucifix before the eyes of the scourged and derided people, and promising them up above, after death, all the joys of Heaven.

It is perhaps just because the great men on this earth are so sure of their superior power and have decided in their hearts to abuse it forever to our misfortune that they are convinced of the necessity of Christianity for their peoples, and it is really a tender, humane impulse that prompts them to take such pains to preserve this religion!

The ultimate fate of Christianity thus depends on whether we still need it. For eighteen centuries this religion was a blessing for suffering humanity; it was providential, divine, holy. Every contribution it has made to civilization by curbing the strong and strengthening the weak, by uniting the peoples through a common sentiment and a common language, and all else that its apologists have urged in its praise—all this is as nothing compared with that great consolation which it has bestowed on human beings by its very nature. Everlasting praise is due the symbol of that suffering God, the Saviour with the crown of thorns, the crucified Christ whose blood was as a soothing balm flowing down into the wound of mankind. The poet in particular will acknowledge with reverence the awesome sublimity of this symbol. The whole system of symbols expressed in the art and life of the Middle Ages will always arouse the admiration of poets. What colossal consistency there really is in Christian art, especially in its architecture! The Gothic cathedrals—how they harmonize with the ceremonies of worship, and how the idea of the Church itself is revealed in them! Everything about them strives upward, everything is transubstantiated; the stone buds forth into branches and foliage and becomes a tree; the fruit of the vine and the ear of corn become blood and flesh; man becomes God; God becomes pure spirit! Christian life in the Middle Ages is a fertile and inexhaustibly precious material for poets. Only through Christianity could there develop in this world conditions which include such bold contrasts, such motley sorrows, and such marvelous beauty that one would think the like could never have existed in the real world and that it was all a vast hallucination, the hallucination of a delirious deity. In those times Nature itself seems to have assumed fantastic disguises; yet though man, absorbed in abstract subtleties, turned away from her with annoyance, she nonetheless often roused him with a voice so uncannily sweet, so terrifyingly tender, so powerfully enchanting that he listened instinctively and smiled and was frightened and even fell sick unto death. The story of the nightingale of Basle comes to my mind here, and as you probably do not know it, I will relate it.

In May, 1433, at the time of the Council of Basle, a group of clerics composed of prelates, doctors, and monks of all orders, were walking in a woods near the city, debating about points of theological controversy, differentiating and arguing, or quarreling about annates, prospects of obtaining a certain office, and provisos, or inquiring whether Thomas Aquinas was a greater philosopher than Bonaventura, and Heaven knows what else. But suddenly, in the midst of their dogmatic and abstract discussions, they fell silent and stopped as if rooted to the spot before a blossoming linden tree in which a nightingale sat exulting and sobbing in its most melodious and tenderest melodies. The learned gentlemen began to feel strangely blissful as the warm tones of spring penetrated their scholastic hearts so limited by provisos; their emotions awoke from their torpid hibernation, and they looked at each other in marveling ecstasy. At last one of them remarked shrewdly that there was something queer about this, that the nightingale might well be a devil, trying with his sweet strains to divert them from their Christian converse and to entice them into lust and other alluring sins, and he proceeded to exorcise the evil spirit, probably with the customary formula of that time: *Adjuro te per eum, qui venturus est, judicare vivos et mortuos,*[15] etc., etc. To this exorcism, they say, the bird replied, "Yes, I am an evil spirit," and flew away laughing. Those, however, who had heard its song are said to have fallen ill that very same day and died shortly thereafter.

This story needs no commentary. It bears the dreadful impress of a time when all that was sweet and lovely was decried as the

15. I command you in the name of Him who will come to judge the quick and the dead.

work of the devil. Even the nightingale was slandered, and people crossed themselves when it sang. The true Christian walked about amidst verdant nature like an abstract ghost, with senses apprehensively sealed. I shall perhaps deal in more detail with this relationship of the Christian to nature in a later work, where, in order to further the understanding of modern romantic literature, I must discuss thoroughly German folk superstitions. For the present I can only remark that French writers, misled by German authorities, are greatly mistaken in assuming that popular superstitions during the Middle Ages were the same everywhere in Europe. It was only with regard to the principle of good, the Kingdom of Christ, that the same views were entertained in all of Europe. The Church of Rome saw to this, and anyone who deviated on this point from the prescribed opinion was a heretic. But with regard to the principle of evil, the realm of Satan, different opinions prevailed in the various countries. In the Teutonic North people had entirely different conceptions of it from those in the Latin countries of the South. This difference arose from the fact that the Christian priesthood did not reject the old national gods it met with there as idle phantoms, but conceded to them a real existence, maintaining, however, at the same time, that all these gods were merely male or female devils who, because of Christ's triumph, had lost their power over men and were now trying to lure them into sin through lust and deceit. All Olympus now became an aerial hell, and no matter how finely a poet of the Middle Ages celebrated in song the Greek tales of the gods, the devout Christian still saw in them only spooks and devils. This gloomy illusion of the monks hit poor Venus hardest; she, most especially, was considered to be a daughter of Beelzebub, and the good knight Tannhäuser tells her right to her face:

> O Venus, lovely lady mine,
> You're nothing but a devil![16]

You see, she had enticed Tannhäuser into that marvelous cavern called the Mountain of Venus, in which, so the legend went, amidst pastime and dancing, the beautiful goddess, with her maidens and lovers, led the most dissolute life. Even poor Diana, despite her

16. My translation.

chastity, was not exempt from a similar fate, and was described passing through the woods by night with her nymphs—hence the legend of the fierce host of hunters and the wild chase.[17] Here we still see intact the gnostic concept of the deterioration of what was previously divine, and in this transformation of an earlier national religion the idea of Christianity manifests itself most profoundly.

National religion in Europe, much more markedly in the North than in the South, was pantheistic. Its mysteries and symbols were related to a worship of nature; in every element the people worshipped marvelous beings; a divinity breathed in every tree; all the phenomena of the universe were permeated by a divine spirit. Christianity reversed this view, and a diabolized nature took the place of a nature permeated by divinity. But the serene figures of Greek mythology that reigned in the South together with Roman civilization, their beauty enhanced by art, could not be transformed into ugly, gruesome, satanic ghouls so easily as the Teutonic gods, whom, to be sure, no particular feeling for art had helped to fashion and who were already as depressed and dreary as the North itself. Thus in France you could produce no such gloomy and terrible realm of Satan as we did in Germany, and the world of apparitions and sorcery itself assumed with you a cheerful aspect. How beautiful, clear, and colorful your folk legends are in comparison with ours, these monstrosities of blood and mist that sneer at us so somberly and cruelly. Our medieval poets, usually selecting materials that you, in Brittany and Normandy, had either invented or treated first, gave their works, perhaps intentionally, as much as possible of the serene spirit of ancient France. But in our national literature and in our folk legends of oral tradition the gloomy northern spirit remained, a spirit of which you can scarcely conceive. Like us, you have various types of nature-spirits, but ours are as different from yours as a German from a Frenchman. How brightly colored and especially how pure are the demons in your *fabliaux* and romances of sorcery in comparison with our dismal and very often filthy rabble of spirits! Your fairies and nature-spirits, wher-

17. The legend of the host of spirits, souls of the dead, led by "the wild huntsman," which rides through the air at night. Any traveler who encounters them must throw himself on the ground and give no greeting; otherwise he is doomed to join the spirits in their hunt until Judgment Day.

ever you took them from, whether from Cornwall or from Arabia,[18] are completely at home with you and a French spirit differs from a German much as a dandy wearing yellow kid gloves and sauntering along the Coblence Boulevard differs from a clumsy German porter. Your water sprites, such as Melusine,[19] are just as different from ours as a princess from a washerwoman. How frightened Morgan le Fay[20] would be if she chanced to meet a German witch, naked, smeared with ointment, riding to the Brocken on a broomstick! This mountain is no fair Avalon, but a rendezvous for everything abominable and hideous. On the summit of the mountain sits Satan in the form of a black billy goat. Each of the witches approaches him with a candle in her hand and kisses him behind where his back ends. After that the infamous sisterhood dances around him singing, *"Donderemus, donderemus!"* The billy goat bleats, the infernal cancan[21] triumphs. It is a bad omen for a witch to lose a shoe in this dance; it means she will be burned that very same year. Yet the mad sabbat-music,[22] pure Berlioz, overpowers all foreboding anxiety, and when the poor witch awakens in the morning from her intoxication, she finds herself lying naked and exhausted in the ashes by the dying hearth fire.

The best information concerning these witches is found in the *Demonology* of the honorable and most learned Doctor Nicholas Remigius,[23] criminal judge to His Serene Highness, the Duke of Lorraine. This keen-witted man certainly had the best opportunity to become acquainted with the doings of witches, since he prepared the cases against them, and at his time eight hundred women ascended the funeral pyre in Lorraine alone after having been convicted of witchcraft. The proof of their guilt usually consisted in tying their hands and feet together and throwing them into the

18. The ultimate source of Arthurian legends is probably Wales, and Oriental legends became popular and more familiar through the Crusades.

19. The story of the nymph who fell in love with a mortal.

20. Sister of King Arthur and pupil of Merlin, the magician.

21. Heine uses here a Germanized form of the French word *chahut,* meaning "din" or "uproar," but both Elster and Walzel state that the word means "cancan," the French dance. I have accepted their explanation, hesitating to question the accuracy of two such serious scholars.

22. Sabbat is a term for the midnight assembly of witches and sorcerers held in medieval times on certain occasions such as Walpurgis Night or Halloween, hence the expression witches' sabbath.

23. Remigius published a book on demonolatry in 1598.

water. If they sank and drowned, they were innocent; if they stayed above water and swam, they were declared guilty and were burned. Such was the logic of those times.

We see as the main trait in the character of German demons that they are stripped of any ideal features and that they are a mixture of the vulgar and the monstrous. The more crudely familiar the form in which they appear to us, the more horrible is the effect they have. Nothing is more uncanny than our hobgoblins, kobolds, and pixies. In his *Anthropodemus* Praetorius has a passage on this subject which I quote here from Dobeneck.[24]

"The ancients could not conceive of hobgoblins as other than real human beings, in stature like small children, wearing brightly colored coats or dresses. Some add that a number of them are said to have knives sticking in their backs; others appeared in different and very frightening forms, depending on what instrument they had formerly been murdered with. For the superstitious believe them to be the souls of former occupants of their houses, murdered there long ago. And they tell many stories about how the kobolds had done the maids and cooks good service for a time in the house and had won their favor, how many a wench had thus been seized with such affection for the kobolds that they also ardently wished to see the little servants and demanded this of them, which longing, however, the spirits would never willingly gratify, making the excuse that no one could see them without being terrified. If the lustful maids still would not yield, the kobolds are said to have told them one place in the house where they would present themselves in the flesh, but the maids were to bring with them a pail of cold water. Whereupon it happened that one of the kobolds would lie down naked, perhaps on the floor, on a cushion, with a butcher knife sticking in his back. Many a maid was so frightened by this that she fell into a faint. Thereupon the creature immediately sprang up, took the water, and doused the wench with it thoroughly in order to bring her to her senses. After this the maids lost their desire and never asked to see dear Chimgen[25] again. To wit, all

24. Ferdinand von Dobeneck's *German Popular Superstitions and Heroic Legends of the Middle Ages (Des deutschen Mittelalters Volksglauben und Heroensagen)*, published in 1815, was Heine's main source for all the material on folk superstitions that he gives in this work. Praetorius' book appeared in 1666–1667.
25. A dialectal diminutive form of *Joachimchen* (little Joachim).

the kobolds are said to have individual names too, although generally called Chim. It is also said that they do all the housework for the men and maid servants to whom they are devoted, currying and feeding the horses, cleaning the stable, scrubbing up everything, keeping the kitchen clean, and taking great pains to do whatever else is necessary in the house, and the cattle are said to grow fat and thrive under their care. In return the kobolds must be toadied to; the domestics must never give them the slightest offense, either by laughing at them or neglecting to feed them well. If, for instance, a cook has once accepted such a creature as her secret helper in the house, she must put out every day at a certain time and at a definite place in the house a little dish she has prepared for him full of good food and then go away again; afterward she can be idle if she likes and go to bed betimes; yet early in the morning she will find her work done. But if she once forgets her duty, perhaps neglecting to put out the food, she has to do her work again by herself and has all sorts of mishaps, either burning herself with hot water, breaking pots and dishes, spilling food or letting it drop, and so on, so that as punishment she has to be scolded by the mistress or master of the house, at which, they say, the kobold is often heard giggling or laughing. And such a kobold is said always to remain in the same house even though the servants are changed. Indeed, a maid, when leaving a house, had to recommend the kobold most highly to her successor in order that the latter might wait on it in the same fashion. If the new servant happened not to want to, she had no lack of perpetual misfortune and very soon had to leave."

The following anecdote[26] is perhaps one of the most dreadful of such stories:

A maid servant had for many years an invisible family spirit sitting beside her by the hearth, where she had given him his own little place and where she conversed with him during the long winter evenings. Now once the maid asked Heinzchen (for this was the name she gave him) to let her see him in his natural form just once, but Heinzchen refused. Finally, however, he consented and told her to go down into the cellar and there she would see

26. Also from Dobeneck, who had taken it from Luther's *Tischreden (Table Talks)*.

him. Taking a candle, the maid goes down into the cellar, and there in an open cask she sees a dead infant swimming in its blood. Now many years before, this maid had given birth to an illegitimate child and had secretly murdered it and concealed it in a cask. Such is the nature of the Germans, however, that they frequently seek in the horrible itself their best jokes, and the folk legends about kobolds are often full of delightful touches. The stories about Hüdeken are particularly amusing. He was a kobold who played his pranks in Hildesheim in the twelfth century and of whom there is so much talk in our spinning rooms and in our ghost stories. A passage from an old chronicle,[27] already often printed, gives the following information about him:

"About the year 1132 there appeared over quite a long time to many persons in the bishopric of Hildesheim an evil spirit in the form of a peasant with a hat on his head, for which reason the peasants called him in the Saxon language Hüdeken.[28] This spirit took pleasure in associating with people, sometimes being visible to them, sometimes invisible, asking and answering questions. He offended no one without cause. If, however, anyone laughed at him or otherwise insulted him, he amply repaid the injury done him. When Count Burchard of Luka was killed by Count Hermann of Wiesenburg and the latter's land was in danger of becoming the booty of the victim's avengers, Hüdeken woke Bishop Bernhard of Hildesheim out of his sleep and addressed him as follows: 'Get up, bald head. The county of Wiesenburg has been abandoned and is in abeyance because of murder, and so can easily be occupied by you.' The bishop speedily assembled his warriors, fell upon the land of the guilty count, and united it, with the Emperor's consent, to his bishopric. The spirit frequently warned the said bishop voluntarily of impending dangers and appeared particularly often in the court kitchen, where he conversed with the cooks and rendered them all manner of services. The servants having gradually become familiar with Hüdeken, one kitchen-boy was daring enough to tease him and even to douse him with dirty water every time he appeared. The spirit requested the chief cook or steward of the kitchen to forbid the naughty lad his mischief. The chief cook

27. Heine's source is again Dobeneck.
28. Little hat.

responded, 'You are a spirit and are afraid of a mere boy!' whereupon Hüdeken replied menacingly, 'Since you won't punish the boy, I will show you in a few days how much I fear him.' Soon afterward the boy who had insulted the spirit sat sleeping all alone in the kitchen. In this condition the spirit seized him, strangled him, tore the body into pieces, and put these in pots on the fire. When the cook discovered this prank, he cursed the spirit, so the next day Hüdeken spoiled all the roasts that were on the spit by pouring the venom and blood of toads over them. Desire for revenge called forth new insults from the cook, after which the spirit finally led him onto a non-existent phantom bridge and plunged him into a deep moat. All the while Hüdeken industriously made the rounds of the walls and towers of the town the whole night long, compelling the sentinels to constant watchfulness. A man who had an unfaithful wife once said as a jest when he was about to take a trip, 'Hüdeken, good friend, I commend my wife to your care. Guard her carefully.' As soon as her husband was gone, the adulterous woman allowed one lover after another to visit her. But Hüdeken would not permit any of them to join her, throwing them all out of the bed onto the floor. When the husband returned from his journey, the spirit went a long distance to meet him and said to the returning traveler, 'I am very glad you are here, so that I shall be free of the burdensome duty you imposed on me. I have with indescribable difficulty preserved your wife from actual faithlessness. But I beg you never to entrust her to me again. I would rather keep watch over all the pigs in the whole of Saxony than over a woman who tries by trickery to get to the arms of her lovers.'"

For the sake of accuracy I must note that Hüdeken's head covering differs from the ordinary costume of the kobolds. They are usually dressed in gray and wear a little red cap. At least this is the way they look in Denmark, where they are said to be most numerous nowadays. I used to think the kobolds liked so much to live in Denmark because red groats were their favorite dish. But a young Danish poet, Mr. Andersen,[29] whom I had the pleasure of seeing here in Paris this summer, assured me very definitely that the *nissen*, as the kobolds are called in Denmark, like best porridge

---

29. Hans Christian Andersen, the well-known author of fairy tales.

with butter. Once these kobolds have settled in a house, they are not readily inclined to leave it. They never come unannounced, however, and when they wish to live somewhere, they notify the master of the house of their intention in the following manner:— They carry into the house by night a large quantity of wood chips and scatter cattle dung in the milk cans. If the master of the house does not throw out the wood chips or if he and his family drink the befouled milk, then the kobolds remain permanently in his house. For many a person this has become extremely unpleasant. A poor Jutlander at last became so annoyed at the companionship of such a kobold that he was even willing to give up his house. Loading all his possessions on a cart, he drove to the nearest village in order to settle there. On the way, however, when he happened to look back, he saw, peering out of one of the empty tubs, the little red-capped head of the kobold, who called to him affably, "*Wi flütten!*"[30]

I have perhaps lingered too long over these small demons, and it is time to return to the big ones. But all these stories illustrate the beliefs and the character of the German people. In past centuries these beliefs were just as powerful as the creed of the Church. When the learned Dr. Remigius had completed his large work on witchcraft, he believed himself to be so well informed on his subject that he fancied he could now practice sorcery himself; and, conscientious man that he was, he did not fail to denounce himself to the tribunals as a sorcerer, and in consequence of this denunciation he was burned for the crime.

These atrocities did not originate directly from the Christian Church, but indirectly they did, for the Church had so cunningly perverted the old Teutonic religion that it transformed the pantheistic cosmogony of the Germans into a pandemonic cosmogony and changed things previously held sacred by the people into hideous demonism. Yet human beings do not willingly relinquish what was precious and dear to them and their forefathers, and their affections secretly cling to it firmly even if it has been corrupted and distorted. Hence these perverted folk beliefs in Germany may perhaps outlive Christianity, which, unlike them, is not rooted in national tradition. At the time of the Reformation the belief in

30. Low German dialect meaning "We're moving."

Catholic legends of saints disappeared very rapidly, but not so the belief in magic and sorcery.

Luther no longer believed in Catholic miracles, but he still believed in devils. His *Table Talks* are full of curious anecdotes about Satanic arts, kobolds, and witches. In periods of distress he himself often thought he was struggling with the devil in person. At the Wartburg, where he translated the New Testament, he was so much disturbed by the devil that he threw the inkstand at his head. Ever since then the devil has had a great dread of ink, but a still greater dread of printers' ink. In the *Table Talks* just mentioned many delightful anecdotes are told about the devil's cunning, and I can't resist giving one of them.

"Doctor Martin Luther related that one day some good comrades were sitting together in a tavern. Now among them was a wild, dissolute fellow who had said that if anyone were to offer him enough wine for a good drinking bout, he would sell him his soul for it.

"Not long afterward a man came into the room and, going to him, seated himself beside him, drank with him, and, among other things, said to the one who had been so rash:

"'Listen, didn't you say just now that if anyone gave you wine for a drinking bout you would sell him your soul for it?'

"Then the other said once more, 'Yes, and I'll do it. Just let me drink and carouse today to the limit and be happy.'

"The man, who was the devil, said, 'Yes,' and soon afterward stole away again. Now when the carouser had been merry all day and finally also became drunk, the above-mentioned man, the devil, returned, sat down beside him, and asked the other topers, 'Good gentlemen, what is your opinion? When someone buys a horse, don't the saddle and bridle belong to him too?' They were all frightened. At last the man said, 'Well, answer me straightway.' Then they admitted it was so and said, 'Yes, saddle and bridle belong to him too.' At this the devil seized the wild, rough fellow and carried him off through the roof so that no one knew where he had disappeared to."

Although I entertain the highest respect for our great master, Martin Luther, still I can't help thinking that he completely misunderstood the nature of Satan, who certainly does not look on the body with such contempt as is here indicated. Whatever evil one can say about the devil, no one could ever accuse him of being a spiritualist.

But Martin Luther misjudged the attitude of the pope and the Catholic Church even more than the attitude of the devil. In my strict impartiality I must defend the two, as well as the devil, against the far too zealous man. Indeed, if I were asked in all conscience, I would admit that Pope Leo X was actually much more sensible than Luther, and that Luther had absolutely no understanding of the fundamental principles of the Catholic Church. For Luther had not understood that the idea of Christianity, the annihilation of sensuality, was far too great a contradiction of human nature for it ever to have been completely realized in actual life. He had not understood that Catholicism was, so to speak, a concordat between God and the devil, that is, between spirit and matter, whereby the autocracy of the spirit is pronounced in theory but matter is enabled to exercise in practice all its nullified rights. Hence a clever system of concessions which the Church made for the benefit of the senses, though always in such a form as to stigmatize every act of sensuality and to preserve for the spirit its scornful usurpation of power. You may obey the tender affections of your heart and embrace a pretty girl, but you must confess that it was a disgraceful sin, and you must do penance for this sin. That this penance could be done with money was as advantageous for humanity as it was profitable for the Church. The Church permitted wergild to be paid, so to speak, for any pleasure of the flesh, and a tariff developed for every kind of sin. There were religious pedlars who offered throughout the land, in the name of the Roman Catholic Church, indulgence for every taxable sin, and one such was that Tetzel against whom Luther made his first attack. Our historians are of the opinion that his protest against the traffic in indulgences was an insignificant event and that only through Romish stubbornness had Luther, who at first merely objected passionately to an abuse within the Church, been driven to attack the entire authority of the Church at the very top of the hierarchy. This is simply an error; traffic in indulgences was not an abuse, it was a consequence of the whole ecclesiastical system, and in attacking it, Luther had attacked the Church itself, and the Church was forced to condemn him as a heretic. Leo X, the cultivated Florentine, the disciple of Politian,[31] the friend of Raphael, the Greek philosopher with the Pope's tiara conferred on him by the conclave, possibly because he was suffering from a disease by no means caused by Christian abstinence and at that time still very dangerous—how must this Leo de Medici have smiled at the poor, chaste, simple monk who imagined the Gospel to be the charter of Christendom and this charter to be a truth! He may not even have noticed what Luther wanted, being at that time much too occupied with the construction of St. Peter's, the cost of which was to be met by this very sale of indulgences, so that sin actually provided the money for the building of this church, which thereby became, as it were, a monument to sensual pleasure like that pyramid built by an Egyptian courtesan with the money she had earned from prostitution.[32] One could perhaps assert more truthfully of this house of God than of the cathedral of Cologne that it was built by the devil. This triumph of spiritualism, that sensualism itself was compelled to construct for it its most beautiful temple; that the means for glorifying the spirit were obtained from the many concessions to the flesh—this triumph was incomprehensible in the German North. For here, far more easily than beneath Italy's glowing sky, it was possible to practice a Christianity that makes as few concessions as possible to sensuality. We Northerners are more cold-blooded, and we didn't need as many indulgences for carnal sins as Leo, with fatherly concern, had sent to us. The climate makes the practice of Christian virtues easier for us, and on October 31, 1516,[33] when Luther nailed his theses against indulgences on the door of the Augustine Church, the moat around the city of Wittenberg was perhaps already frozen over, and one could go skating there, a very chilly pleasure and consequently not a sin.

In the above I have already used the words spiritualism and sensualism several times. These words, however, do not refer here, as they do with the French philosophers, to the two different sources of our knowledge; on the contrary, I use them, as is always clear of itself just from the sense of my argument, to designate those two different modes of thought of which the one attempts to glorify the spirit by striving to destroy matter, whereas the other

31. Angelo Poliziano, Italian poet and scholar, friend of Lorenzo de Medici.
32. The pyramid of Rhodope.
33. The incorrect date is Heine's mistake.

seeks to vindicate the natural rights of matter against the domination of the spirit.

I must also call your particular attention to the above-mentioned beginnings of the Lutheran Reformation—beginnings that already reveal the whole spirit of it—since here in France people entertain the old misconceptions about the Reformation which Bossuet propagated in his *Histoire des variations*[34] and which make their influence felt even among present-day writers. The French understood only the negative side of the Reformation. They saw in it merely a battle against Catholicism and often believed that this battle had always been conducted on the other side of the Rhine for the same reasons as a similar struggle on this side, in France. But the motives there were totally different and contradictory to the motives here. The struggle against Catholicism in Germany was nothing but a war which spiritualism began when it realized that it possessed only the title of authority and ruled only *de jure,* while sensualism, by means of a fraud of long tradition, was exercising actual sovereignty and governing *de facto.* The dealers in indulgences were driven off, the pretty concubines of the priests were exchanged for frigid wives, the charming images of the Madonna were dashed to pieces, and here and there a Puritanism developed that was utterly hostile to all sensuous pleasures. The struggle against Catholicism in France in the seventeenth and eighteenth centuries, on the other hand, was a war which sensualism began when it saw that it ruled *de facto* and yet that every act of its sovereign authority was derided as illegitimate and denounced in the most cruel manner by a spiritualism which maintained that it reigned *de jure.* Instead of battling with chaste seriousness, as in Germany, in France they fought with obscene jokes, and instead of carrying on a theological discussion, as in Germany, they wrote funny satires. The object of these satires was usually to demonstrate the conflict that arises in a human being when he tries to be completely spiritual; hence the flowering of the most priceless stories of pious men involuntarily succumbing to their animal natures or even trying to preserve the appearance of sanctity and

---

34. Jacques Bénigne Bossuet (1627–1704) wrote a *Histoire des variations des Églises protestantes (History of the Variations of the Protestant Churches)* and other works in the hope of bringing Protestants back to the Catholic Church.

taking refuge in hypocrisy. The Queen of Navarre[35] had already portrayed such abuses in her novellas. The relationship between monks and women is her customary theme, and her aim is not merely to convulse with laughter but to shake monasticism to its foundations. Molière's *Tartuffe* is undoubtedly the most malicious gem of such comical polemic, for it is not directed simply against the Jesuitism of its age, but against Christianity itself, indeed, against the idea of Christianity, against spiritualism. Tartuffe's ostentatious display of fear of Dorine's naked bosom, the words

> *Le ciel défend, de vrai, certains contentements,*
> *Mais on trouve avec lui des accomodements*—[36]

these things ridicule not only ordinary hypocrisy, but also the universal falsehood that necessarily arises from the impossibility of putting the Christian idea into practice, as well as the whole system of concessions that spiritualism was forced to make to sensualism. In fact, Jansenism[37] had far more reason than Jesuitism to feel insulted at the performance of *Tartuffe,* and Molière may still be as offensive to the Methodists of our day as he was to the Catholic devotees of his own time. It is just this which makes Molière so great, that, like Aristophanes and Cervantes, he ridicules not merely contemporary incidents, but the eternal absurdities, the original weaknesses of mankind. Voltaire, who always attacked only things temporary and unessential, is in this respect inferior to Molière.

This kind of ridicule, however, especially the Voltairean, has fulfilled its mission in France, and any attempt to continue it would be both untimely and unwise. For if the last visible remains of Catholicism were to be destroyed, it might easily happen that the idea of Catholicism would take refuge in a new form, assume, so to speak, a new body, and, laying aside the very name of Christianity,

35. Margaret of Navarre (1492–1549) wrote a number of novellas, which were published under the title *Heptaméron des nouvelles.* Both title and content are reminiscent of Boccaccio's *Decameron.*

36. Tartuffe speaking to Elmire, Act IV, Scene 5: "Heaven forbids certain pleasures, it is true,/But you can come to some sort of compromise with it."

37. A Roman Catholic movement originating from the work of the Dutch theologian, Cornelius Jansen. Its purpose was a reform of Christian life by a return to greater personal holiness, hence the characteristic mystical trend in Jansenist writings.

might in this transformation harass us far more vexatiously than in its present shattered, ruined, and universally discredited form. Yes, there is a certain advantage in the fact that spiritualism is represented by a religion that has already lost the better part of its strength and by a priesthood that stands in direct opposition to all the enthusiasm for freedom that is characteristic of our time. But why then is spiritualism so very repugnant to us? Is it something so bad? Not at all. Attar of roses is a precious thing, and a small flask of it is refreshing for those who must pass their days mournfully in the locked chambers of a harem. But nonetheless we don't want all the roses of this life to be crushed and trampled in order to obtain a few drops of attar of roses, however comforting their effect. We resemble rather the nightingales that delight in the roses themselves and are enraptured by their blushing blossoms as by their invisible fragrance.

I have stated above that it was actually spiritualism which attacked Catholicism in Germany. But this applies only to the beginning of the Reformation. As soon as spiritualism had made a breach in the ancient structure of the Church, sensualism rushed forth with all its long restrained passion, and Germany became the most tumultuous arena for the intoxication with liberty and sensual pleasures. The oppressed peasants had found in the new doctrine spiritual weapons with which to wage war against the aristocracy; the desire for such a war had already existed for a century and a half. In Münster sensualism, in the person of John of Leiden,[38] ran naked through the streets and lay down with its twelve wives on that huge bedstead still to be seen today in the town hall there. Everywhere the portals of cloisters flew open, and nuns and monks rushed billing and cooing into each other's arms. Yes, the external history of that period consists almost entirely of sensual mutinies. We shall see later how few results remained; how spiritualism again suppressed those rioters; how it gradually made its authority secure in the North, but was mortally wounded by an enemy it had nurtured in its own bosom, namely, by philosophy. It is a very complicated history, difficult to unravel. For the Catholic party it is easy to stress at will the worst motives, and to hear them talk

38. A Dutch Anabaptist leader (c. 1509–1536). He moved to Münster, where in 1534 the Anabaptists took up arms and deposed the civil and religious authorities.

one might think the only motives were to legitimize the most brazen sensuality and to plunder Church property. To be sure, in order to gain the victory, spiritual interests must always form an alliance with material interests. But the devil had shuffled the cards so strangely that it is now impossible to state with certainty anything about the intentions.

The illustrious personages assembled in the Diet Hall at Worms in the year 1521 may well have borne in their hearts thoughts that were at odds with the words on their lips. There sat a young Emperor,[39] wrapping himself in his new crimson mantel with youthful delight in power and secretly rejoicing that the proud Roman who had so often mistreated his imperial predecessors and had still not abandoned his arrogant pretensions had now received a very effectual reprimand. The representative of that Roman, on his part, felt a secret joy that dissension was arising among those Germans who, like drunken barbarians, had so often invaded and plundered beautiful Italy and were still threatening it with fresh invasions and plunderings. The secular princes were glad that they could appropriate the new doctrine and at the same time the old Church domains. The high prelates were already considering whether they might not marry their cooks and bequeath their electoral dominions, bishoprics, and abbeys to their male offspring. The deputies of the towns rejoiced at a further extension of their independence. Everyone had something to gain here and was secretly thinking of earthly advantages.

Yet there was *one* man there who, I am convinced, was not thinking of himself but only of the divine interests which he was to represent. This man was Martin Luther, the poor monk chosen by Providence to destroy the world empire of Rome, against which even the most powerful emperors and the boldest sages had struggled in vain. But Providence is well aware upon what shoulders it lays it burdens; here not only spiritual, but also physical strength was necessary. There was need of a body steeled from youth by monastic rigor and chastity to endure the hardships of such a duty. At that time our dear master was still thin and looked very pale, so that the ruddy, well-fed lords of the Imperial Diet gazed down almost

---

39. As an ardent Spanish Catholic, Charles V was strongly opposed to Luther and used his influence to have him condemned as a heretic.

with compassion at the wretched man in the black cowl. But he was nonetheless quite healthy, and his nerves were so steady that the glittering throng did not intimidate him in the least. Even his lungs must have been strong, for after having delivered his long defense, he had to repeat it in Latin because the Emperor did not understand High German.[40] I get angry whenever I think of it, for our dear master was standing beside an open window, exposed to the draft, while sweat dripped from his forehead. He was probably exhausted from speaking so long, and his mouth had probably gotten a little dry. The Duke of Brunswick certainly must have thought, "The man must be very thirsty"; at any rate, we read that he sent Martin Luther in his inn three jugs of the best Eimbeck beer. I shall never forget this noble deed of the House of Brunswick.

Just as people in France have very wrong ideas about the Reformation, so also about its heroes. The immediate cause of this lack of understanding is probably that Luther is not merely the greatest, but also the most *German,* man in our history, that in his character are united most magnificently all the virtues and the defects of the Germans, and that he represents in his own person the wonderful country of Germany. He also possessed qualities that we seldom find combined but usually encounter as hostile antitheses. He was both a dreamy mystic and a practical man of action. His thought not only had wings but also hands; he spoke and he acted. He was not merely the tongue but also the sword of his time. He was both a cold, scholastic quibbler and an inspired prophet intoxicated by the Divinity. After working laboriously all day at his dogmatic distinctions, in the evening he would take his flute and go out to watch the stars, and he would dissolve in melody and worship. The same man who could scold like a fishwife could also be as gentle as a tender girl. He was often as fierce as the storm that uproots the oak, and then again he was as mild as the breeze that caresses the violets. He was full of the most awesome piety, full of self-sacrificing devotion to the Holy Spirit; he could lose himself completely in pure spirituality. And yet he was well acquainted with the glories of this earth and knew how to appreciate

40. Not High German in the modern use of the phrase, meaning the standard German spoken by educated Germans. At that time there was as yet no standard German language used and understood by all German-speaking people. Latin was still the lingua franca in Germany and between European countries.

them, and from his lips came the famous saying: "Who loves not woman, wine, and song, remains a fool his whole life long." He was a complete man, I might say an absolute man, in whom matter and spirit are not separate. To call him a spiritualist, therefore, would be just as wrong as to call him a sensualist. How shall I say it?—he had something primordial, incomprehensible, miraculous in him such as we find in all men sent by Providence, something terrifyingly naive, something boorishly wise, something sublimely provincial, something invincibly demonic.

Luther's father was a miner in Mansfeld, and the boy was often with him in his subterranean workshop, where the mighty metals grow and the lively parent springs ripple, and his young heart had perhaps unconsciously absorbed the most mysterious forces of Nature or was even protected from harm by the magic powers of the mountain spirits. This may also be the reason why so much earthiness, so much of the dross of passion still clung to him, a reproach often enough made against him. But the reproach is unjust, for without that admixture of earthiness he could not have been a man of action. Pure spirits cannot act. Don't we learn from Jung Stilling's[41] *Theory of Ghosts* that spirits can in fact make themselves visible in color and distinct form, and can walk, run, dance, and bear themselves otherwise just like living human beings, but that they cannot move any material object, not even the smallest nightstand, from its place?

Praise be to Luther! Eternal praise for the dear man to whom we owe the salvation of our noblest possessions and from whose benefactions we still live today! It little becomes us to complain of the narrowness of his views. The dwarf standing on the shoulders of the giant can of course see farther than the giant himself, especially if he puts on glasses, but the elevated perspective lacks the noble emotion, the giant heart that we cannot lay claim to. It becomes us still less to pronounce harsh judgment of his failings; these failings have benefited us more than the virtues of a thousand others. Neither the subtlety of Erasmus nor the gentleness of Melanchthon would ever have gotten us as far as, occasionally, the godly brutality of Brother Martin. Yes, the error in regard to

---

41. Johann Heinrich Jung, known as Jung-Stilling (1740–1817), a well-known Pietist and mystic who wrote a number of widely read works on ghosts.

the beginning, as I mentioned before, has borne very precious fruits, fruits from which all mankind derives strength. From the day of the Diet, when Luther denied the authority of the Pope and openly declared "that his doctrine could be refuted only by the word of the Bible itself or on rational grounds," a new era began in Germany. The chain with which Saint Boniface had bound the German church to Rome was cut asunder. This church, which had hitherto formed an integral part of the great hierarchy, split into religious democracies. Religion itself underwent a change; the Indo-Gnostic element disappeared, and we see the Judaic-Deistic element again becoming prominent. Evangelical Christianity emerged. Because the most essential claims of matter were not merely respected but also legitimized, religion once more became a truth. The priest became a human being and took a wife and begot children, as God has ordained. On the other hand, God Himself became once more a celestial bachelor without a family; the legitimacy of His Son was disputed; the saints were deposed; the angels' wings were clipped; the Blessed Virgin lost all claims to the crown of heaven and was forbidden to perform miracles. From this time on, especially once the natural sciences began making such great progress, miracles ceased altogether. Whether it be that the dear Lord is annoyed when the physicists view His activities with such distrust, or that He doesn't like to compete with Bosco,[42] certain it is that even in most recent times, when religion is in such very great danger, He has disdained to support it by any sort of dazzling miracle. Perhaps from now on, with all the new religions that He introduces on this earth, He will have nothing more to do with any holy tricks and will always demonstrate the truths of the new doctrines by means of reason, which is indeed the most sensible thing. At any rate, in the case of Saint-Simonism,[43] the newest religion, not a single miracle has occurred, except possibly that an old tailor's bill Saint-Simon still owed when he died was paid in cash by his disciples

42. Bartolommeo Bosco, a famous Italian magician who caused quite a stir in Europe after 1814.
43. Count Claude Henri Saint-Simon (1760–1825) was a French social philosopher whose ideas were taken up by his followers after his death and developed into the movement known as Saint-Simonism. It aimed at social, economic, and religious reform, and some aspects were to influence later sociologists, e.g., Comte. What appealed to Heine was not so much social reform as the so-called "emancipation of the senses."

ten years after his death. I can still see the worthy Père Olinde[44] rise enthusiastically in the Taitbout Hall, holding up before the astonished congregation the receipted tailor's bill. Young grocers were taken aback at such evidence of the supernatural. The tailors, however, immediately began to have faith!

Yet though we in Germany lost the old miracles because of Protestantism and much else that was poetic, we gained various compensations. People became nobler and more virtuous. Protestantism had the most beneficial influence on that purity of manners and that strictness in the performance of duties which we usually call morality; indeed, in many communities Protestantism took a direction that ultimately caused it to become completely identical with this morality, and the Gospel remains valid only as a beautiful parable. We now notice especially a refreshing change in the life of the clergy. The debauchery and vices of the monks vanished together with celibacy. Among the Protestant clergy it is not unusual to find extremely virtuous men, men for whom even the ancient Stoics would have had respect. One has to travel on foot, as a poor student, through North Germany[45] to discover how much virtue and, to give this word "virtue" a beautiful epithet, how much evangelical virtue is often to be found in a modest parsonage. How often, on a winter evening, I found there a hospitable welcome, I, a stranger bringing no recommendation other than that I was hungry and tired. When I had then eaten well and slept soundly and was about to go on my way the next morning, the old pastor would appear in his dressing gown to bestow his blessing on my journey—a thing that never brought me misfortune. And his kindly, garrulous wife would put into my pocket some slices of buttered bread, which were no less comforting to me. And at a distance, silent, stood the pastor's lovely daughters with their blushing cheeks and violet eyes; their shy ardor, remaining in my memory, kept my heart warm the whole winter day.

When Luther declared that his doctrine could be refuted only by the Bible itself or on grounds of reason, human reason was granted the right to explain the Scriptures, and reason was acknowledged as the supreme judge in all religious controversies. Thus there arose

---

44. One of the leaders among the Saint-Simonists.
45. North Germany was then predominantly Protestant, South Germany predominantly Catholic.

in Germany so-called spiritual freedom or, as it is also called, freedom of thought. Thought became a right, and the authority of reason became legitimate. To be sure, for several centuries already one had been able to think and speak with considerable freedom, and the scholastics disputed about matters which we can scarcely conceive even being mentioned in the Middle Ages. But this came about through the distinction made between theological and philosophical truth, a distinction whereby one explicitly protected himself against heresy; and such controversies took place only in the lecture rooms of the universities and in a Latin gothically abstruse, which the people could not understand a word of, so that little harm to the Church was to be feared. Nevertheless, the Church had never really sanctioned such proceedings, and now and then it actually did burn a poor scholastic at the stake. Since Luther, however, no distinction was any longer made between theological and philosophical truth, and people disputed in the public marketplace and in the German language, without hesitation or fear. The princes who accepted the Reformation made this freedom of thought legitimate, and an important, internationally important result is German philosophy.

In fact, from the middle of the last century until the French invasion, nowhere, not even in Greece, could the human mind express itself so freely as in Germany. In Prussia especially an unrestrained freedom of thought prevailed. The Marquis of Brandenburg had understood that he, who could be a legitimate king of Prussia only because of Protestant principles, also had to preserve Protestant freedom of thought.

Since then, to be sure, things have changed, and the natural protector of our Protestant freedom of thought has come to an understanding with the Ultramontane party to suppress that liberty, and for this purpose he often uses the weapon first invented and directed against us by the Papacy: censorship.

Strange! We Germans are the strongest and cleverest of peoples. Princes of our race sit on all the thrones of Europe, our Rothschilds dominate all the exchanges in the world, our scholars reign supreme in all the sciences, we invented gunpowder and the printing-press— and yet anyone who fires a pistol in our country pays a fine of three taler, and if we want to announce in the *Hamburger Korrespondent:* "My dear spouse has given birth to a daughter as beautiful as Liberty!," Dr. Hoffmann[46] immediately seizes his red pencil and crosses out "Liberty."

Can this continue much longer? I do not know. But I know that the question of the freedom of the press, at present so vehemently discussed in Germany, is significantly connected with the reflections outlined above, and I believe its solution is not difficult if one considers that freedom of the press is nothing other than a consequence of freedom of thought and hence a Protestant right. The Germans have already given their best blood for rights of this kind, and they may well be brought to the point of entering the lists once more.

The same remarks apply to the question of academic freedom, now so passionately rousing people in Germany. Since the supposed discovery that political agitation, that is, love of liberty, is most rampant in the universities, intimations come from all sides to the rulers that these institutions should be suppressed or at least converted into ordinary instructional institutions. Plans are now being concocted, and pros and cons discussed. But the avowed opponents of the universities do not seem to understand the fundamental principles of the question any better than the avowed defenders whom we have heard from so far. The former do not understand that youth everywhere and under all forms of disciplines will be enthusiastic about liberty and that, if the universities are suppressed, these enthusiastic young people will find expression all the more energetically elsewhere, perhaps in an alliance with the youth of the commercial and industrial classes. The defenders seek only to prove that with the closing of the universities the flower of German scholarship would be destroyed, that it is precisely academic freedom that is so valuable for these studies, providing the youth with such a fine opportunity to develop in many and varied ways, etc. As if a few Greek phrases or a few crude actions, more or less, had anything to do with the matter!

And what use would all science, study, or culture be to the princes if the sacred security of their thrones were endangered! They were heroic enough to sacrifice all those relative benefits for the one absolute good, their absolute sovereignty. For this has been

46. The censor in Hamburg. Needless to say, this paragraph, the one before it, and the one following, did not appear in the early German editions of this work.

entrusted to them by God, and where Heaven commands, all earthly considerations must yield.

There is also misunderstanding of the question on the part of the poor professors who appear publicly as representatives of the universities as well as on the part of the government officials who appear as opponents of them. It is only Catholic propaganda in Germany that comprehends the significance of the universities. These pious obscurantists are the most dangerous enemies of our university system, treacherously working against it with lies and deception, and whenever one of them makes a kindly pretence of saying a good word for the universities, some Jesuit intrigue is revealed. These cowardly hypocrites know very well what gains are at stake here. For with the destruction of the universities the Protestant Church will also fall, a Church that since the Reformation has had its roots so exclusively in the universities that the whole history of the Protestant Church for the last centuries consists almost entirely of theological disputes among the university scholars of Wittenberg, Leipzig, Tübingen, and Halle. The consistories are only a feeble reflection of the theological faculty; if the latter should disappear, they will lose all support and character and will sink into a desolate dependence on the ministries of the government or even on the police.

But let us not give these melancholy reflections too much space, especially since we still have to speak of the providential man who did such great things for the German people. I have shown above how through him we achieved the broadest freedom of thought. But this Martin Luther gave us not merely freedom of movement, but also the means to move, that is, he gave the spirit a body. He put the thought into words. He created the German language.

He did this by translating the Bible.

As a matter of fact, the Divine Author of this book seems to have known as well as anyone else that it is by no means unimportant who the translator is, and He Himself chose His translator and bestowed on him the marvelous power to translate a dead language which was already buried, so to speak, into another language which had not yet come into existence.

We have the Vulgate, of course, which people understood, as well as the Septuagint, which by that time could also be understood. But the knowledge of Hebrew had completely died out in the

Christian world. Only the Jews, who kept themselves hidden here
and there in some corner or other of the earth, still preserved the
traditions of this language. Like a ghost that watches over a treasure
once entrusted to it, this massacred people, this ghost of a people,
sat in their ghettos and guarded the Hebrew Bible. And into these
hiding places of ill repute German scholars could be seen stealthily
creeping down to unearth the treasure in order to acquire a
knowledge of Hebrew. When the Catholic clergy noticed the danger
thus threatening them, that the people might by this bypath arrive
at the true Word of God and discover the Romish falsifications,
they would have liked to suppress the Jewish tradition as well.
They set to work to destroy all Hebrew books, and on the Rhine
there began that book-persecution against which our admirable
Dr. Reuchlin fought so gloriously.[47] The Cologne theologians who
were active at that time, especially Hochstraaten, were by no means
so stupid as Reuchlin's valiant fellow-combatant, the knight Ulrich
von Hutten, portrays them in his *Litterae Obscurorum Virorum*.[48]
Their aim was the suppression of the Hebrew language. When
Reuchlin gained the victory, Luther was able to begin his work. In
a letter he wrote to Reuchlin at this time, he seems already to sense
the importance of the victory Reuchlin had won—a victory won
by a man in a dependent and difficult position—whereas he, as an
Augustinian monk, was completely independent. Very naively
Luther says in this letter, *"Ego nihil timeo, quia nihil habeo."*[49]

But how Luther arrived at the language into which he translated
the Bible is a mystery to me even now. The old Swabian dialect
had totally disappeared with the chivalric literature of the Hohen-
staufen imperial era. The old Saxon dialect, so-called Low German,
was in use only in one portion of North Germany and, despite all

47. Johann Reuchlin (1455–1522), a German humanist, scholar of Greek and
the best Hebrew scholar among the Christians of his day. Johann Pfefferkorn, a
converted Jew, advocated the destruction of all Hebrew books. Emperor Maximilian
requested Reuchlin's opinion on the matter, and when Reuchlin suggested that only
Hebrew books calumniating Christianity should be suppressed, he was violently
attacked by bigots and obscurantists.
48. The first word of the Latin title was *Epistolae. Letters of Obscure Men*,
published anonymously, the first series in 1515–1517, was a witty and satirical
defense of Reuchlin's liberal attitude and a humanistic attack upon the Church
party. Hutten contributed a few letters, but Johann Jäger (Crotus Rubianus) seems
to have had the chief share in the book.
49. "I fear nothing because I possess nothing." Heine's quotation is not quite
accurate, but the sense is the same.

attempts that were made, never proved to be suitable for literary purposes. If Luther had taken for his translation of the Bible the language then spoken in present-day Saxony, Adelung[50] would have been right in maintaining that the Saxon dialect, particularly that of Meissen, was our actual High German, that is, our literary language. But this error has long since been refuted, and I must call attention to it here all the more pointedly because it is still current in France. Present-day Saxon was never a dialect of the German people, any more than Silesian was, for the latter, like the former, was in its origins strongly tinged with Slavic.[51] I therefore frankly confess that I do not know how the language we find in the Lutheran Bible originated. But I know that through this Bible, of which the newly invented press, the black art, hurled thousands of copies among the people, the Lutheran language spread in a few years over all of Germany and was elevated to the rank of the common written language. This written language still prevails in Germany and gives that politically and religiously dismembered country a literary unity. Such a priceless gain may well make amends to us for the fact that this language in its modern development lacks something of that inner warmth which we usually find in languages originating from a single dialect. The language in Luther's Bible, however, is far from lacking such inner warmth, and this ancient book is a perennial source of rejuvenation for our language. Every expression and every turn of phrase in the Lutheran Bible is German; an author can still use them without hesitation; and since this book is in the hands of the poorest people, they need no special scholarly instruction in order to be able to express themselves in a literary fashion.

This circumstance will have most remarkable consequences when political revolution breaks out in Germany. Liberty will be able to speak everywhere, and its language will be Biblical.

Luther's original writings have also contributed to standardizing the German language. Owing to their polemical passionateness they penetrated deeply into the heart of his time. Their tone is not always delicate, but you can't make even a religious revolution out of orange blossoms. Coarseness must often be countered with

50. Johann Adelung (1732–1806), well-known German grammarian.
51. Heine's comments on the origin of High German and of these dialects are wrong, but the history of their origins is too complicated to be summarized adequately in a footnote.

coarseness. In the Bible Luther's language is always restrained within the bounds of a certain dignity out of reverence for the ever-present spirit of God. In his polemical writings, on the other hand, he abandons himself to a plebeian vulgarity that is often as repulsive as it is magnificent. His expressions and his images then resemble those gigantic stone figures which we find in Hindu or Egyptian temple grottos and whose gaudy coloring and fantastic ugliness both repel and attract us. Because of this baroque granite style the bold monk sometimes seems to us like a religious Danton, a preacher of the mountain, who, from its peak, hurls down his motley word-boulders onto the heads of his adversaries.

More remarkable and more significant than these prose works are Luther's poems, the songs that sprang from his heart in the midst of conflict and distress. Often they resemble a flower growing on a rocky cliff, often a moonbeam quivering across a tossing sea. Luther loved music; he even wrote a treatise on this art; and his lyrics are therefore unusually melodious. In this respect also he deserves the name: the Swan of Eisleben.[52] He was, however, anything but a gentle swan in many songs in which he rouses the courage of his followers and inspires himself with wildest ardor for the combat. That defiant song with which he and his companions entered Worms[53] was a battle song. The old cathedral trembled at these novel tones, and the ravens started up in terror in their obscure nests in the towers. This song, the Marseillaise Hymn of the Reformation, has retained its power of inspiration right up to the present time.[54]

> A mighty fortress is our God,
> A bulwark never failing;
> Our helper He amid the flood
> Of mortal ills prevailing.
> For still our ancient foe
> Doth seek to work us woe;
> His craft and and power are great,
> And, armed with cruel hate,
> On earth is not his equal.

52. Luther was born in Eisleben, and he gave himself this name.
53. It is doubtful that this song was written so early.
54. I use here the widely known translation by Frederick H. Hedge.

Did we in our own strength confide,
Our striving would be losing,
Were not the right Man on our side,
The Man of God's own choosing.
Dost ask Who that may be?
Christ Jesus, it is He,
Lord Sabaoth His name,
From age to age the same,
And He must win the battle.

And though this world, with devils filled,
Should threaten to undo us,
We will not fear, for God hath willed
His truth to triumph through us.
The Prince of Darkness grim,
We tremble not for him;
His rage we can endure,
For lo! his doom is sure,
One little word shall fell him.

That word above all earthly powers,
No thanks to them, abideth;
The spirit and the gifts are ours
Through Him Who with us sideth.
Let goods and kindred go,
This mortal life also;
The body they may kill;
God's truth abideth still,
His kingdom is forever.

I have shown that we owe our beloved Doctor Martin Luther the intellectual freedom that modern literature needed for its development. I have shown how he also created for us the word, the language, in which this new literature could express itself. I have now only to add that he is himself the originator of this literature; that our belles-lettres in the real sense begin with Luther; that his religious songs prove to be the first significant manifestations of our modern literature and already reveal its distinctive character. Anyone wishing to speak about modern German literature must therefore commence with Luther and not, for instance, with a certain Nürnberg philistine by the name of Hans Sachs,[55] as has been done with deceitful malice by some writers of the Romantic School. Hans Sachs, the troubadour of the honorable guild of shoemakers, whose Meistergesang was only a silly parody of the earlier Minnelieder[56] and whose plays were mere clumsy travesties of the old mystery plays,—this pedantic buffoon who painfully imitates the natural naivete of the Middle Ages can perhaps be regarded as the last poet of the older period but certainly not as the first poet of the modern age. No further proof will be needed for this than to discuss in specific terms the contrast between our modern literature and earlier literature.

If we examine the German literature that flourished before Luther, we find:

1) Its material, its content, is, like the life of the Middle Ages itself, a combination of two heterogeneous elements which wrestled so mightily with each other in a long duel that they finally blended together, namely, Germanic national character and Hindu-Gnostic, so-called Catholic, Christianity.

2) The treatment of the subject matter, or rather the spirit of the treatment, in this earlier literature is romantic. The same term, "romantic," is also applied incorrectly to the content of that literature and to all the aspects of the Middle Ages that originated through the blending of the two elements just mentioned, Germanic national character and Catholic Christianity. For just as certain poets of the Middle Ages treated Greek history and mythology in a fashion truly romantic, so also medieval customs and legends can be presented in classical form. The terms "classical" and "romantic" thus apply only to the spirit of the treatment.[57] The treatment is classical when the form of what is represented is completely identical with the idea of what is to be represented, as is the case in the art works of the Greeks, in which therefore the greatest harmony between form and idea can be found in this

55. See above, p. 68, note 135.
56. The German Minnesang, cultivated from about the middle of the twelfth century until into the fourteenth century, was, broadly speaking, the lyric of courtly love belonging to the feudal tradition. Hans Sachs' poems may have followed the form of the Minnesang, but the content derives from a different world. His poetry is not chivalric love poetry, but religious, didactic, and, as Heine said, philistine or middle-class.
57. The following ideas can also be found in *The Romantic School*, pp. 8f.

identity. The treatment is romantic when the form does not reveal the idea by means of identity but makes it possible by means of a parable to divine this idea. I prefer to use here the word "parable" rather than the word "symbol." Greek mythology possessed an array of deities, each one of which, despite all identity of form and idea, could nevertheless be given a symbolic meaning. But in this Greek religion only the form of the gods was fixed; everything else, their lives and their activities, was left to the fancy of the poets to treat as they pleased. In the Christian religion, however, there are no such definite figures but rather definite facts, definite sacred events and deeds to which the creative spirit of man could lend a parabolic significance. It has been said that Homer invented the Greek gods. This is not true; they already existed in definite outlines, but he invented the stories about them. The artists of the Middle Ages, however, never dared to invent the slightest detail in the historical portion of their religion; the fall of man, the incarnation, the baptism, the crucifixion, and the like, were unimpeachable facts which could not be reshaped, but to which the creative spirit of man could lend a parabolic significance. All the arts of the Middle Ages were actually treated in this parabolic spirit, and their treatment is romantic. Hence the mystical universality in the poetry of the Middle Ages; the figures are so shadowy, what they do is so vague, everything about them has a twilight air as if illuminated only fitfully by moonlight. The idea is hinted at in the form only as a puzzle, and we see here a vague form such as was quite appropriate for a spiritualistic literature. There is no obvious harmony between form and idea as with the Greeks; on the contrary, the idea often transcends the given form, which strives despairingly to attain the same level, and we see then bizarre, fantastic sublimity. Sometimes the form completely outgrows the idea, a trivial little thought is dragged along in a colossal form, and we see grotesque farce. Almost always we find deformity.

3) The universal character of this literature was that in all its productions there was manifested the firm, secure faith which then prevailed in all secular and spiritual matters. All opinions of the period were based on authorities; the poet walked with the confidence of a mule along the abysses of doubt, and in his works prevail an intrepid serenity, a blissful trust, such as was impossible later when the chief of those authorities, namely the authority of

the Pope, was overthrown and all other authorities fell in its wake. All literary works of the Middle Ages thus have the same character, as if not an individual person but the whole people had created them; they are objective, epic, and naive.

In the literature, however, which burst into flower under Luther's influence we find just the opposite:

1) Its material, the content that is to be dealt with, is the struggle between the interests and views of the Reformation and the old order of things. To the new spirit of the age the mongrel creed that originated, as mentioned, from two elements, Germanic national character and Hindu-Gnostic Christianity, was completely repugnant. The latter almost seemed to it to be heathen idolatry, which must be replaced by the true religion of the Judaic-Deistic gospel. A new order of things takes shape; the intellect makes inventions that further the success of material things; through the prospering of industry and through philosophy, spiritualism is discredited in public opinion; the third estate emerges; the Revolution is already rumbling in hearts and heads; and what the age feels and thinks and needs and wants is expressed, and this is the content of modern literature.

2) The spirit of the treatment is no longer romantic, but classical. Due to the revival of ancient literature, a joyful enthusiasm for Greek and Roman writers spread over all of Europe, and scholars, the only people then writing, tried to appropriate the spirit of classical antiquity or at least to imitate classical art forms in their writings. Though, unlike the Greeks, they failed to achieve harmony between form and idea, they clung all the more rigidly to the externals of the Greek treatment. They distinguished, according to Greek precepts, among the various genres, refrained from any romantic extravagance, and in this respect we call them classical.

3) The universal characteristic of modern literature is the predominance of individuality and scepticism. The authorities have collapsed; reason alone is now the only lamp man has, and his conscience is his only staff in the dark labyrinths of this life. Man now stands alone face to face with his Creator and sings his song to Him. Hence this literature begins with religious songs. But even later, when literature becomes secular, there prevails in it the most intense self-awareness, the sense of personality. Poetry is now no longer objective, epic, and naive, but subjective, lyric, and reflective.

BOOK TWO

In the previous book we dealt with the great religious revolution represented in Germany by Martin Luther. Now we must speak of the philosophical revolution that arose out of it and indeed is nothing else but the last consequence of Protestantism. But before relating how the outbreak of this revolution was caused by Immanuel Kant, it is necessary to mention the philosophical developments in other countries, the significance of Spinoza, the fate of Leibnitz's philosophy, the mutual relations, discords, and dissensions between this philosophy and religion, and the like. We shall, however, constantly keep in view those philosophical questions to which we attribute a social significance and towards whose solution philosophy competes with religion.

We shall deal first with the question of the nature of God. "God is the beginning and the end of all wisdom," say the believers in their humility, and the philosopher, in all the pride of his knowledge, is compelled to agree with this pious axiom.

Not Bacon,[58] as we are usually taught, but René Descartes[59] is the father of modern philosophy, and we shall demonstrate very clearly to what degree German philosophy is derived from him.

René Descartes is a Frenchman, and here too the glory of the initiative belongs to great France. But great France, the noisy, lively, loquacious land of the French, has never been a suitable soil for philosophy, which perhaps will never flourish there, and René Descartes felt this and went to Holland, the peaceful, silent land of *trekschuiten*[60] and Dutchmen, and there he wrote his philosophical works. Only there could he free his spirit from traditional formalism and construct a complete system of philosophy from pure thought that is borrowed neither from faith nor from empiricism—a method since then required of any genuine philosophy. Only there could he plunge so deeply into the abysses of thought that he chanced upon it in the ultimate grounds of self-awareness

---

58. Francis Bacon (1561–1626), founder of empiricism.
59. French philosopher of the seventeenth century (1596–1650) who took issue with the belief in traditionally accepted knowledge and developed a philosophical system based on the cognitive process, thus breaking with religious tradition.
60. The small boats on canals in Holland pulled along by men or horses.

and was able to substantiate self-awareness by means of thought itself in the world-famous axiom, *Cogito, ergo sum.*[61]

But also perhaps nowhere else than in Holland could Descartes have dared to teach a philosophy that conflicted quite obviously with all traditions of the past. To him is due the honor of having established the autonomy of philosophy; it no longer needed to beg from theology permission to think; it could now take its place beside the latter as an independent science. I do not say in opposition to the latter, for at that time it was an acknowledged principle that the truths at which we arrive through philosophy are ultimately the same as those transmitted by religion. The scholastics, as I have already remarked, had, on the contrary, not only conceded to religion the supremacy over philosophy, but had also declared philosophy to be a worthless pastime, a vain haggling, the instant it came into conflict with the dogmas of religion. The scholastics were concerned only with expressing their thoughts, no matter under what conditions. They said, "One times one is one," and proved it; but they added with a smile, "This is another error of human reason, which always errs when it comes into conflict with the decision of the Ecumenical Councils; 'One times one is three,' and this is the real truth, long since revealed to us in the name of the Father, the Son, and the Holy Ghost!" In private the scholastics formed a philosophical opposition to the Church. But publicly they feigned the greatest submissiveness, in many instances they even fought for the Church, and during processions they paraded among its followers, somewhat as the French deputies of the opposition paraded at the ceremonies of the Restoration. The comedy of the scholastics lasted more than six centuries and became more and more trivial. In destroying scholasticism Descartes likewise destroyed the superannuated opposition of the Middle Ages. The old brooms had worn out from long sweeping, too much rubbish was sticking to them, and the new age required new brooms. After every revolution the former opposition must abdicate; otherwise great follies are committed. We have seen this ourselves. In the times I am writing about, it was not so much the Catholic Church as her old adversaries, the rear-guard of the scholastics, who first

61. I think, therefore I exist.

took up arms against the Cartesian philosophy. Not until 1663 did the Pope ban this philosophy.

I can assume that Frenchmen have an adequate and sufficient acquaintance with the philosophy of their great countryman, and it is not necessary for me to show here how the most contradictory doctrines could borrow from it material they needed. I refer to idealism and materialism.

Since these two doctrines, especially in France, are called spiritualism and sensualism, and since I use these latter terms in a different fashion, I shall have to discuss in more detail the above-mentioned expressions to avoid confusion of ideas.

From the earliest times there have been two opposing views regarding the nature of human thought, that is, regarding the ultimate sources of intellectual cognition, regarding the origin of ideas. Some maintain that we acquire ideas only from without, that our mind is only an empty receptacle in which the impressions gulped down by the senses are digested, much as the foods we eat are digested in the stomach. To use a better image, these persons view our mind as a *tabula rasa,* on which experience subsequently writes something new every day according to definite principles of composition.

Others, holding the opposite view, maintain that ideas are innate in man, that the human mind is the original seat of ideas, and that the external world, experience, and the mediating senses only lead us to the knowledge of what was already present in the mind, only awaken there the dormant ideas.

The first view has been called sensualism, sometimes also empiricism; the other was called spiritualism, sometimes also rationalism. From these terms, however, misunderstandings can easily result, since we have for some time been using these names, as I mentioned in the previous book, to designate those two social systems which make themselves felt in every manifestation of existence. Hence we shall assign the name spiritualism to that outrageous arrogance of the human spirit which, striving for exclusive self-glorification, attempts to trample matter under foot, or at least to vilify it. And we give the name sensualism to that opposition which, in passionate revolt, aims at rehabilitating that matter and vindicates the rights of the senses without denying the rights of the spirit or even its supremacy. To the philosophical opinions concerning the nature of knowledge, however, I prefer to give the names idealism and materialism; and I shall designate with the former the theory of innate ideas, of ideas *a priori*, and with the second term I shall designate the theory of cognition through experience, through the senses, the theory of ideas *a posteriori*.

It is significant that the idealistic side of Cartesian philosophy was never a success in France. Several famous Jansenists pursued this direction for a time, but they soon went astray into Christian spiritualism. It may have been this circumstance that brought discredit on idealism in France. Nations have an instinctive presentiment of what they need in order to fulfill their mission. The French were already on the way toward that political revolution which did not break out until the end of the eighteenth century and for which they needed an axe and a philosophy equally cold and sharp and materialistic. Christian spiritualism stood as a fellow-combatant in the ranks of their enemies; hence sensualism became their natural ally. French sensualists being ordinarily materialists, the erroneous idea arose that sensualism was but a product of materialism. No, sensualism can just as well claim to be the result of pantheism, and as such it appears beautiful and splendid. It is by no means our intention, however, to deny French materialism its merits. French materialism was a good antidote against the evil of the past, a desperate remedy for a desperate disease, mercury[62] for an infected people. French philosophers chose John Locke as their master. He was the saviour they needed. His *Essay Concerning Human Understanding* became their gospel, and they swore by it. John Locke had gone to school to Descartes and from him had learned everything that an Englishman can learn—mechanics, the analytical method, deduction, synthesizing, and arithmetic. There was only one thing he could not comprehend, namely, innate ideas. He therefore perfected the doctrine that we acquire our knowledge from without, by means of experience. He turned the human mind into a kind of calculating machine; the whole human being became an English machine. The same thing applies to man as constructed by Locke's disciples, though they tried to distinguish themselves from one another by the use of different terminology. They were

62. Heine is probably referring to mercury chloride, one form of which was and is used as an anti-syphilitic.

all afraid of the ultimate inferences of their leading principle, and the disciple of Condillac[63] was horrified at being put into the same category with a Helvétius,[64] or, worse, with a Holbach, [65] or perhaps, worst of all, with a La Mettrie.[66] Yet such a classification is inevitable, and I can therefore characterize the French philosophers of the eighteenth century and their present-day successors, one and all, as materialists. *L'homme machine* is the most consistent product of French philosophy; and even the title reveals the last word of their whole concept of the universe.

Most of these materialists were also adherents of deism, for a machine presupposes a mechanic, and it is part of the highest perfection of such a machine to recognize and appreciate the technical skills of such an artificer, as seen in its own construction or in his other works.

Materialism has fulfilled its mission in France. It is perhaps now completing the same task in England, and the revolutionary factions there, especially the Benthamites,[67] the preachers of utility, are based on Locke. These latter are men of powerful intellect who have grasped the right lever for setting John Bull in motion. John Bull is a born materialist, and his Christian spiritualism is for the most part traditional hypocrisy or even just material dullness—his flesh is resigned because the spirit does not come to its aid. In Germany it is different, and the German revolutionaries are mistaken if they think that a materialistic philosophy is advantageous for their aims. Indeed, no general revolution is possible there at all unless its principles have been deduced from a more rational, more religious, and more German philosophy which has come to prevail through their power. What philosophy is this? We shall discuss it later with all candor. I say "with all candor," for I am counting on Germans reading these pages too.

63. Particularly in his *Traité de sensations,* Étienne Bonnot de Condillac (1715–1780) demonstrated that sensuous perception is the only source of knowledge and that thinking is only the result of perceptions derived from sensory experience.
64. Claude Adrien Helvétius (1715–1771) dealt primarily with ethical questions. Self-interest was for him the only reliable guide for action, though a certain training was necessary to bring it into conformity with the common good.
65. Paul Henri Thiry, Baron d'Holbach (1723–1789), was a materialistic philosopher whose main work was his *Système de la nature.*
66. Julien Offray de La Mettrie (1709–1751) was a radical materialist and atheist. His best-known work was *L'homme machine.*
67. Jeremy Bentham (1748–1832) was the founder of utilitarianism.

Germany has always shown a dislike for materialism and hence became for a century and a half the true arena of idealism. The Germans also went to the school of Descartes, and the name of his great disciple was Gottfried Wilhelm Leibnitz. As Locke followed the materialistic direction of his master, Leibnitz followed the idealistic direction. In Leibnitz we find the doctrine of innate ideas in its most decisive form. In his *Nouveaux essays sur l'entendement humain*[68] he opposed Locke. With Leibnitz there sprang up among the Germans a great passion for philosophical studies. He awakened their minds and directed them into new paths. Because of the inherent kindliness, the religious feeling that animated his writings, even his opponents became reconciled in some measure to their boldness, and their effect was enormous. The boldness of this thinker is shown particularly in his theory of monads, one of the most remarkable hypotheses that ever originated from the mind of a philosopher. It is also the best thing he produced, for in it there already dawns the perception of the most important laws that have been accepted by modern philosophy. The theory of monads was perhaps only a crude formulation of these laws, which have now been expressed in better formulas by the philosophers of nature. Actually, instead of the word "law," I ought to say here simply "formula," for Newton is quite right when he remarks that what we call laws of nature does not really exist, that these are only formulas which help our power of comprehension to explain a succession of phenomena in nature. Of all the writings of Leibnitz', the *Theodicy* is the one that has been most discussed in Germany. Yet it is his weakest work. This book, like several other writings in which Leibnitz' religious spirit finds expression, exposed him to many a malicious rumor and much cruel misunderstanding. His enemies accused him of maudlin silliness; his friends, defending him, made him out to be a sly hypocrite. Leibnitz' character remained a subject of controversy among us for a long time. The fairest critics could not absolve him from the accusation of duplicity. The freethinkers and men of enlightenment reviled him most. How could they forgive a philosopher for having defended the Trinity, eternal punishment in Hell, and, worst of all, the divinity of Christ! Their tolerance did not go so far as that. But Leibnitz was neither

68. *New Essays Concerning Human Understanding.*

a fool nor a knave, and from his serene heights he could very well defend the whole of Christianity. I say the whole of Christianity, for he defended it against semi-Christianity. He demonstrated the consistency of the orthodox as opposed to the halfheartedness of their adversaries. More than this he never intended. And thus he stood at that neutral point of equilibrium where the most diverse systems seem to be merely different sides of the same truth. Mr. Schelling later also recognized this neutral point, and Hegel established it scientifically as a system of systems. In the same manner Leibnitz tried to reconcile Plato and Aristotle. Even in subsequent times this attempt has been made often enough in Germany. Has the problem been solved?

No, certainly not! For this problem is nothing less than a settlement of the struggle between idealism and materialism. Plato is an idealist through and through and recognizes only inborn or rather co-born ideas; man brings ideas with him into the world, and when he becomes conscious of them, they seem to him like recollections of a former state of existence. Hence the vagueness and mysticism of Plato; his recollections are sometimes more clear, sometimes less. With Aristotle, however, everything is clear, intelligible, certain; for his perceptions are not revelations connected with any pre-existence; he draws everything from experience and can classify everything with the utmost precision. He therefore remains a model for all empiricists, and they cannot thank God enough that He made him Alexander's teacher, that due to his lord's conquests Aristotle found so many opportunities for the advancement of science, and that his victorious pupil gave him so many thousand talents of gold for zoological research.[69] The old master used this money conscientiously, and with it was able to dissect a respectable number of mammals and to stuff a like number of birds, and in so doing made very important observations. But the great beast which he had right before his eyes, which he had reared himself, and which was far more remarkable than the whole world-menagerie of that time, he overlooked, alas, and failed to investigate. He has indeed left us totally without information about the nature of that youthful king whose life and deeds we still marvel at as wonder and enigma. Who was Alexander? What did

69. Aristotle wrote a *History of Animals*.

he want? Was he a madman or a god? To this day we do not know. But Aristotle gives us all the more complete information about Babylonian monkeys, Indian parrots, and Greek tragedies, the last of which he also dissected.[70]

Plato and Aristotle! These are not merely the two systems but also the representatives of two different types of human beings who have opposed each other more or less hostilely in many different guises since time immemorial. Especially throughout the entire Middle Ages and right up to the present day this conflict raged, and it is the most essential part of the history of the Christian church. The discussion is always about Plato and Aristotle, though under other names. Visionary, mystical, Platonic natures reveal from the depths of their being Christian ideas and the corresponding symbols. Practical, orderly, Aristotelian natures construct out of these ideas and symbols a solid system, a dogma, and a cult. The Church ultimately embraces both natures, the one group usually entrenching itself within the clergy, the other within monasticism, yet feuding with each other incessantly. The same struggle is evident in the Protestant church, the conflict between Pietists and Orthodox, who correspond after a fashion to the Catholic mystics and dogmatists. The Protestant Pietists are mystics without imagination, and the orthodox Protestants are dogmatists without intelligence.

We find these two Protestant groups engaged in bitter combat at the time of Leibnitz, whose philosophy intervened later when Christian Wolf made himself master of it, adapted it to contemporary needs, and, most important of all, lectured on it in German.[71] Before giving more information about this pupil of Leibnitz, however, about the effects of his endeavors, and about the subsequent fate of Lutheranism, we must mention the providential man who, at the same time as Locke and Leibnitz, had educated himself in the school of Descartes, had for a long time been viewed only with scorn and hatred, and who nevertheless today is rising to exclusive supremacy in the world of intellect.

I am speaking about Benedict Spinoza.

One great genius shapes himself by means of another, less through assimilation than through friction. One diamond polishes

70. In his *Poetics*.
71. Until 1688 all professors at German universities lectured in Latin.

the other. Thus Descartes' philosophy did not originate, but merely furthered, Spinoza's. Hence we find in the pupil, first of all, the method of the master; this is a great gain. We also find in Spinoza, as in Descartes, a method of demonstration borrowed from mathematics. This is a great defect. The mathematical form gives Spinoza's work a harsh exterior. But this is like the hard shell of the almond; the kernel is all the more delightful. On reading Spinoza we are seized by an emotion similar to that which we feel at the sight of great Nature in her most animated composure. A forest of heaven-aspiring thoughts whose blossoming treetops are tossing like waves, while the immovable trunks are rooted in the eternal earth. There is a certain mysterious aura about Spinoza's writings. The air of the future seems to flow over us. Perhaps the spirit of the Hebrew prophets still hovered over their late-born descendant. There is, withal, a seriousness in him, a confident pride, a solemn dignity of thought, which also seem to be a part of his inheritance; for Spinoza belonged to one of those martyr families exiled from Spain by the most Catholic of kings. Added to this is the patience of the Hollander, which was always revealed in the life of the man as well as in his writings.

It is a fact that Spinoza'a life was beyond reproach and pure and spotless as the life of his divine cousin, Jesus Christ. Like Him, he too suffered for his teachings; like Him he wore the crown of thorns. Wherever a great mind expresses its thought, *there* is Golgotha.

Dear reader, if you go to Amsterdam sometime, have a guide show you the Spanish synagogue. It is a beautiful building. The roof rests on four colossal pillars, and in the center stands the pulpit from which excommunication was pronounced on the man who despised the Mosaic law, the hidalgo Don Benedict de Spinoza. On such an occasion a ram's horn called the shophar was blown. There must be something very frightening about this horn. For, as I once read in the life of Salomon Maimon,[72] when the rabbi of Altona once tried to lead him, the pupil of Kant, back again to the old faith, and when he stubbornly persisted in his philosophical heresies, the rabbi resorted to threats, showed him the shophar,

72. A Jewish philosopher (1754–1800) and pupil of Kant, who, however, differed with his teacher on some important issues.

and asked sinisterly, "Do you know what this is?" But when Kant's pupil replied with calm indifference, "It is a ram's horn," the rabbi fell flat on his back from horror.

The excommunication of Spinoza was accompanied by the sound of this horn; he was solemnly expelled from the communion of Israel and declared unworthy henceforth of bearing the name of Jew. His Christian enemies were magnanimous enough to leave him the name. The Jews, however, the Swiss guard of deism, were inexorable, and the place is still pointed out in front of the Spanish synagogue in Amsterdam where they once tried to stab Spinoza with their long daggers.

I could not refrain from calling particular attention to these personal misfortunes of the man. It was not merely schooling that shaped him, but life as well. In this he is different from most philosophers, and in his writings we recognize the indirect influence of his own life. Theology was for him not simply a branch of knowledge. Nor was politics. This too he became acquainted with through experience. His fiancée's father was hung in the Netherlands for political offenses. And nowhere in the world are people so badly hung as in the Netherlands. You have no idea what innumerable preparations and ceremonies are connected with the procedure. The delinquent dies of boredom while these are going on, and the spectator has plenty of time for reflection. So I am convinced that Benedict Spinoza reflected a great deal on the execution of old Van Ende, and just as he had previously learned to understand religion by its daggers, so now he learned to understand politics by its ropes. His *Tractatus politicus* gives evidence of this.

My aim is merely to point out how the philosophers are related to each other, and whether more or less closely, and I shall show only the degrees of relationship and the genealogy. The philosophy of Spinoza, the third son on René Descartes, as he teaches it in his main work, the *Ethics,* is as remote from the materialism of his brother Locke as from the idealism of his brother Leibnitz. Spinoza does not torment himself with analytical inquiry into the ultimate grounds of our knowledge. He gives us his grand synthesis, his explanation of the Deity.

Benedict Spinoza teaches: there is only one substance, and that is God. This one substance is infinite; it is absolute. All finite substances originate from it, are contained in it, arise out of it, are immersed in it; they have only a relative, transient, accidental existence. The absolute substance is revealed to us both in the form of infinite thought and in the form of infinite dimension. These two, infinite thought and infinite dimension, are the two attributes of the absolute substance. We recognize only these two attributes, but it is possible that God, the absolute substance, has other attributes that we do not know. *"Non dico, me deum omnino cognoscere, sed me quaedam ejus attributa, non autem omnia, neque maximam intelligere partem."*[73]

Only stupidity and malice could attach to this doctrine the epithet "atheistic." No one has ever spoken more sublimely of the Deity than Spinoza. Instead of saying that he denied God, one might say that he denied man. All finite things are to him only *modi*[74] of the infinite substance. All finite things are contained in God; the human mind is but a light-ray of infinite thought; the human body is but a particle of the infinite dimension. God is the infinite cause of both, of spirits and of bodies, *natura naturans.*[75]

In a letter to Madame du Deffant[76] Voltaire professes himself quite delighted at a sally of this lady's, who had said that everything man can know absolutely nothing about is certainly of such a nature that knowledge about it would be of no use to him. I would like to apply this remark to the passage from Spinoza just quoted in his own words, according to which not only the two knowable attributes, thought and dimension, pertain to the Deity, but also possibly other attributes that we cannot know. What we cannot know has no value for us, at least no value from a social point of view, where the important thing is to bring to realization as a corporeal phenomenon what the intellect perceives. In our explanation of the nature of God, therefore, we refer only to these two knowable attributes. And besides, everything we call an attribute of God is ultimately but a different form of our intuition, and these different forms are identical in the absolute substance. Thought is,

73. I do not say that I know God completely, but that I understand certain of his attributes, though not all and certainly not the greatest part of them.

74. Manifestations.

75. As Spinoza uses the phrase, it means nature in its unity, as the creative principle which determines the multiplicity of its modes or manifestations.

76. Marquise du Deffand, a French woman of letters whose salon was frequented by many important writers and scholars.

after all, only invisible dimension, and dimension is only visible thought. Here we come to the main point of the German Philosophy of Identity,[77] which in essence differs in no way from the doctrine of Spinoza. No matter how violently Mr. Schelling may protest that his philosophy is different from Spinozism, that it is rather "a living amalgam of the ideal and the real," that it differs from Spinozism "as the perfection of Greek sculpture differs from the rigid Egyptian originals," nevertheless I must declare most emphatically that in his earlier period, when he was still a philosopher, Mr. Schelling did not differ in the slightest from Spinoza. He merely arrived at the same philosophy by a different path. I shall illustrate this later when I tell how Kant entered on a new path, how Fichte followed him, how Mr. Schelling in turn continued in Fichte's footsteps and, wandering lost in the forest darkness of nature philosophy, finally found himself face to face with the great figure of Spinoza.

The only merit of modern nature philosophy is that it demonstrated most ingeniously the eternal parallelism between spirit and matter. I say spirit and matter, and I use these terms as equivalents for what Spinoza calls thought and dimension. These terms are also, to some extent, synonymous with what our nature philosophers call spirit and nature or the ideal and the real.

In what follows I shall designate by the name Pantheism not so much Spinoza's system as his way of viewing things. Pantheism, like Deism, assumes the unity of God. But the god of the pantheist is in the world itself, not by permeating it with his divinity in the manner which St. Augustine tried to illustrate by comparing God to a large lake and the world to a large sponge lying in the middle of it and absorbing the Deity—no, the world is not merely God-imbued, God-impregnated; it is identical with God. "God," called by Spinoza the one and only substance, and by German philosophers the absolute, "is everything that exists"; He is matter as well as spirit, both are equally divine, and whoever insults the sanctity of matter is just as sinful as he who sins against the Holy Ghost.

The god of the pantheist is thus distinguished from the god of the deist by the fact that he is in the world itself, whereas the latter

77. According to this philosophy, represented here by Schelling, spiritual and corporeal phenomena are identical, two aspects of the entity of being. Spinoza calls this entity "the substance," Schelling calls it "the absolute."

is completely outside of it or, what is the same thing, above it. The god of the deist rules the world from above as an establishment separate from him. The deists differ among themselves only with regard to the type of rule. The Hebrews conceive of God as a thundering tyrant; the Christians, as a loving father; the disciples of Rousseau, the whole Geneva school, conceive him as a knowledgeable artist, who constructed the world somewhat as their fathers constructed watches, and as connoisseurs they admire the work and praise the master high above.

To the deist, who assumes an extra-mundane or supra-mundane god, only the spirit is holy, since he views it, so to speak, as the divine breath which the creator breathed into the human body, the work of his hands kneaded out of clay. Hence the Jews looked on the body as something inferior, as a wretched cloak for the *ruach hakodasch,* the holy breath, the spirit, and only to the latter did they award their attention, their reverence, their worship. They therefore became in a very special sense *the* people of the spirit, chaste, temperate, serious, abstract, obstinate, capable of martyrdom; and their sublimest flower is Jesus Christ. He is, in the true sense of the word, spirit incarnate, and it is a beautiful legend and profoundly significant, that He was brought into the world by an immaculate virgin, conceived only by the spirit.

But if the Jews regarded the body merely with contempt, the Christians went much farther on this road and regarded it as something objectionable, something bad, as evil itself. Thus, several centuries after the birth of Christ, we see a religion arise that will forever amaze mankind and will cow the latest generations into the most terrified admiration. Yes, it is a great, a holy religion, full of infinite bliss, a religion that sought to conquer for the spirit the most absolute domination on earth. But this religion was all too sublime, all too pure, all too good for this earth, where the idea of it could only be proclaimed in theory, but could never be realized in practice. The attempt to realize this idea has produced countless splendid manifestations in history, and poets of all times will celebrate them in song and tale for ages to come. As we shall see in the end, however, the attempt to realize the idea of Christianity failed miserably, and this unfortunate attempt has cost mankind incalculable sacrifices, one distressing result of them being the present social disorder in all of Europe. If, as many believe, humanity is still in its adolescence, then Christianity was, so to speak, among its most extravagant illusions of youth, which do far more credit to their hearts than to their intelligence. Christianity relinquished temporal things to the hands of Caesar and his Jewish chamberlains[78] and contented itself with denying the supremacy of the former and with stigmatizing the latter in the opinion of the public—but behold! the sword they hated and the money they despised gained supreme power in the end, and the representatives of the spirit had to come to an understanding with them. Indeed, out of this understanding there has even developed a joint alliance. Not just the Roman priests, but also the English, the Prussian, in short, all privileged clergy, have allied themselves with Caesar and his confederates for the oppression of the peoples. But due to this alliance the religion of spiritualism will perish all the more speedily. Certain priests already understand this, and in order to save religion, they pretend to renounce this ruinous alliance, and they come over to our side, put on red caps, swear death and hatred for all kings, the seven bloodsuckers, they demand equality of wealth on this earth, and they curse even more than Marat and Robespierre.— Just between us, if you observe them closely, you will see that they read the Mass in the language of Jacobinism, and just as they once gave Caesar poison concealed in the Host, they try now to give the people their consecrated wafers by concealing them in the poison of Revolution; for they know we love this poison.

But all your efforts are in vain! Mankind is weary of all Eucharistic wafers and longs for more nourishing food, for real bread and good meat. Mankind smiles pityingly at those youthful ideals which it could not realize despite all efforts and is becoming manfully practical. Mankind now worships a worldly system of utilitarianism and is considering seriously the establishment of middle-class prosperity, sensible management of funds, and comfort in its old age. There is certainly no more talk about leaving the sword in Caesar's hands and certainly not of leaving the money bag in the hands of his servants. Service to royalty is stripped of privilege and honor, and industry is freed from its ancient lack of respectability. The next task is to become healthy, for our limbs still feel very

78. The term *Kammerknechte* derives from German medieval history and refers to Jews under the protection of the Emperor and paying tribute to him.

weak. The holy vampires of the Middle Ages have sucked so much life-blood out of us. And after this, great sacrifices must be offered upon the altar of matter to atone for old offenses against it. It might even be advisable to institute festivals and to bestow on matter still more extraordinary honors as compensation. For Christianity, unable to annihilate matter, has always denounced it. Christianity has degraded the noblest pleasures, the senses were forced to play the hypocrite, and the result was deceit and sin. We must clothe our women in new garments and in new ideas, and we must fumigate all our emotions, as if we had survived a plague.

Thus the immediate aim of all our new institutions is the rehabilitation of matter, its restoration to dignity, its moral recognition, its religious sanctification, its reconciliation with the spirit. Purusha is re-wedded to Prakriti.[79] Due to their enforced separation, as the Indian myth relates so ingeniously, the great rupture of the world, evil, originated.

Do you know what evil is? The spiritualists have always reproached us because in the pantheistic view there is no distinction between good and evil. But evil is in part only an illusory concept of their own philosophy of life, and in part it is an actual result of their own world-order. According to their philosophy of life, matter is evil in and of itself, which is surely nothing less than calumny and dreadful blasphemy. Matter becomes evil only when it is forced to conspire secretly against the domination of the spirit, when the spirit has stigmatized it and it prostitutes itself out of self-contempt, or when matter goes so far as to take revenge on the spirit with the hatred born of despair. Hence evil becomes only a result of the spiritualistic world-order.

God is identical with the world. He manifests himself in plants, which unconsciously lead a cosmic-magnetic life. He manifests himself in animals, which, in their sensuous, dreamlike life, have a feeling of their more or less vague existence. But he manifests himself most magnificently in man, who both feels and thinks, who is able to distinguish himself as an individual from objective nature and already possesses in his intellect the ideas that present themselves to him in the world of phenomena. In man the deity attains self-

79. In Indian philosophy *purusha* is pure consciousness, or in Heine's terms, spirit; *prakriti* is nature, or in Heine's terms, matter.

consciousness and reveals this self-consciousness again through man. This process does not take place in and through the individual human being, but in and through collective humanity, the result being that every human being comprehends and represents only one portion of the divine universe, whereas collective humanity will comprehend and represent the totality of the divine universe in idea and in reality. Perhaps each nation has the mission of recognizing and making known a certain part of this divine universe, of comprehending a series of phenomena and bringing to realization a series of ideas, and of transmitting the result to succeeding races on whom a similar mission is imposed. God is therefore the real hero of universal history, which is but his never-ending thought, his never-ending action, his word, his deed; and we can rightly say of all mankind that it is an incarnation of God.

It is wrong to think that this religion, Pantheism, leads men to indifference. On the contrary, the consciousness of his divinity will inspire man to bear witness to it, and only then will the really noble achievements of true heroism glorify this earth.

The political revolution that is based on the principles of French materialism will find in the pantheists not opponents, but allies, allies, however, who have drawn their convictions from a deeper source, from a religious synthesis. We promote the welfare of matter, the material happiness of the peoples, not, like the materialists, because we despise the spirit, but because we know that the divinity of man is also revealed in his corporeal form, that misery destroys or debases the body, God's image, and that as a result the spirit likewise perishes. The great maxim of the Revolution pronounced by St. Just,[80] "*Le pain est le droit du peuple,*"[81] is translated by us, "*Le pain est le droit divin de l'homme.*"[82] We are fighting not for the human rights of the people, but for the divine rights of mankind. In this and in many other things we differ from the men of the Revolution. We do not want to be sansculottes, nor simple citizens, nor venal presidents; we want to found a democracy of gods, equal in majesty, in sanctity, and in bliss. You demand simple dress, austere morals, and unspiced pleasures, but we demand

80. Louis Antoine Saint-Just was a French revolutionist, a friend of Robespierre, and was executed at the same time.
81. Bread is the right of the people.
82. Bread is the divine right of man.

nectar and ambrosia, crimson robes, costly perfumes, luxury and splendor, the dancing of laughing nymphs, music and comedies. Don't be angry with us because of this, you virtuous Republicans. To your censorious reproaches we will respond in the words of one of Shakespeare's fools: "Dost thou think because thou art virtuous, there shall be no more nice cakes and sweet champagne in this world?"[83]

The Saint-Simonists understood and desired something of the sort, but the soil they stood on was unfavorable, and the surrounding materialism repressed them, for the time at least. In Germany they were more highly regarded. For Germany is the most fertile soil for pantheism. This is the religion of our greatest thinkers, of our best artists, and in Germany deism, as I shall presently explain, was long ago overthrown in theory. Like many other things, it still maintains its position only among the mindless masses, a position without rational justification. No one says it, but everyone knows that pantheism is an open secret in Germany. We have, in fact, outgrown deism. We are free and don't want any thundering tyrant. We are of age and need no paternal care. Nor are we the botches of any great mechanic. Deism is a religion for servants, for children, for the Genevese, for watchmakers.

Pantheism is the clandestine religion of Germany, and those German writers who fifty years ago railed against Spinoza foresaw that this would happen. The most furious of these opponents of Spinoza was F.H. Jacobi,[84] who is occasionally honored by being classed among German philosophers. He was nothing but a quarrelsome sneak, who disguised himself in the cloak of philosophy and insinuated himself among the philosophers, first whimpering to them ever so much about his affection and softheartedness, then letting loose a tirade against reason. His perpetual refrain was that philosophy, knowledge acquired by reason, was a vain illusion; that reason itself did not know where it was going; that it led mankind into a dark labyrinth of error and contradiction; and that faith alone could guide man safely. Mole that he was, he could not

83. From *Twelfth Night,* Act II, Scene 3, speech by Sir Toby. Heine adapts Shakespeare's text to German taste. The last part of the quotation reads in the original, "there shall be no more cakes and ale."
84. Friedrich Heinrich Jacobi (1743–1819), a religious philosopher who recognized the logic of Spinoza's philosophy but opposed it on religious grounds.

see that reason resembles the eternal sun which, pursuing its appointed course through the heavens above, illumines its path with its own light. Nothing resembles the pious, unrestrained hatred of the little Jacobi toward the great Spinoza.

It is a curious thing, how the most diverse parties battled against Spinoza. They form an army whose motley composition is a very amusing sight. Next to a swarm of black and white Capuchins with crosses and smoking censers marches the phalanx of the Encyclopedists, who also rail at this *penseur téméraire*.[85] Beside the rabbi of the Amsterdam synagogue, who sounds the attack with the ram's horn of faith, walks Arouet de Voltaire playing the piccolo of irony for the benefit of Deism. In between whines the old milksop Jacobi, the camp follower of this army of the faith.

Let us escape as quickly as possible from this caterwauling. Returning from our pantheistic excursion, we shall go back to Leibnitz' philosophy and relate its subsequent fortunes.

Leibnitz had written his works, which are familiar to you, partly in Latin, partly in French. Christian Wolf is the name of the excellent man who not merely systematized Leibnitz' ideas, but also lectured on them in German. His real merit consists not in having fitted Leibnitz' ideas into a firm system, still less in having made them accessible to a wider public by the use of the German language; his merit lies in having stimulated us to philosophizing in our mother tongue. Until Luther's time we could treat theology only in Latin; until the time of Wolf we were able to deal with philosophy only in that language. The example of a very few scholars who had previously lectured on such subjects in German had no effect, but the literary historian must call them to mind with special praise. We therefore mention here particularly Johannes Tauler,[86] a Dominican monk who was born on the Rhine at the beginning of the fourteenth century and who died there, I believe in Strassburg, in 1361. He was a devout man, one of those mystics whom I have named the Platonic party of the Middle Ages. In the last years of his life this man, renouncing all scholarly arrogance, was not ashamed to preach in the humble language of the people, and these sermons, which he wrote down, together with German

85. Daring thinker.
86. One of the most important German mystics (1290–1361).

translations of some of his earlier Latin sermons, are among the most remarkable documents in the German language. For here German already shows that it is not merely adequate for metaphysical investigations but is far more suitable than Latin. The latter, the language of the Romans, can never belie its origin. It is a language for generals' orders, a language for administrators' decrees, a legal language for usurers, a lapidary language for the stone-hard Roman people. It became the appropriate language for materialism. Though Christianity, with truly Christian patience, struggled for more than a thousand years to spiritualize this language, it did not succeed; when Johannes Tauler sought to fathom the most terrifying abysses of thought, and when his heart was overflowing with the holiest emotions, he was compelled to speak German. His speech is like a mountain spring bursting forth from solid rock with the strange aromatic fragrance of unknown herbs and mysterious metallic virtues. Not until recent times, however, did the usefulness of the German language for philosophy become fully apparent. In no other language than in our beloved German mother tongue could Nature have revealed her most secret workings. Only on the sturdy oak could the sacred mistletoe thrive.

This would probably be the fitting place to discuss Paracelsus, or, as he called himself, Theophrastus Paracelsus Bombastus of Hohenheim.[87] For he too usually wrote in German. But I shall have occasion to speak of him later in an even more significant context. His philosophy was what today we call nature philosophy, and such a doctrine of nature animated by ideas, so mysteriously appealing to the German mind, would have developed among us already at that time had not, through a chance influence, the inanimate, mechanistic physics of the Cartesians become universally dominant. Paracelsus was a great charlatan, always wore a scarlet coat and breeches, red stockings and a red hat, and claimed to be able to create *homunculi*, little men; at any rate he was on familiar footing with invisible beings that dwell in the various elements. Yet he was also one of those very profound naturalists who, with truly German ardor for scholarly investigation, understood pre-

---

87. Paracelsus (1493–1541) was a well-known physician, chemist, and alchemist, of great influence on his own and succeeding centuries.

Christian popular beliefs, German pantheism, and what they did not know they very accurately divined.

I really ought to say something here about Jakob Böhme as well.[88] He too used German for philosophical expositions for which he has been much praised. But I have never yet been able to bring myself to read him. I don't like to be made a fool of. You see, I suspect the eulogists of this mystic of trying to mystify the public. As to the content of his works, Saint-Martin[89] has given you a sample in French. His works have also been translated into English. Charles I had so high an opinion of this theosophical shoemaker that he sent a learned man to him in Görlitz for the express purpose of studying him. This scholar was more fortunate than his royal master. For while the latter lost his head at Whitehall under Cromwell's axe, the former merely lost his mind at Görlitz through Jakob Böhme's theosophy.

As I have already said, Christian Wolf first successfully established the German language in the field of philosophy. His least merit was his systematizing and popularizing of Leibnitz' ideas. Both undertakings have incurred the gravest censure, and we must speak of this at least in passing. His systematizing was merely empty illusion, and the most important aspect of Leibnitz' philosophy was sacrificed to this illusion, for instance, the best part of the theory of monads. To be sure, Leibnitz had left behind him no systematic body of theory, only the ideas necessary for its construction. A giant was needed to fit together the colossal blocks and columns that a giant had raised from the depths of the marble quarries and delicately chiseled out. It might have become a beautiful temple. Christian Wolf, however, was of very short stature and was able to master only a portion of these materials, which he worked up into a wretched tabernacle of deism. Wolf had a mind more encyclopedic than systematic, and he could not comprehend the unity of a doctrine except as a complete whole. He was satisfied with a certain framework in which the compartments are arranged in perfect order, filled to the brim, and provided with unambiguous labels. Hence he gave us an "encyclopedia of the philosophical

88. A religious mystic of the early seventeenth century whose influence was felt not only in Germany but also in Holland and England.
89. Louis Claude St.-Martin (1743–1804), French author and mystic. He was influenced by Böhme and translated several of his works.

sciences." Naturally, as the grandson of Descartes, he inherited his grandfather's form of mathematical demonstration of proof. I have already criticized this mathematical form in Spinoza's works, and due to Wolf it caused a great deal of trouble. In his disciples it degenerated into the most insufferable schematicism and a ridiculous mania for demonstrating everything in mathematical form. Thus arose the so-called Wolfian dogmatism. Any investigation of a more profound character ceased, and a tedious zeal for distinctness took its place. Wolf's philosophy became more and more watery and finally flooded all Germany. Traces of this deluge are still visible today, and here and there, at our greatest universities, old fossils from the Wolf school are still found.

Christian Wolf was born in Breslau in 1678 and died in Halle in 1754. His intellectual domination of Germany lasted more than half a century. We must mention particularly his relationship with the theologians of his time, and in so doing we will supplement our remarks about the fate of Lutheranism.

In the whole history of the Church there is no portion more complicated than the quarrels of Protestant theologians since the Thirty Years' War. Only the sophistical wrangling of the Byzantines can be compared with them, but it was not so boring, for behind it were concealed major court intrigues of concern to the state, whereas Protestant polemics usually had their origin in the pedantry of provincial scholars and academicians. The universities, especially Tübingen, Wittenberg, Leipzig, and Halle, were the arenas for these theological struggles. The two parties which we saw fighting in Catholic garb during the entire Middle Ages merely changed costumes and continued to feud with each other just as before. They were the Pietists and the Orthodox, whom I mentioned earlier and defined as mystics without imagination and dogmatists without intelligence. Johannes Spener[90] was the Scotus Erigena[91] of Protestantism, and as the latter, by his translation of the legendary Dionysus the Areopagite, founded Catholic mysticism, the former founded Protestant mysticism by his Assemblies for Worship,

90. Philipp Jakob Spener (1635–1705), founder of Pietism.
91. John Scotus Erigena (c. 810–880), scholastic philosopher. He translated the writings of Pseudo-Dionysus and developed a religious philosophy which contained the origins of both Catholic scholasticism and mysticism.

colloquia pietatis,[92] from which, perhaps, the name "Pietists" fell to his disciples. He was a devout man—all honor to his memory. A Berlin Pietist, Mr. Franz Horn, has produced a good biography of him. Spener's life was an incessant martyrdom for the Christian idea. In this respect he was superior to his contemporaries. He demanded good works and piety and was a preacher of the spirit rather than of the letter. His homiletic nature was laudable, considering the times. For all theology, as taught at the universities just mentioned, consisted only in strait-laced dogmatism and hair-splitting polemics. Exegesis and church history were completely neglected.

A pupil of Spener's, Hermann Francke,[93] began to lecture at Leipzig, following his teacher's example and ideas. He lectured in German, a merit we are always glad to mention with appreciation. The approbation these lectures received aroused the envy of his colleagues, who accordingly made our poor Pietist's life miserable. He was forced to quit the field and went to Halle, where he taught Christianity by word and deed. His memory is imperishable there, for he was the founder of the Halle Orphanage. The University of Halle now became populated with Pietists, who were called "the Orphanage Party." Incidentally, this group has been preserved there until the present day; Halle is as yet still the *taupinière*[94] of the Pietists, and just a few years ago their quarrels with the Protestant rationalists created a scandal that spread its stench through all of Germany. You fortunate Frenchmen, who have heard nothing about this! You have remained ignorant of even the existence of those Evangelical scandal sheets in which the pious fishwives of the Protestant Church insulted each other roundly. Fortunate Frenchmen, who have no idea how maliciously, pettily, and disgustingly our Evangelical clergy can slander one another. You know that I am no partisan of Catholicism. Among my present religious convictions there still survives not indeed the dogma, but nevertheless the spirit of Protestantism. Thus I am still partial to

92. A misprint in all Heine editions for *collegia pietatis*, due either to the carelessness of the printers or to an oversight on Heine's part. (A similar mistake is the name "Johannes," found in all editions as Spener's first name.) These meetings for fellowship and Bible study led to a religious revival in Germany.

93. August Hermann Francke (1663–1727) was the founder of the well-known home for orphans in Halle.

94. Mole-hill.

the Protestant Church. And yet I must in all honesty confess that nowhere in the annals of the Papacy have I found anything so contemptible as appeared in *The Berlin Evangelical Church Journal* during the scandal just mentioned. The most dastardly knavery of the monks, the meanest intrigues of the cloister are still noble and generous in comparison with the Christian heroics of our pietist and orthodox Protestants in combating the hated rationalists. You French have no conception of the hatred that is displayed on such occasions. The Germans are in general more vindictive than the Latin peoples.

The reason is that they are idealists even in their hatred. We do not hate each other, as you French do, because of external things, perhaps because of wounded vanity, perhaps on account of an epigram or a visiting-card to which there was no response,—no, we hate in our enemies the most profound, most basic characteristic they have, their thought. You French are frivolous and superficial in hatred as well as in love. We Germans hate thoroughly, permanently; too honest and also too inept to avenge ourselves with speedy perfidy, we hate until our dying breath.

"I know this German calmness, sir," a lady said recently, looking at me with wide-eyed incredulity and anxiety; "I know that you Germans use the same word for forgiving and for poisoning." And as a matter of fact, she is right; the word *vergeben* has this double meaning.

If I am not mistaken, it was the orthodox of Halle who, in their struggle against the pietist settlers, called to their assistance Wolf's philosophy. For religion, when it can no longer burn us, comes to beg us for alms. Yet all our donations profit it little. The garment of mathematical demonstration in which Wolf had affectionately clothed poor Religion fitted her so badly that she felt even more constrained, and in this constraint made herself very ridiculous. Weak seams burst open everywhere. Especially the organ of shame, original sin, appeared in its most glaring nakedness. Here a logical fig-leaf was of no avail. Christian-Lutheran original sin and Leibnitz-Wolfian optimism are incompatible. The French raillery at optimism was thus least displeasing to our theologians. Voltaire's wit came to the aid of naked original sin, but the German Pangloss[95] lost

95. Voltaire's *Candide, ou l'optimisme* was a satire directed against Leibnitz'

much by the destruction of optimism and searched long for a similar doctrine that would be consoling, until the Hegelian statement, "Everything that is is reasonable!," offered him a partial equivalent.

From the moment when a religion requires the aid of philosophy, its downfall is inevitable. Attempting a defense, it chatters itself more and more deeply into destruction. Religion, like any absolutism, must not try to justify itself. Prometheus is chained to the rock by silent force. Indeed, Aeschylus does not allow personified Force to utter a single word.[96] It must remain mute. As soon as religion prints a catechism supported by arguments, as soon as political absolutism publishes an official newspaper, both are done for. But this is precisely our triumph; we have forced our adversaries to speak, and they must justify themselves.

It certainly cannot be denied that religious, as well as political, absolutism has found very powerful organs of expression. Still, let us not be alarmed by this. If the word is alive, it may be carried by dwarfs; if the word is dead, not even giants can support it.

Now, as I said above, since Religion looked to Philosophy for aid, German scholars, besides providing new clothing, made innumerable experiments with her. They wanted to furnish her a new youth, and in doing this they acted somewhat like Medea at the rejuvenation of King Aeson.[97] First she was bled, and all superstitious blood was slowly drained out of her. To express myself without metaphors, the attempt was made to remove from Christianity all historical content and to retain only the moral portion. By this process Christianity was transformed into pure deism. Christ ceased to be God's co-regent; He was mediatized, so to speak, and only as a private person did He still receive appreciative recognition. His moral character was extolled beyond measure. There was no end to the eulogies describing what a splendid man He had been. As for the miracles He performed, they were either explained according to the laws of nature or were given as little

---

optimistic belief that this world is the best of all conceivable worlds. Pangloss is young Candide's tutor.

96. In *Prometheus Bound* Force does not speak.

97. Heine refers here to Ovid's description in his *Metamorphoses*, Book 7. By means of her magic powers Medea transformed Jason's aged father, Aeson, into a man of forty.

attention as possible. Miracles, said some, were necessary in those superstitious times, and a sensible man having a truth of any kind to proclaim made use of them about as one would use an advertisement. Those theologians who eliminated the historical element from Christianity are called Rationalists, and against them was directed the wrath of both Pietists and Orthodox, who since then have quarreled with each other less violently and not infrequently joined forces as allies. A common hatred of the Rationalists succeeded in doing what love could not.

This tendency in Protestant theology began with the peaceful Semler,[98] whom you do not know, rose to a disquieting height with the lucid Teller,[99] whom you don't know either, and reached its peak with the shallow Bahrdt,[100] by the lack of whose acquaintance you have lost nothing. The strongest stimulus came from Berlin, where Frederick the Great and the book dealer Nicolai[101] ruled.

About the first, crowned materialism, you are sufficiently informed. You know that he wrote poetry in French, played the flute very well, won the battle of Rossbach, took quantities of snuff, and believed in nothing but cannons. Some of you have doubtless also visited Sans Souci, and the old disabled veteran who is the warden there has pointed out to you in the library the French novels which Frederick, when crown prince, used to read in church and which he had bound in black morocco so that his stern father would think he was reading the Lutheran hymnal. You know him, that royal philosopher whom you have called the Solomon of the North. France was the Ophir of this northern Solomon, and from there he obtained his poets and philosophers, for whom he cherished a great partiality, like the Solomon of the South, who, as you can read in the first book of Kings, chapter ten, ordered through his friend Hiram whole shiploads of gold, ivory, poets, and philosophers

98. Johann Salomo Semler, professor of theology in Halle from 1752 until his death in 1791.
99. Wilhelm Abraham Teller, from 1767 on a pastor and member of the high consistorial court in Berlin.
100. Karl Friedrich Bahrdt, professor of theology at various universities, but always shocking people by his aggressiveness and his dissolute life. He later became an innkeeper in the vicinity of Halle and was a notorious representative of Rationalism.
101. See above, p. 14 and note 35 on that page, also pp. 62 f.

from Ophir. To be sure, this preference for foreign talent prevented Frederick the Great from gaining any considerable influence over the German mind. On the contrary, he insulted and wounded German national feeling. The contempt he displayed for our literature cannot but offend us even today, the descendants of those writers. Except for old Gellert[102] not one of them enjoyed any sign of his most gracious favor. The interview he had with Gellert is remarkable.[103]

But if Frederick the Great jeered at us without supporting us, the book dealer Nicolai supported us all the more, without our having on that account any scruples about jeering at him. His whole life long he was unceasingly active for the welfare of his country, he spared neither pains nor money when he hoped to further a good cause, and yet never has anyone in Germany been so brutally, so relentlessly, so devastatingly ridiculed as this very man. Although we, a later generation, know very well that old Nicolai, the friend of Enlightenment, was definitely not in error about essentials, though we know that it was chiefly our own enemies, the obscurantists, who wrecked him with their abuse, still we cannot think of him with a perfectly straight face. Old Nicolai tried to do in Germany the same thing that the French philosophers had done in France; he tried to destroy the past in the mind of the people, a laudable preliminary, without which no radical revolution can take place. But in vain—he was not equal to such a task. The ancient ruins still stood too securely and the ghosts arose from them and mocked him; but then he became very cross and struck out at them blindly, and the spectators laughed when the bats whizzed about his ears and got entangled in his well-powdered wig. At times it also happened that he mistook windmills for giants and fought them. But he fared still worse when he occasionally mistook real giants for mere windmills, for instance, a Wolfgang Goethe. He wrote a satire on Goethe's *Werther*[104] in which he displayed the grossest misunderstanding of all the author's inten-

102. Christian Fürchtegott Gellert (1715–1769), from 1751 professor of philosophy at the University of Leipzig, popular with students and with the large public that knew and applauded his writings. To a later generation, like Heine's, he must have seemed very naive and old-fashioned in his approach to literature and scholarship.
103. This took place in Leipzig on December 18, 1760.
104. *The Sorrows of Young Werther,* 1773, Goethe's first novel.

tions. Yet about essentials he was always right. Even though he did not understand what Goethe really meant with his *Werther,* he nonetheless understood very well its effect—the effeminate dreaminess, the barren sentimentality which came into vogue because of this novel and which were in hostile contradiction to every sensible attitude that we needed. In this, Nicolai was in complete agreement with Lessing, who wrote to a friend the following opinion about *Werther:*

"If such a fervent production is not to do more harm than good, don't you think it should have appended to it a brief, dispassionate epilogue, a few hints as to how Werther came to have such a strange character, and how some other young man on whom nature had bestowed a similar tendency could protect himself against it? Do you think that a Greek or Roman youth would ever have killed himself in such a manner and for the same reason? Certainly not. They knew how to protect themselves from the extravagancies of love in quite a different way; and at Socrates' time even a *girl* would scarcely have been forgiven for such transports of love as drive a man to venture something so unnatural. It was reserved for Christian training, which understands so wonderfully how to transform a physical need into a spiritual perfection, to produce eccentrics at once so mean and so great, so contemptible and so estimable. So, dear Goethe, give us another chapter as a brief conclusion, and the more cynical, the better."

In accordance with this suggestion friend Nicolai actually did publish a different *Werther.* In his version the hero did not shoot himself, but merely befouled himself with chicken blood, for the pistol was loaded with it instead of lead. Werther makes himself ridiculous, keeps on living, marries Charlotte—in short, he ends even more tragically than in Goethe's original.

The *Allgemeine deutsche Bibliothek* is the name of the journal Nicolai founded and in which he and his friends fought against superstition, Jesuits, court lackeys, and the like. It cannot be denied that many a blow directed against superstition unfortunately struck poetry itself. Nicolai fought, for instance, against the rising partiality for old German folksongs. But essentially he was once more in the right. Despite all their excellence, the songs did contain many recollections that were anything but up-to-date; these ancient strains of the Alpine cowherds of the Middle Ages could lure the hearts of the people back into the stables of a bygone faith. Like Ulysses, Nicolai tried to stop the ears of his companions so that they would not hear the songs of the sirens, not caring that they then also became deaf to the innocent tones of the nightingale. In order to clear the field of the present completely of all weeds, this practical man hardly scrupled at pulling up the flowers as well. But the party of the flowers and the nightingales, with all that belonged to it, beauty, grace, wit, and playfulness, rose up in arms against this, and poor Nicolai was defeated.

In present-day Germany circumstances have changed, and the party of the flowers and the nightingales is closely allied with the Revolution. To us belongs the future, and already the morning glow of victory is dawning. When in time this beautiful day sheds its light on our whole fatherland, then we will also remember the dead. We will then certainly remember you, old Nicolai, poor martyr of reason; we will bear your ashes to the German Pantheon, the sarcophagus surrounded by an exultant triumphal procession and accompanied by a band of players among whose wind instruments there shall certainly not be a flute; we will place on your bier a most befitting laurel wreath, and while so doing we will try very hard not to laugh.

Since I would like to give an idea of the philosophical and religious conditions of that time, I must also mention here those thinkers who, in more or less intimate association with Nicolai, were active in Berlin and formed, as it were, a *juste milieu* between philosophers and belles-lettres. They had no definite system, merely a definite tendency. In style and in basic principles they resembled the English moralists.[105] They used no strict scientific form in their writing; moral awareness was the sole source of their knowledge. Their tendency was the same as that of the French Philanthropists.[106] In religion they were rationalists. In politics they were cosmopolitans. In morals they were human beings, noble, virtuous human beings, strict in regard to themselves, tolerant toward others. As

105. A reference to the didactic element in much English literature of the eighteenth century, but most particularly to newspapers such as Addison's and Steele's, which had great influence in Germany and were widely imitated.

106. French writers and thinkers such as Voltaire, Montesquieu, Diderot, Rousseau, and others, liberals who condemned all forms of despotism and believed in the best ideals of the eighteenth century, tolerance, social justice and equality, and political freedom.

for talent, Mendelssohn,[107] Sulzer,[108] Abbt,[109] Moritz,[110] Garve,[111] Engel,[112] and Biester[113] might be named as the most distinguished. I like Moritz best. He accomplished a great deal in experimental psychology. He had a delightful naivete little appreciated by his friends. His autobiography is one of the most important documents of that time. Mendelssohn, however, has great social significance beyond all the others. He was the reformer of the German Israelites, his co-religionists; he destroyed the authority of Talmudism and founded pure Mosaism. This man, whom his contemporaries called the German Socrates and whom they admired so reverently for his nobility of spirit and vigor of intellect, was the son of a poor sexton at the synagogue, in Dessau. In addition to this misfortune of birth, Providence had also afflicted him with a hunchback, as if to teach the common people in a very vivid way that one should judge a person not by his outward appearance but by his intrinsic worth. Or did Providence assign him a hunchback with benevolent foresight, so that he could attribute many an insult of the masses to a misfortune for which a wise man can readily console himself?

As Luther had overthrown the Papacy, so Mendelssohn overthrew the Talmud, and in the very same way, namely, by repudiating tradition, by declaring the Bible to be the source of religion, and by translating the most important part of it. By so doing he destroyed Judaic catholicism, as Luther had destroyed Christian catholicism. The Talmud is, in fact, the catholicism of the Jews. It is a Gothic cathedral, which, to be sure, is overloaded with childish and superfluous ornament, yet nevertheless astounds us with its heaven-aspiring, gigantic proportions. It is a hierarchy of religious

107. Moses Mendelssohn (1729–1786), the well-known Jewish philosopher, one of Lessing's best friends.
108. Johann Georg Sulzer (1720–1779), prominent esthetician of the time, for many years a professor at the University of Berlin.
109. Thomas Abbt (1738–1766), journalist and writer, of considerable influence on the young Herder.
110. Karl Philipp Moritz (1757–1793), author of an autobiographical novel *Anton Reiser, a Psychological Novel,* and of two books on his travels in England and Italy. The novel is the autobiography referred to by Heine in what follows.
111. Christian Garve (1742–1798), popular moral philosopher.
112. Johann Jakob Engel (1741–1802), writer, editor, and theater director in Berlin.
113. Johann Erich Biester (1749–1816), librarian at the Royal Library in Berlin, editor of various journals.

laws, often dealing with the quaintest, most absurd subtleties, but so ingeniously superimposed and subordinated, each part supporting and sustaining another, and so formidably consistent in their collective effect as to form an awesomely bold, colossal whole.

After the downfall of Christian catholicism, Jewish catholicism, the Talmud, also had perforce to decline. For the Talmud had now lost its significance. It served simply as a bulwark against Rome, and the Jews owe it to the Talmud that they were able to resist Christian Rome just as heroically as they had formerly resisted pagan Rome. And they did not merely resist; they were victorious. The poor Rabbi of Nazareth, over whose dying head the pagan Roman wrote the sardonic words "King of the Jews"—it was precisely this thorn-crowned mock-king of the Jews, decked out in ironic scarlet, who finally became the God of the Romans, and they had to kneel down before Him! Like heathen Rome, Christian Rome was also defeated and even had to pay tribute. If you, dear reader, during the first days of the trimester, will betake yourself to Lafitte Street, to the hotel at no. 15, you will see there in front of a tall gate a lumbering carriage from which a stout man will descend. He will go upstairs to a small room where a blond young man is sitting, actually older than he probably looks, in whose elegant, grand-seignorial nonchalance there is yet something as solid, something as positive, something as absolute as if he had all the money in this world in his pocket. And indeed he *has* all the money in this world in his pocket, and his name is Mr. James Rothschild, and the stout man is Monsignor Grimbaldi, legate of His Holiness the Pope, and he is bringing in the latter's name the interest on the Roman loan, the tribute from Rome.

But of what use is the Talmud now?

Moses Mendelssohn thus deserves great praise for having overthrown this Jewish catholicism, at least in Germany. For anything superfluous is harmful. Rejecting tradition, he nonetheless tried to preserve the Mosaic ceremonial law as religious obligation. Was this cowardice or prudence? Was it a melancholy nostalgia that kept him from laying a destructive hand on objects that were most sacred to his forefathers and for which so much martyrs' blood and tears had flowed? I think not. Like the sovereigns of material kingdoms, the sovereigns of the spirit must also harden their hearts against family affections; even on the throne of thought one must not give way to tender sentiments. Therefore I am rather of the opinion that Moses Mendolssohn saw in pure Mosaism an institution that could serve as a last entrenchment for deism, so to speak. For deism was his innermost faith and his deepest conviction. When his friend Lessing died and was accused of being a follower of Spinoza, he defended him 'with the most anxious fervor and worried himself to death over the incident.

I have already mentioned for the second time the name no German can utter without rousing in his bosom an echo more or less loud. Since Luther, Germany has produced no greater nor better man than Gotthold Ephraim Lessing. These two are our pride and our delight. In the gloom of the present we look up to their comforting figures, and they nod in affirmation of a brilliant promise. Yes, the third man will also come, who will complete what Luther began, what Lessing continued, and what the German fatherland needs so much—the third emancipator!—I can already see his golden armor shining through his imperial crimson cloak "like the sun through the rosy dawn"!

Like Luther, Lessing was influential not only because he did something definite but because he roused the German people to its very depth and because he brought about a beneficial intellectual movement by his criticism and by his polemics. He was the living criticism of his time, and his whole life was a polemic. His criticism made itself felt throughout the whole range of thought and of feeling, in religion, in science, in art. His polemics overcame every adversary and grew more vigorous with every victory. Lessing, as he himself admitted, simply had to have conflict for his own intellectual development. He was just like that legendary Norman who inherited the talents, knowledge, and powers of the men he slew in combat and thus was ultimately endowed with all possible merits and excellencies. It is understandable that such a pugnacious warrior caused no small stir in Germany, in peaceful Germany, where in those days an even greater Sabbath-like peace reigned than today. The majority were dumfounded at his literary boldness. But it was this very quality that came to his aid, for *oser*[114] is the secret of success in literature as in revolution—and in love. Everyone trembled before Lessing's sword. No head was safe from it. Indeed,

114. To dare.

he even struck off many a skull out of sheer high spirits, and then was malicious enough to lift it up from the ground and show the public that it was empty inside. The man whom his sword could not reach he slew with the arrows of his wit. His friends admired the brightly colored feathers of these arrows; his enemies felt the points in their breasts. Lessing's wit bears no resemblance to that *enjouement*,[115] that *gaieté*,[116] those bounding *saillies*[117] so familiar here in France. His wit was not a little French lapdog[118] chasing its own shadow; it was more like a big German tomcat playing with a mouse before strangling it.

Yes, polemic was Lessing's delight, and for this reason he never thought very much about whether his opponent was worthy of him. With his polemic he snatched many a name from well-deserved oblivion. He wove a web, as it were, of the wittiest mockery, the most delightful humor, about not a few paltry scribblers, who are now preserved for all time in Lessing's works like insects embedded in a piece of amber. While slaying his adversaries, he made them immortal. Who among us would ever have heard anything about that Klotz[119] on whom Lessing lavished so much derision and ingenuity! The boulders which he hurled at this wretched antiquarian and with which he crushed him are now an indestructible monument to his victim.

It is remarkable that this man, the wittest in Germany, was also the most honest man. There is nothing comparable to his love of truth. Lessing made not the slightest concession to a lie, even if by doing so, in the usual manner of the worldy-wise, he might promote the triumph of truth. He could do anything for the truth except lie. Anyone, he once said, who plans to display truth with all sorts of make-up and disguises might well be the pander, but has never been the lover, of truth.

115. Sprightliness.
116. Gaiety.
117. Sallies.
118. In German the word is *Windhündchen*, the diminutive of *Windhund*, which means "greyhound." According to Grimm's *Wörterbuch*, after the introduction of dogs as luxury articles, the word was also used to represent weakness. As far as I know, the English word has no such connotation, hence my use of an equivalent rather than a literal translation.
119. Christian Adolf Klotz (1738–1771), professor of classical literature at Halle. Lessing attacked him violently in his *Briefe antiquarischen Inhalts (Letters Concerning Antiquarian Questions)*.

The nice saying of Buffon's, "The style is the man himself," can be applied to no one better that to Lessing. His style of writing is just like his character, genuine, stable, unadorned, beautiful, and imposing by virtue of its inherent vigor. His style is altogether like that of Roman architecture; the greatest solidity and at the same time the greatest simplicity; the sentences rest one upon the other like square-hewn blocks of stone, and just as with the latter the law of gravity, so with the former logical reasoning is the invisible cement. For this reason we find in Lessing's prose so few of those expletives and rhetorical arts which we employ as mortar, so to speak, in constructing our sentences. Still less do we find in it those caryatides of thought which you French call *la belle phrase*.[120]

You will readily understand that a man like Lessing could never be happy. Even if he had not loved truth, even if he had not defended it obstinately on every occasion, he would still perforce have been unhappy, for he was a genius. "People will forgive you anything," said a poet recently, with a sigh, "they will forgive you your wealth, they will forgive you your noble birth, they will forgive you your fine figure, they won't even mind if you are talented, but they are pitiless toward a genius." And alas! even though he may not encounter ill will from without, a genius would still find within himself the enemy preparing misery for him. Thus the history of great men is always a martyrology; even when they did not suffer for the great human race, they suffered for their own greatness, for the grand mold of their existence, for their antipathy to philistinism, for their discomfort in the presence of vulgarity, of grinning baseness of their surroundings, a discomfort that naturally leads them to extravagances, to the theater, for example, or even to the casino, as happened to poor Lessing.

But malicious rumor has not been able to charge him with anything worse than this, and from his biography we learn only that pretty actresses seemed to him more amusing than Hamburg clergymen and that speechless cards afforded him better entertainment than babbling Wolfian philosophers.

It is heartrending to read in this biography how fate denied him any joy whatsoever and would not even permit him to relax from his daily conflicts in the peace of the family circle. Only once did

120. A fine phrase.

fortune seem to wish to smile on him; it gave him a beloved wife and a child—but this happiness was like the sunbeam that gilds the wings of a bird flying past, for it vanished just as quickly. His wife died as a result of childbirth, and the child very soon after birth. To a friend he wrote about his child the bitterly witty words: "My joy was but brief. And I lost him with such regret, this son! For he possessed so much intelligence—so much intelligence! Don't think that my few hours of paternity made me such an ape of a father. I know what I am saying. Didn't it show intelligence on his part that he had to be brought into the world with iron forceps, and that he smelled a rat so soon? Wasn't it intelligence that he seized the first opportunity to take to his heels again? I wanted for once to have things as good as other people, but it cost me dearly."

There was one misfortune which Lessing never spoke to his friends about; this was his terrible loneliness, his intellectual solitariness. Some of his contemporaries loved him; none understood him. Mendelssohn, his best friend, defended him zealously against the charge of Spinozism. Defense and zeal were as absurd as they were superfluous. Rest easy in your grave, old Moses. Your Lessing was, to be sure, on the way to that dreadful error, that wretched misfortune, namely, to Spinozism—but the Almighty, our Father in heaven, saved him by death just at the right moment. Rest easy, your Lessing was not a Spinozist, as slander maintained; he died a good deist like you and Nicolai and Teller and the *Allgemeine deutsche Bibliothek!*

Lessing was merely the prophet who pointed out the way from the second to the third Testament.[121] I have called him Luther's continuator, and it is actually in this relation that I must discuss him here. I can speak only later of his significance for German art. In this he brought about a salutary reform, not merely by his criticism but also by his example, and this side of his activity is usually the one most emphasized and analyzed. We, however, are considering him from a different standpoint, and his philosophical and theological battles are more important for us than his dramaturgy and his plays. Yet the latter, like all his writings, have a social significance, and *Nathan the Wise* is not only a good comedy, but also a philosophical-theological treatise on behalf of pure deism.

---

121. As, for instance, in his late work *The Education of the Human Race.*

For Lessing art was also a rostrum, and when he was pushed down from the pulpit or driven from the lecture room, he leaped to the theater and spoke there even more plainly and gained an even more numerous audience.

I say that Lessing continued Luther's work. After Luther had liberated us from tradition and had set up the Bible as the one and only source of Christianity, there arose, as I have already related previously, a rigid literalism, and the letter of the Bible ruled just as tyrannically as tradition had once ruled. Lessing contributed the most to liberation from this tyrannical letter. Just as Luther was not the only one who battled tradition, so, to be sure, Lessing was not the only, but still the most valiant, warrior against the letter. Here his battle cry resounds loudest. Here he wields his sword most joyfully, and it flashes and slays. But it is here also that Lessing is most sorely beset by the black legion, and in such straits he once cried out:

"*O sancta simplicitas!* But I am not yet at the place where the good man who cried out thus could still utter only these words. (Huss cried out thus when burned at the stake.) We must first be heard; we must first be judged by those who can and wish to hear and judge.

"O, if *he* could only do so, he whom I would most like to have as my judge! You, Luther! Great, misunderstood man! And misunderstood by no one more than by those obstinate persons who, your slippers in their hands, dawdle along the path you made for them, clamorous but indifferent. You saved us from the yoke of tradition. Who will save us from the more intolerable yoke of the letter? Who will at last bring us a Christianity such as you would teach today, such as Christ Himself would teach?"

Yes, the letter, said Lessing, is the last veil enveloping Christianity, and only after its destruction will the spirit of Christianity stand revealed. This spirit, however, is none other that what the Wolfian philosophers meant to demonstrate, what the Philanthropists felt in their hearts, what Mendelssohn found in Mosaism, what Freemasons chanted, what poets sang, what at that time was making itself felt in Germany in all manner of ways—pure Deism.

Lessing died in Brunswick in 1781, misunderstood, hated, and denounced. In the same year Immanuel Kant's *Critique of Pure Reason* appeared in Königsberg. With this book, which due to a strange delay did not become generally known until the end of the decade, there began in Germany an intellectual revolution which presents the most striking analogies to the material revolution in France and which must seem to more profound thinkers just as important. It went through the same phases of development, and the most remarkable parallelism exists between both revolutions. On both sides of the Rhine we see the same break with the past; all respect for tradition has been renounced. Just as here in France every privilege must be justified, so, in Germany, must every thought be justified, and just as here the monarchy, the keystone of the old social order, so there deism, the keystone of the old intellectual regime, has fallen.

Of this catastrophe, deism's 21st of January,[122] we shall speak in the following section. A peculiar awe, a mysterious piety, prevents our writing more today. Our heart is filled with shuddering compassion—it is ancient Jehovah himself who is preparing for death. We knew him so well, from his cradle in Egypt, where he was reared among divine calves and crocodiles, sacred onions, ibis, and cats. We saw him as he bade farewell to these playmates of his childhood and to the obelisks and sphinxes of his native Nile valley and became a little god-king in Palestine among a poor shepherd people and lived in his own temple-palace. We saw him later when he came in contact with Assyrian-Babylonian civilization and put aside his all too human passions, no longer spitting nothing but wrath and vengeance, at least no longer thundering at every trifle. We saw him emigrate to Rome, the capital, where he renounced all national prejudices and proclaimed the divine equality of all nations, and with such fine phrases established an opposition to old Jupiter, and intrigued until he gained supreme authority and from the Capitol ruled the city and the world, *urbem et orbem*. We saw how he became even more spiritual, how he whimpered in bland bliss, becoming a loving father, a universal friend of man, a world benefactor, a philanthropist—but all this could avail him nothing—

Do you hear the little bell ringing? Kneel down. They are bringing the sacraments to a dying god.

122. Louis XVI was beheaded on January 21, 1793.

BOOK THREE

The tales goes that an English inventor, who had already invented the most ingenious machines, finally hit on the idea of constructing a human being. In the end he succeeded; the work of his hands could behave and act just like a man; it even bore within its leathern breast a sort of human feeling differing not too greatly from the usual feelings of the English; it could communicate its emotions by articulate sounds, and it was precisely the noise of the wheels inside, of springs and screws, which was then audible, that lent these sounds a genuinely English pronunciation. In short, this automaton was a perfect gentleman, and nothing was missing to make it a real human being except a soul. This, however, the English inventor could not give him, and the poor creature, aware of its deficiency, tormented its creator day and night with the plea to give it a soul. This request, repeated day after day with growing urgency, at last became so unendurable to the poor artist that he ran away to escape from his own masterpiece. But the automaton immediately took a special coach, followed him to the continent, traveled incessantly at his heels, sometimes caught up with him, and then rattled and grunted at him, "Give me a soul." These two figures may now be met in every country, and only he who knows their particular relationship understands their strange haste and their anxious discontent. But as soon as we know about this particular relationship, we recognize in it something of a general nature; we see how one part of the English people is weary of its mechanical existence and demands a soul, whereas the other part, out of anxiety at such a desire, is driven about in all directions, and neither can endure things at home any longer.

This is a dreadful story. It is terrifying when the bodies we have created demand from us a soul. It is far more dreadful, terrifying, uncanny, however, when we have created a soul and it demands from us its body and pursues us with this demand. The thought we have conceived is such a soul, and it leaves us no peace until we have given it its body, until we have helped it to become a material phenomenon. Thought strives to become action, the word to become flesh. And marvelous to relate, man, like God in the Bible, needs only to express his thought, and the world takes shape, there is light or there is darkness, the waters separate from the dry land, or it may even be that wild beasts appear. The world is the symbol of the word.

Take note of this, you proud men of action. You are nothing but unconscious handymen for the men of thought who, often in the humblest quiet, have prescribed with the utmost precision all your actions. Maximilian Robespierre was nothing but the hand of Jean Jacques Rousseau, the bloody hand that drew forth from the womb of time the body whose soul Rousseau had created. Did not, perhaps, the restless anxiety that embittered the life of Jean Jacques stem from a premonition in his spirit as to what sort of accoucheur his thoughts would need in order to enter the world in corporal form?

Old Fontenelle[123] may have been right when he said, "If I held all the ideas of this world in my hand, I would be very careful not to open it." For my part, I think differently. If I held all the ideas of this world in my hand, I would perhaps beg you to cut off my hand immediately; under no circumstances would I keep it closed so long. I was not made to be a jailer of ideas. By God, I would set them free. Even though they should materialize into the most hazardous realities, though they should storm through all lands like a mad bacchanalian procession, though they should crush our most innocent flowers with their thyrsi, though they should break into our hospitals and chase the sick old world from its bed—my heart would sorrow, to be sure, and I myself would come to grief! For alas, I too am part of this sick old world, and the poet says rightly, even though you make fun of your crutches, you can't walk any better for it. I am the sickest of all, and am the more to be pitied since I know what health is. But you—you don't know, you enviable ones! You are capable of dying without even noticing it. Yes, many of you are long since dead and maintain that your real life is only now beginning. When I contradict such a delusion, you get mad at me and revile me—and—a horrible thing!—the corpses rush at me and insult me, and still more annoying than their insults is the smell of their putrefaction. Away, you ghosts! I shall now speak of a man whose very name has the power of an exorcism. I shall speak of Immanuel Kant.

123. Bernard Le Bovier de Fontenelle (1657–1757), a writer, nephew of Corneille.

It is said that nocturnal spirits are terrified at the sight of the executioner's sword. How terrified they must then be when someone holds up to them Kant's *Critique of Pure Reason*! This book is the sword with which deism was executed in Germany.

To speak frankly, you French are tame and moderate compared with us Germans. The most you could do was kill a king, and he had already lost his head before you beheaded him. And in doing this you had to drum and shriek so much and stamp your feet till the whole universe trembled. Truly, it does Maximilian Robespierre too much honor to compare him with Immanuel Kant. Maximilian Robespierre, the great bourgeois of the Rue Saint Honoré, did indeed have his attacks of destructive rage when it was a question of the monarchy, and his convulsions were frightful enough in his regicidal epilepsy; but as soon as there was any mention of the Supreme Being, he washed the white froth from his mouth and the blood from his hands, put on his blue Sunday coat with the shiny buttons, and, what's more, stuck a nosegay in the front of his broad vest.

The history of Immanuel Kant's life is difficult to portray, for he had neither life nor history. He led a mechanically ordered, almost abstract bachelor existence in a quiet, remote little street in Königsberg, an old town on the northeastern border of Germany. I do not believe that the great clock of the cathedral there performed more dispassionately and methodically its outward routine of the day than did its fellow countryman Immanuel Kant. Getting up in the morning, drinking coffee, writing, giving lectures, eating, walking, everything had its appointed time, and the neighbors knew for certain that it was half-past three when Immanuel Kant, in his gray frock-coat, his Spanish cane in his hand, stepped out of his house and strolled to the little linden avenue called after him to this day the "Philosopher's Path." Eight times he walked up and down it, in every season of the year, and when the sky was overcast, or gray clouds announced a rain coming, old Lampe, his servant, was seen walking anxiously behind him with a big umbrella under his arm, like an image of Providence.

What a strange contrast between the outward life of the man and his destructive, world-crushing thoughts! Truly, if the citizens of Königsberg had had any premonition of the full significance of his ideas, they would have felt a far more terrifying dread at the presence of this man than at the sight of an executioner, an executioner who merely executes people. But the good folk saw in him nothing but a professor of philosophy, and as he passed by at his customary hour, they gave him a friendly greeting and perhaps set their watches by him.

If, however, Immanuel Kant, the arch-destroyer in the realm of ideas, far surpassed Maximilian Robespierre in terrorism, yet he possessed many similarities with the latter which invite comparison of the two men. In the first place, we find in both the same stubborn, keen, unpoetic, sober integrity. We also find in both the same talent for suspicion, only that the one directs his suspicion toward ideas and calls it criticism, while the other applies it to people and entitles it republican virtue. But both represented in the highest degree the type of the provincial bourgeois. Nature had destined them to weigh coffee and sugar, but Fate determined that they should weigh other things and placed on the scales of the one a king, on the scales of the other a god.

And they gave the correct weight!

The *Critique of Pure Reason* is Kant's chief work, and we must give preference to it in our discussion. None of all his other works has greater significance. This book, as already mentioned, appeared in 1781 but did not become generally known until 1789.[124] In the beginning it was completely overlooked, only two insignificant reviews of it appeared at that time, and only late, with articles by Schütz, Schulz, and Reinhold, was the attention of the public directed to this great work. The reason for the tardy recognition probably lies in the unusual form and bad style in which the book is written. As to his style, Kant deserves more severe censure than any other philosopher, all the more when we consider the better style of his earlier writing. The recently published collection of his minor works contains his first attempts, and we are surprised at the fine and often very witty style. While Kant was working out in his mind his great work, he hummed to himself these little essays. In them he is smiling like a soldier calmly arming himself for a battle he feels certain of winning. Especially remarkable among them are the *General Natural History and Theory of the Heavens,* written as early as 1755; *Observations on the Emotions*

124. It was the second edition, in 1787, that caused a stir in Germany.

of the Beautiful and the Sublime, written ten years later; and *Dreams of a Spirit-Seer,* full of fine wit after the manner of the French essay. The wit of a Kant, as displayed in these lesser works, is something extremely individual. The wit clings to the thought, and despite its weakness is thus able to achieve a refreshing height. Without such support, to be sure, not even the most fertile wit can succeed; like the grapevine that lacks a stake, it must then creep wretchedly along on the ground and rot together with all its most precious fruits.

But why did Kant write his *Critique of Pure Reason* in such a colorless, dry, wrapping-paper style? I think he feared that because he had rejected the mathematical form of the Cartesian-Leibnitzian-Wolfian philosophers, science might lose something of its dignity if it were expressed in a light, pleasantly cheerful tone. Hence he gave it a stiff, abstract form which coldly repelled any familiarity on the part of intellects of the lower order. He wanted to separate himself superciliously from the contemporary popular philosophers, who strove for the plainest clarity, and he clothed his ideas in a courtly, frigid, bureaucratic language. In this he shows himself to be a true philistine. Possibly, however, Kant also needed for his carefully calculated sequence of ideas a language that was similarly calculated, and he was not capable of creating a better one. Only a genius possesses for a new idea a new word as well. But Immanuel Kant was not a genius. Conscious of this deficiency, like the worthy Maximilian, Kant was all the more suspicious of genius, and in his *Critique of Judgment* he even maintained that a genius had no function in the pursuit of scientific knowledge, that his effectiveness belonged to the realm of art.

Due to the ponderous, pedantic style of his main work, Kant did an enormous amount of damage. For his brainless imitators aped him in this external characteristic, and hence there arose among the Germans the superstition that you can't be a philosopher if you write well. After Kant, however, the mathematical form could no longer prevail in philosophy. In his *Critique of Pure Reason* he quite mercilessly pronounced the sentence of death on this form. The mathematical form in philosophy, he said, produced nothing but houses of cards, just as the philosophical form in mathematics produces only vain prattle. For in philosophy there can be no definitions such as in mathematics, where definitions are not discursive but intuitive, that is, they can be demonstrated by perception; what are called definitions in philosophy are put forth only experimentally and hypothetically, the truly correct definition appearing only at the end, as result.

Why is it that philosophers show such a great preference for the mathematical form? This preference begins as early as Pythagoras, who designated the principles of things by numbers. This was a brilliant idea. In a number the material and the finite are cast aside, and yet the number designates something definite and also the relationship of this definite thing to another definite thing, which last, if it is likewise designated by a number, has assumed the same dematerialized and infinite character. In this respect a number resembles ideas that have the same character and the same relationship to each other. Ideas, as they appear in our minds and in nature, can be designated very precisely by numbers; but the number nonetheless always remains a symbol for the idea, not the idea itself. The master is always aware of this difference, but the pupil forgets it and passes on to future pupils only a hieroglyphic of numbers, mere ciphers whose living significance no one knows any longer and which are repeated parrot-fashion with schoolboy-pride. This also applies to the other principles of mathematical demonstration. The intellectual process in its perpetual activity does not permit any fixity; it cannot be fixed by line, triangle, square, or circle any more than by numbers. Thought can neither be calculated nor measured.

Since I am chiefly interested in facilitating the study of German philosophy in France, I always discuss principally those external characteristics that can easily discourage a foreigner if he has not been informed about them in advance. I want particularly to call the attention of men of letters who wish to adapt Kant for the French public to the fact that they can omit that part of his philosophy which serves merely to combat the absurdities of Wolfian philosophy. This polemic, constantly reappearing, can create only confusion in the minds of the French and can be of no benefit to them. I hear that Dr. Schön, a German scholar living in Paris, is preparing a French edition of Kant. I have too much respect for the philosophical views of this man that I would consider it necessary to address the above admonition to him. I expect from him, rather, a book which is just as useful as it is significant.

As I have already said, the *Critique of Pure Reason* is Kant's chief work, and his other writings can to some extent be viewed as superfluous or at any rate as commentaries. The social significance contained in that chief work will become clear from what follows.

Philosophers before Kant did, to be sure, ponder the origin of our cognitions and, as we have already shown, followed two different paths, depending on whether they assumed ideas as *a priori* or as *a posteriori*. There has been less reflection on the faculty of knowing itself, on the scope or on the limits of this faculty. This now became Kant's task; he subjected our faculty of knowing to a ruthless examination; he sounded all the depths of this faculty and established all its limits. He found, to be sure, that we can know nothing at all about a great many things with which we previously believed ourselves to have the most intimate acquaintance. This was extremely annoying. But it has always been useful to know what things we cannot know anything about. He who warns us about useless roads does us just as good a service as he who shows us the right road. Kant proved to us that we can know nothing about things as they are in and of themselves, but that we know something about them only in so far as they are reflected in our minds. Thus we are just like the prisoners of whom Plato paints such a depressing picture in the seventh book of his *Republic*. These unfortunate beings, fettered at their necks and thighs so that they cannot turn their heads, are seated in a dungeon open at the top, and they get some light from above. This light, however, comes from a fire burning on a height behind them, and indeed is separated from them by a low wall. Along this wall walk people carrying all sorts of statues, images made of wood or stone, and talking with one another. Now the poor prisoners can see nothing at all of these people, who are not so tall as the wall, and of the statues carried past, which tower above the wall, they see only the shadows which move along on the wall opposite them. They take these shadows to be the real objects, and, deceived by the echo of their dungeon, they think it is the shadows that are talking with one another.

Earlier philosophy, which ran about sniffing at things and collecting and classifying their characteristics, came to an end when Kant appeared. He directed investigation back to the human mind and examined what was to be found there. Hence he compared his philosophy, and not without reason, with Copernicus' procedure. Previously, when the world was made to stand still and the sun to revolve around it, astronomical calculations did not agree very well. Then Copernicus made the sun stand still and the earth revolve around it, and behold, everything now functioned splendidly. Previously reason, like the sun, moved around the physical world and tried to illumine it, but Kant made reason, the sun, stand still, and the physical world revolves around it and is illumined wherever it comes within the realm of this sun.

After these few words, with which I have indicated Kant's mission, everyone will understand why I consider that section of his book in which he deals with the so-called phenomena and noumena the most important part, the center, of his philosophy. For Kant distinguishes between the appearances of things and things themselves. Since we can know nothing about things except in so far as they manifest themselves to us through their appearance, and since, therefore, things, as they are in and of themselves, are not revealed to us, Kant called things as they appear to be, phenomena, and things in and of themselves, noumena. We can know something only about things as phenomena, but we can know nothing about things as noumena. The latter are purely problematic. We can neither say that they exist nor that they do not exist. Indeed, the word noumenon is paired with the word phenomenon only so that one can speak about things, in as far as they are accessible to our knowledge, without touching, in our judgment, upon things not accessible to our knowledge.

Thus Kant did not, as do many teachers whom I do not care to name, divide things into phenomena and noumena, into things that exist for us and things that do not exist for us. This would be an Irish bull in philosophy. His intention was simply to give a concept of limitation.

According to Kant, God is a noumenon. As a result of his argument, this transcendental ideal being which we have hitherto called God is nothing but a fiction. It arose from a natural illusion. Yes, Kant shows that we can know nothing at all about this noumenon, about God, and that even any future proof of his existence will be impossible. We shall write Dante's words, "Leave hope behind,"[125] at the head of this section of the *Critique of Pure Reason.*

I believe you will gladly exempt me from attempting a discussion for the general public of this section which deals with "the arguments of speculative reason in favor of the existence of a supreme being." Although the actual refutation of these arguments does not occupy much space and does not appear until the second half of the book, it is quite deliberately prepared for from the very beginning and is one of the main points of the work. Upon this follows the "Critique of All Speculative Theology," in which the remaining phantoms of the deists are destroyed. I cannot help remarking that in attacking the three principal types of proof for the existence of God, namely, the ontological, the cosmological, and the physicotheological, Kant succeeded, in my opinion, in destroying the last two but not the first. I do not know whether the above terms are understood here in France, and I therefore quote the passage from the *Critique of Pure Reason* in which Kant formulates the differences:

"Only three kinds of proof of the existence of God are possible on the basis of speculative reason. All the paths that may be taken with this aim in view start either from definite experience and the particular nature of the material world as revealed by experience and ascend from this world according to the laws of causality up to the supreme first cause beyond the world; or they are based merely on an indefinite experience, on some sort of existence or being; or, lastly, they make an abstraction from all experience and arrive at the conclusion, entirely *a priori* from pure ideas, of the existence of a supreme first cause. The first proof is the physicotheological, the second the cosmological, and the third the ontological. There are no other proofs, nor can others exist."

After repeated and thorough study of Kant's chief work I fancied I perceived everywhere his polemic against the existent proofs of the existence of God, and I would discuss it at greater length were I not restrained by religious sentiment. The mere fact that I see someone discussing the existence of God arouses in me a strange anxiety, a dismal dejection, such as I once experienced at New

125. A reference to the inscription above the gate of Hell in Dante's *Divine Comedy*. It begins: "All hope abandon, ye who enter here."

Bedlam[126] in London when I lost sight of my guide and found myself surrounded by nothing but madmen. "God is all that is," and doubt of His existence is doubt of life itself, is death.

As objectionable as any dispute about the existence of God may be, all the more praiseworthy is reflection on the nature of God. This reflection is true worship of God; the spirit is thereby diverted from the transitory and finite and attains to consciousness of innate love and of eternal harmony. In prayer or in the contemplation of spiritual symbols this consciousness thrills the man of feeling; the thinker finds this holy fervor in the exercise of that sublime faculty of the mind called reason, whose highest function is to inquire into the nature of God. People of specially religious bent occupy themselves with this task from childhood on; as early as the first stirring of reason they are mysteriously obsessed by it. The author of these pages is most thankfully aware of having possessed this early primitive religiosity, and it has never deserted him. God was always the beginning and the end of all my thoughts. I now ask: what is God? what is His nature?, but even as a small child I used to ask: what is God like? how does He look? And at that time I could gaze up into the sky for days on end and in the evening was very sad that I had not once caught sight of God's most holy countenance but had seen only silly, grotesque faces in the gray clouds. Information about astronomy, which then, in the Age of Enlightenment, not even the youngest children were spared, confused me completely, and I was astonished no end that all those thousands of millions of stars were spheres just as large and beautiful as ours and that over all this sparkling throng of worlds a single god ruled. Once in a dream, I remember, I saw God, far above in the remotest distance. He was looking contentedly out of a little window in the sky, a pious old man's face with a little Jewish beard, and scattering quantities of seeds which, as they fell down from heaven, sprouted, as it were, in infinite space and expanded to vast dimensions until they became gleaming, blossoming, populated worlds, each as large as our own earth. I have never been able to forget that face; afterwards in dreams I often saw the cheerful old man pouring down from his little window in the sky the seeds of the universe; once I even saw him clucking like our

126. An insane asylum.

servant girl when she threw the hens their barley feed. I could see only how the falling seeds always expanded into huge, sparkling globes, but the huge hens that were perhaps waiting somewhere impatiently with beaks wide open in order to be fed with the scattered globes I could not see.

You smile, dear reader, at the huge hens. But this childish notion is not so very far removed from the view of the most advanced deists. Orient and Occident have exhausted themselves with childish hyperboles in order to provide a conception of an extramundane god. The imagination of the deists, however, has exerted itself to no purpose in dealing with the infinity of space and time. It is here that their impotence, the emptiness of their world view, of their conception of the nature of God, becomes fully apparent. Hence we are not greatly disturbed when this conception is destroyed. Kant did indeed inflict this injury on them by refuting their proofs of the existence of God.

A vindication of the ontological proof would not particularly benefit deism, for this proof can also be used for pantheism. To make this easier to understand, let me note that the ontological proof is the one which Descartes put forward and which long before that, in the Middle Ages, had been expressed in the form of a moving[127] prayer by Anselm of Canterbury. Indeed, one might say that St. Augustine already established the ontological proof in the second book of *De libro arbitrio*.[128]

I shall refrain, as I have said, from any discussion for the benefit of the general public of Kant's polemic against these proofs. I shall content myself with assuring you that since then deism has vanished from the realm of speculative reason. It may perhaps take several centuries before this sad death notice gets into general circulation— we, however, have long since put on mourning. *De profundis!*

You think we can go home now? Not on your life! There is another play still to be performed. After the tragedy comes the farce. Up to this point Immanuel Kant presents the picture of the relentless philosopher; he stormed heaven, put the whole garrison to the sword, the sovereign of the world swam unproven in his own blood, there was now no all-mercifulness, no paternal kindness,

127. I follow here Strodtmann's reading of *rührenden* instead of *ruhenden* ("testing" or "peaceful"), as in the editions by Elster and Walzel.
128. *On Free Will.*

no reward in the other world for renunciation in this, the immortality of the soul lay in its last throes—you could hear its groans and death rattle; and old Lampe stood there, a mournful spectator, his umbrella under his arm, cold sweat and tears pouring from his face. Then Immanuel Kant relented and showed that he was not simply a great philosopher but also a good man, and he deliberated and said, half good-naturedly and half ironically, "Old Lampe must have a God, otherwise the poor fellow can't be happy. But man ought to be happy in this world—practical reason says so—that's certainly all right with me—then let practical reason also guarantee the existence of God." As a result of this argument Kant distinguished between theoretical reason and practical reason, and by means of the latter, as with a magician's wand, he revived the corpse of Deism, which theoretical reason had killed.

But did Kant perhaps undertake this resurrection, not simply for old Lampe's sake, but also because of the police? Or did he really act out of conviction? Did he perhaps, just by destroying all the proofs for the existence of God, intend to show us clearly how awkward it is not to be able to know anything about the existence of God? In this matter he acted almost as wisely as a Westphalian friend of mine who had smashed all the lamps in Grohnder Street and then, standing in the dark, delivered a long lecture to us on the practical necessity of lamps, which he had broken scientifically only in order to show us that we could see nothing without them.

I have already mentioned that when it appeared, the *Critique of Pure Reason* did not create the slightest sensation. Not until several years later, when certain perceptive philosophers had written commentaries on it, did it arouse public attention, and in 1789 nothing was talked of in Germany but Kant's philosophy, and it received an abundance of commentaries, chrestomathies, interpretations, criticisms, apologies, etc. One needs only to glance at the first philosophic catalogue at hand, and the legion of works about Kant published at that time testifies adequately to the intellectual stimulus that originated with this single man. Some showed a bubbling enthusiasm, others bitter annoyance, many a gaping curiosity about the result of this intellectual revolution. We had riots in the intellectual world just as you had in the material world, and we became just as excited over the demolition of ancient dogmatism as you did over the storming of the Bastille. There was also but a handful of the totally disabled, all old, left for the defense of dogmatism, that is, the philosophy of Wolf. It was a revolution, and there was no lack of atrocities. In the party of tradition the really good Christians were the least indignant at these atrocities. In fact, they desired still worse ones so that patience might be exhausted and the counterrevolution take place more speedily as an inevitable reaction. We had pessimists in philosophy as you had in politics. Many of our pessimists went so far in their self-deception as to believe that Kant was in secret alliance with them and that he had destroyed the previous proofs of the existence of God merely in order that the world might realize that one can never arrive at a knowledge of God by the use of reason and must therefore, in this matter, adhere to revealed religion.

Kant brought about this great intellectual movement less by the content of his writings than by the critical spirit that pervaded them and now made its way into all branches of knowledge. All disciplines were affected by it. Yes, even poetry did not escape its influence. Schiller, for instance, was a strong Kantian, and his views on art are impregnated with the spirit of Kantian philosophy. Because of its dry, abstract character this philosophy was extremely harmful to belles-lettres and fine arts. Fortunately it did not interfere with the art of cooking.

The German people is not easily set in motion; but once it has been directed to a certain path, it will follow this path with the most dogged perseverance to the very end. We showed this trait in matters of religion. We also showed it in philosophy. Will we continue to advance as consistently in politics?

Germany had been drawn by Kant onto the path of philosophy, and philosophy became a national cause. A sizeable troop of great thinkers suddenly emerged from German soil as if conjured up by magic. If some day German philosophy finds, as the French Revolution found, its Thiers and its Mignet,[129] its history will provide just as remarkable reading, and Germans will read it with pride and Frenchmen with admiration.

Among Kant's followers Johann Gottlieb Fichte rose to prominence at an early stage.

129. François Mignet, French historian and journalist. He and his friend Thiers played an important part in the liberal opposition to the government of Charles X.

I almost despair of being able to convey an accurate idea of the importance of this man. In the case of Kant we had only a book to examine. But here, besides the book we have to examine the man. In this man thought and conviction were one, and in this magnificent unity they influenced the contemporary world. Thus we have not only a philosophy to discuss but a personality by which that philosophy is conditioned, so to speak, and in order to understand the influence of both, a description of the contemporary state of affairs would be necessary. What an extensive task! We shall surely be fully exonerated for offering here only meager information.

It is extremely difficult to give an account even of Fichte's ideas. We encounter peculiar difficulties, difficulties connected not merely with the subject matter but also with the form and method of presentation, two things with which we would like to make the foreigner acquainted at the very outset. First, then, concerning Fichte's method. Originally it was borrowed entirely from Kant, but it soon underwent a change because of the nature of the subject. Kant had only to put forward a critique, that is, something negative, whereas Fichte had, later on, to set up a system, consequently, something positive. Because of the lack of a definite system Kant's philosophy was sometimes denied the name "philosophy." As regards Immanuel Kant himself, this was correct, but certainly not as regards the Kantians, who constructed from Kant's propositions a quite sufficient number of definite systems. In his earlier writings Fichte remained, as I have said, entirely faithful to Kant's method, so much so that his first treatise, published anonymously, was understandably thought to be a work of Kant's. But when Fichte later set up a system, he was seized with an ardent and headstrong passion for construction, and after constructing the whole universe, he began, just as ardently and obstinately, to prove every detail of these constructions. In this constructing and proving Fichte manifests, so to speak, a passion for the abstract. As in his system itself, subjectivity also soon prevailed in his exposition. Kant, on the other hand, laid a thought before him, and dissected it, and analyzed it down to its most minute fibers, and his *Critique of Pure Reason* is a kind of anatomical theater of the intellect. During the dissection he himself remained cold and unfeeling, like a true surgeon.

The form of Fichte's works resembles the method. It is full of life, but it also has all the defects of life: it is unbalanced and confusing. In order to remain lively Fichte rejected the usual terminology of philosophers, which he felt to be dead, but this makes him still more difficult to understand. He had, after all, quite peculiar ideas about intelligibility. When Reinhold[130] shared an opinion with him, Fichte declared that no one understood him better than Reinhold. But when afterward the latter differed with him, Fichte declared that Reinhold had never understood him. When Fichte disagreed with Kant, he published the statement that Kant did not understand himself. I am here touching only on the comical aspect of our philosophers. They are forever complaining about not being understood. When Hegel was lying on his deathbed, he said, "Only one person has understood me," but immediately afterward he added crossly, "and even he didn't understand me."

As far as content alone is concerned, Fichte's philosophy is not of great importance. It provided no fruits for society. Only insofar as it is one of the most remarkable phases of all German philosophy, only insofar as it attests to the sterility of idealistic philosophy in its final consequences, and only insofar as it forms the necessary transition to present-day nature philosophy, is the content of Fichte's doctrine of some interest. Since this content is thus more important historically and scientifically than socially, I shall sketch it only very briefly.

The task that Fichte set himself was: what reasons do we have for assuming that there are objects external to us which correspond to our ideas of them? And to this question he gave the answer: all things have reality only in our minds.

Just as the *Critique of Pure Reason* is Kant's chief work, the *Science of Knowledge* is Fichte's. The latter work is a kind of continuation of the former. The *Science of Knowledge* likewise directs the mind back to itself. But where Kant analyzes, Fichte constructs. The *Science of Knowledge* begins with an abstract equation ($I = I$); it creates the world out of the depths of the mind; it reunites the fragmented parts; it retraces its course along the road of abstraction until it reaches the world of phenomena. The

130. Karl Leonhard Reinhold (1758–1823), for a long time professor at the University of Jena, was the first to call the attention of a wider public to Kant's philosophy.

mind can then declare the phenomenal world to be a necessary operation of the intelligence.

With Fichte there is also the special difficulty that he attributes to the mind the ability to observe itself while it is active. The ego is supposed to reflect on its intellectual activities while performing them. Thought is to spy upon itself while it thinks, while it gradually becomes warm, then warmer, and is finally cooked to a turn. This operation reminds us of the monkey sitting on the hearth in front of a copper kettle, cooking his own tail. For it was his opinion that true culinary art does not consist merely in the objective act of cooking but also in becoming subjectively aware of the process of cooking.

It is a singular circumstance that Fichte's philosophy always had to endure a great deal of satire. I once saw a caricature representing a Fichtean goose. It had such a large liver that it no longer knew whether it was a goose or a liver. On its stomach was written: I = I. Jean Paul has subjected Fichtean philosophy to the most exorbitant ridicule in a book entitled *Clavis Fichteana*. To the general public the fact that idealistic philosophy, pursued consistently to its ultimate conclusions, should end by denying even the reality of matter seemed to be carrying the joke too far. We rather enjoyed making fun of the Fichtean Ego, which created by mere thought the whole physical world. The mockers among us were aided by a misunderstanding that had become too popular to permit me to leave it unmentioned. The great mass of people really thought that the Fichtean Ego was the ego of Johann Gottlieb Fichte, and that this individual ego denied all other existences. "What impudence!" exclaimed the good people, "this fellow doesn't believe that we exist, we who are far more corpulent than he is and, as mayors and magistrates, are actually his superiors!" The ladies asked, "Doesn't he at least believe in the existence of his wife? No? And Madame Fichte doesn't mind?"

The Fichtean Ego, however, is not an individual ego, but the universal world-Ego awakened to self-awareness. The Fichtean process of thought is not the thinking of an individual, of a certain person called Johann Gottlieb Fichte; quite the contrary—it is the universal thought manifesting itself in an individual. Just as we say, "It is raining," "It is lightning," and so on, so Fichte ought not to say, "I think," but "It thinks," "Universal world-thought is thinking in me."

In a comparison between the French Revolution and German philosophy I once, more in jest than in earnest, compared Fichte with Napoleon. But there are, in fact, remarkable similarities between them. After the Kantians had completed their terroristic work of destruction, Fichte appeared, just as Napoleon appeared after the Convention had demolished the whole past, and like the Kantians by using a critique of pure reason. Napoleon and Fichte represent the great inexorable Ego in which thought and action are one, and the colossal structures successfully created by both testify to a colossal will. But due to the boundlessness of this will their structures soon collapsed, and both the *Science of Knowledge* and the Empire disintegrated and vanished as quickly as they arose.

The Empire is now nothing but history, but the agitation which the Emperor produced in the world has not yet subsided, and from this agitation our times still draw their vitality. So it is also with Fichte's philosophy. It has completely perished, but men's minds are still excited by the thoughts that found a voice in Fichte, and the after-effect of his words is incalculable. Even supposing all transcendental idealism was an error, yet Fichte's writings were animated by a proud independence, a love of liberty, a manly dignity that have had a wholesome influence, especially on the young. The Ego of Fichte was in complete accord with his inflexible, stubborn, austere character. The theory of such an all-powerful Ego could perhaps originate only from such a character, and such a character, rooted in such a theory, could not but become still more inflexible, more stubborn, more austere.

How unscrupulous sceptics, frivolous eclectics, and moderates of all shades must have loathed this man! His whole life was a constant battle. The story of his youth, like that of almost all our distinguished men, is a series of afflictions. Poverty sits by their cradles and rocks them to manhood, and this scrawny nurse remains their faithful companion through life.

Nothing is more touching than the sight of the proud-willed Fichte struggling to make his way in the world by being a private tutor. He could not find even this wretched servant's wage in his own country and had to go to Warsaw. There it was the old story. The tutor fails to please the gracious lady of the house, or perhaps even the ungracious lady's maid. His bows are not genteel enough, not French enough, and he is no longer judged worthy of directing the education of a young Polish nobleman. Johann Gottlieb Fichte was dismissed like a lackey, received from his dissatisfied employers scarcely a meager sum for traveling expenses, left Warsaw, and, with youthful enthusiasm, went to Königsberg to make the acquaintance of Kant. The meeting of these two men is interesting in every respect, and I do not think I can illustrate their ways and their circumstances better than by citing a fragment from Fichte's diary, to be found in a biography of him recently published by his son.[131]

"On the 25th of June I set out for Königsberg with a coachman from there and arrived without any particular hazards on the first of July.—On the fourth I visited Kant, who did not, however, receive me with any special attention. I attended a lecture of his at his invitation and again found my expectations disappointed. His delivery is dull. Meantime I have begun this journal.—

"I have long wished for a more serious interview with Kant, but found no way of bringing this about. At last I hit upon the plan of writing a 'Critique of All Revelation' and of presenting it to him instead of a letter of introduction. I began about the thirteenth and since then have been working at it continuously.—On the eighteenth of August I finally sent the completed work to Kant, and on the twenty-third went to call on him to hear his opinion of it. He received me with the most marked kindness and seemed very well satisfied with my essay. We did not get into any detailed scholarly discussion; in regard to my philosophical doubts he referred me to his *Critique of Pure Reason* and to the court chaplain, Schulz, whom I shall look up immediately. On the twenty-sixth I dined with Kant in the company of Professor Sommer, and I found Kant to be a very pleasant and clever man. I now for the first time perceived in him traits worthy of the great intellect that reposes in his writings.

"On the twenty-seventh I brought this journal entry to a close, after having completed the excerpts from Kant's lectures on anthropology, lent me by Mr. von S. At the same time I resolve

131. *Johann Gottlieb Fichte's Life and Literary Correspondence* by Immanuel Hermann Fichte, published 1830–1831.

from now on to continue this journal regularly every evening before going to bed and to record everything of interest that happens to me, but especially traits of character and observations.

"The twenty-eighth, evening. Yesterday I began to revise my 'Critique,' and many good and profound ideas occurred to me which, however, unfortunately convinced me that the first version is completely superficial. Today I wanted to continue my new investigations, but found myself so carried away by my imagination that I have not been able to do anything all day. Alas, in my present position this is not surprising. I have calculated that, counting from today, I can subsist here only fourteen more days.—To be sure, I have been in such straits before, but it was in my own country, and besides, with advancing years and a stronger sense of honor, such circumstances become harder and harder to endure.—I have made no decision, cannot make one.—I don't want to confide in Pastor Borowski, to whom Kant sent me; if I must confide in someone, it will be to no one but Kant himself.

"On the twenty-ninth I visited Borowski and found him to be a truly good and honorable man. He suggested a position for me, but it is not yet absolutely definite and besides, I don't like it. At the same time, by the frankness of his manner, he extorted from me the admission that I was in dire need of finding a position. He advised me to go to Professor W. It has been impossible for me to work.—The following day I did in fact call on W. and afterwards visited the court chaplain, Schulz. The prospects held out by the former are very uncertain; still he mentioned positions as house tutor in Kurland, which certainly nothing but the most extreme necessity will induce me to accept! Afterwards to the court chaplain, where I was received first by his wife. He appeared too, but preoccupied with mathematical circles; afterwards, when he heard my name more clearly, he was all the more amiable because of Kant's recommendation. He has an angular, Prussian face, but honesty and congeniality shine forth from his features. I also met there a Mr. Bräunlich and his ward, Count Dönhof, Mr. Büttner, nephew of the court chaplain, and a young scholar from Nuremberg, Mr. Ehrhard, a fine and decent fellow, but without refinement and worldliness.

"By the first of September I had made a firm decision which I wanted to tell Kant about. A position as private tutor, however reluctantly I might have accepted it, is not to be found, and the uncertainty of my situation prevents me from working here with freedom of mind and benefiting from the instructive association with my friends. So off, and back to my own country! The small loan that I need for this purpose will perhaps be obtained through Kant's good offices. But as I was about to go to him and make my proposal, my courage failed me. I decided to write. For the evening I was invited to the court chaplain's, where I spent a very pleasant evening. On the second I finished the letter to Kant and sent it off."

Despite the remarkableness of this letter, I cannot bring myself to give it here in French. I fancy a red blush mounting to my cheeks, and I feel as if I were relating in the presence of strangers the most humiliating troubles of my own family. In spite of my striving for French urbanity, in spite of the cosmopolitanism of my philosophy, old Germany, with all its petty bourgeois sentiments, still holds its place in my heart.—Enough, I cannot transmit this letter and shall simply relate: Immanuel Kant was so poor that, notwithstanding the pathetic, heartrending tone of the letter, he could not lend Johann Gottlieb Fichte any money. The latter was not in the least annoyed by this, as we can see from the words in his journal which I shall add here:

"On the third of September I was invited to Kant's. He received me with his usual candor, telling me, however, that he had not yet come to a decision about my proposal, that he would not be able to do so for two weeks. What kind frankness! For the rest, he raised objections to my plans which revealed that he is not sufficiently familiar with our situation in Saxony.—During all these days I have done nothing, but I want to set to work again and simply leave the rest to God.—The sixth.—I was invited to Kant's, and he suggested that I sell my manuscript on the 'The Critique of All Revelation' to the publisher Hartung, through the intervention of Pastor Borowski. 'It is well written,' he said, when I spoke of revising it.—Is this true? And yet Kant says so!—I might add that he refused my first request.—On the tenth I had lunch at Kant's. Nothing said about our affair; Magister Gensichen was present, and only general conversation, in part very interesting. And Kant remains the same toward me, completely unchanged.—On the thirteenth, today, I wanted to work, and I get nothing done. I am

overcome by depression. How will this end? How will things be a
week from now? By that time my money will be all gone!"

After much wandering about and after a long stay in Switzerland,
Fichte finally found a permanent position at Jena, and his most
brilliant period dates from this time. Jena and Weimar, two little
Saxon towns only a few hours distant from each other,[132] were
then the center of German intellectual life. At Weimar were the
court and poetry; at Jena, the university and philosophy. *There* we
saw the greatest poets, *here* the greatest scholars of Germany. In
1794 Fichte began his lectures at Jena. The date is significant and
explains the spirit of his writings at this period as well as the
tribulations to which he was exposed from then on and to which,
four years later, he finally succumbed. For in 1798 there were
raised against him the accusations of atheism which brought
insufferable persecutions upon him and were also the cause of his
departure from Jena. This event, the most noteworthy in Fichte's
life, has a general significance too, and we must not pass over it
in silence. This is also the natural place to speak of Fichte's views
concerning the nature of God.

In the periodical *The Philosophical Journal,* of which Fichte was
then the editor, he published an article called "The Development
of the Concept of Religion," sent to him by a certain Forberg, a
schoolteacher in Saalfeld. To this article he appended a short
explanatory essay with the title "Concerning the Basis of Our Belief
in a Divine Government of the Universe."[133]

Both articles were suppressed by the government of the Electorate
of Saxony under the pretext that they contained atheistic doctrine,
and at the same time a requisition was sent from Dresden to the
court of Weimar demanding that it punish Professor Fichte severely.
The court of Weimar had of course not let itself be misled by such
a demand, but since Fichte on this occasion committed the gravest
blunders, namely, writing an appeal to the public[134] without
consulting official authorities, the Weimar government, annoyed
at this action and under pressure from outside, had no alternative

132. Hours by coach or on horseback, of course.
133. In this article Fichte declared that God and the moral order of the universe
were synonymous.
134. "Appeal to the Public. A Work the Public Is Requested to Read Before It
Is Suppressed," published in Jena and Leipzig, 1799.

but to goad with a mild reproof the professor who had been so
indiscreet in expressing his views. Fichte, however, believing himself
to be in the right, had no intention of submitting humbly to such
reproof and left Jena. To judge from his letters written at this time,
he was particularly annoyed at the behavior of two men who, due
to their official positions, had an especially weighty voice in his
affair; these persons were His Reverence the President of the
Consistorial Council, von Herder, and His Excellency the Privy
Councillor, von Goethe. But there is sufficient excuse for both. It
is touching to read in Herder's posthumous letters how much
difficulty the poor man had with the candidates in theology who,
after studying at Jena, came to him in Weimar to undergo
examination as Protestant ministers. He no longer dared to ask
them anything about Christ the Son; he was only glad if they
merely acknowledged the existence of the Father. As for Goethe,
he expressed himself about this occurrence in his memoirs as
follows:

"After Reinhold's departure from Jena, which quite rightly
appeared to be a great loss for the University, Fichte had rashly,
even audaciously, been appointed as his successor, a man who had
expressed himself in his writings with grandeur, but perhaps not
quite properly concerning the most important topics of morality
and politics. He was one of the most able men ever seen, and,
considered in their broader aspects, there was nothing to find fault
with in his views, but how could he conform to a world which he
regarded as his own created possession?

"Objections having been raised to the hours he wanted to use
on weekdays for public lectures, he undertook to give on Sundays
the lectures that had met obstacles. The annoyances arising from
this, some petty, others of more importance, had scarcely been
smoothed over and adjusted, not without inconvenience for the
higher authorities, when his remarks about God and things divine,
about which, to be sure, it is better to maintain profound silence,
brought us protests from outside circles.

"In his *Philosophical Journal* Fichte had ventured to express
himself about God and things divine in a way that seemed to
contradict the traditional language used in dealing with such
mysteries. He was called to account for this; his defense did not
improve matters because he set to work passionately, without any

idea of how well disposed people here were towards him, how well they understood how to interpret his ideas, his language—a thing that couldn't just be explained to him bluntly—and with just as little idea of how people were intending to help him out of the affair with as much lenience as possible. Innumerable discussions, surmises and assertions, corroborations and resolutions, surged confusedly through the university in frequent indecisive deliberations; there was talk of a reproach from the Ministry, of nothing less than a kind of reprimand which Fichte might have to expect. Distraught at hearing this, Fichte considered himself justified in presenting to the Ministry a violent document in which, assuming the certainty of this action against him, he declared vehemently and defiantly that he would never submit to such treatment, that he would rather quit the university without further ado, in which case he would not go alone, as several influential teachers, in agreement with him, were intending to leave the place.

"Because of this all the benevolent intentions that had been entertained in his behalf were now suddenly curbed, indeed paralyzed. No solution, no compromise was possible, and the kindest thing was to dismiss him without delay. Only then, after the affair was beyond remedy, did Fichte hear of the turn his friends had meant to give the matter, and he of course regretted his precipitate action, as we also regret it."

Isn't this the very essence of the ministerial Goethe, smoothing things over and hushing them up? In reality he censures Fichte only for having said what he thought and for not having said it with the customary euphemistic expressions. He finds fault not with the thought, but with the word. That deism, since Kant, had been annihilated in the German intellectual world was, as I have already said, a secret everyone knew, a secret, however, that was not to be shouted from the housetops. Goethe was as little of a deist as Fichte; he was a pantheist. But his very position on the heights of pantheism enabled Goethe, with his sharp eyes, to see through perfectly the untenableness of Fichtean philosophy, and his charitable lips could not but smile at it. To the Jews (and every deist is, after all, a Jew) Fichte's philosophy was necessarily an abomination; to the great pagan it was simply a folly. "The great pagan" is the name bestowed on Goethe in Germany. But this name is not entirely appropriate. Goethe's paganism is strangely modernized. His vigorous pagan nature shows itself in his clear, penetrating interpretation of all external phenomena, of all forms and colors. But at the same time Christianity endowed him with a more profound understanding; in spite of his rebellious antipathy toward it, Christianity initiated him into the mysteries of the spiritual world; he drank of the blood of Christ and thus came to understand the most secret voices of nature, like Siegfried, the hero of the *Nibelungen,* who suddenly understood the language of the birds when a drop of blood from the slain dragon moistened his lips. It is a remarkable thing that Goethe's pagan nature was permeated by our most modern sentimentality, that the antique marble pulsated in such a modern fashion, and that he sympathized just as deeply with the sorrows of a young Werther as with the joys of an ancient Greek god. Goethe's pantheism is therefore very different from pagan pantheism. To express myself briefly, Goethe was the Spinoza of poetry. The whole of Goethe's poetry is filled with the same spirit that is wafted toward us from the writings of Spinoza. There is no doubt whatsoever that Goethe paid undivided allegiance to Spinoza's doctrine. At any rate, he occupied himself with it throughout his entire life; in the first part of his memoirs as well as in the last volume, recently published, he frankly acknowledged this. I don't remember now where I read that Herder once exploded peevishly at the constant preoccupation with Spinoza, "If Goethe would only for once pick up some other Latin book than Spinoza!" But this applies not only to Goethe; quite a number of his friends, who later became more or less well-known as poets, paid homage to pantheism in their youth, and this doctrine flourished actively in German art before it attained supremacy among us as a philosophic theory. Just at Fichte's time, when idealism celebrated its most sublime flowering period in the realm of philosophy, it was being violently destroyed in the realm of art, and there began that famous revolution in art which even now is not at an end and which started with the struggle of the Romanticists, the mutinies of the Schlegel brothers, against the ancient classical regime.

As a matter of fact, our first Romanticists acted out of a pantheistic instinct which they did not themselves understand. The feeling which they took to be nostalgia for the Catholic mother church was of deeper origin than they themselves suspected, and their veneration and partiality for the traditions of the Middle Ages, for the popular beliefs, the Satanism, the sorcery, and the witchcraft of those times—all this was a suddenly awakened, though uncomprehended desire to return to the pantheism of the old Teutons, and what they really loved about it in its despicably befouled and maliciously mutilated form, was the pre-Christian religion of their ancestors. I must remind you here of the first section of this book, where I showed how Christianity absorbed the elements of the old Germanic religion, how these elements, after undergoing the most outrageous transformations, were preserved in the popular beliefs of the Middle Ages in such a way that the old worship of nature came to be regarded as nothing but wicked sorcery, the old gods as nothing but ugly demons, and their chaste priestesses as nothing but profligate witches. From this point of view the aberrations of our first Romanticists can be judged more leniently than is usually the case. They wanted to restore the Catholicism of the Middle Ages because they felt that in it were preserved many of the sacred relics of their earliest ancestors and many of the glories of their earliest national culture. It was these mutilated and desecrated relics that were so sympathetically attractive to their temperaments, and they detested Protestantism and Liberalism, which strove to destroy these relics together with the whole Catholic past.

But I shall return to this subject later. At present it is sufficient merely to mention that even in Fichte's time pantheism was penetrating German art, that even the Catholic Romanticists unconsciously followed this tendency, and that Goethe gave the movement its most definite expression. This is true already in *Werther,* where he yearns for a blissful identification with nature. In *Faust* he tries to establish a relationship with nature by a method boldly mystical and direct: he conjures up the mysterious forces of the earth by the spells from his book of magic. But it is in his lyrics that Goethe's pantheism reveals itself with greatest purity and charm. Spinoza's doctrine has burst out of its mathematical cocoon and flutters about us as Goethean song. Hence the rage of our orthodox believers and pietists against Goethe's lyrics. With their pious bears' paws they grope clumsily for this butterfly that constantly eludes them. It is so delicately ethereal, so airily winged. You French can have no idea of it if you do not know the language. These lyrics of Goethe's have a tantalizing charm that is indescribable. The melodious lines cling to your heart like a dearly beloved; the word embraces you as the thought kisses you.

Thus we do not see in Goethe's behavior toward Fichte any of the base motives characterized in even baser language by many contemporaries. They had not understood the different natures of the two men. The most moderate among them misinterpreted Goethe's passivity when, later, Fichte was sorely pressed and persecuted. They did not take into consideration Goethe's situation. This giant was minister in a lilliputian German state. He could never act naturally. It was said of the seated Jupiter of Phidias at Olympia that he would shatter the dome of the temple if he were suddenly to stand up. This was precisely Goethe's position at Weimar; if he had suddenly jumped to his feet from the tranquility of his sitting posture, he would have shattered the housetop of the state, or, what is more probable, he would have broken his head against it. And was he to risk this for a doctrine that was not merely wrong, but also absurd? The German Jupiter remained calmly seated and allowed himself to be worshipped in peace and perfumed with incense.

It would lead me too far from my subject if I tried, from the standpoint of the artistic interests of that time, to justify even more thoroughly Goethe's conduct on the occasion of the accusation against Fichte. In Fichte's favor there is only the fact that the accusation was in reality a pretext behind which political persecution was concealed. A theologian can certainly be accused of atheism because he has obligated himself to teach certain doctrines. A philosopher, however, has not entered into any such obligation, cannot do so, and his thought remains as free as a bird in the air. It is perhaps unfair of me that, partly to spare my own feelings, partly to spare those of others, I do not state here all the circumstances on which that accusation was founded and justified. I shall quote only one of the dubious passages from the censured essay: "—The living and active moral order is itself God; we need no other God, nor can we comprehend any other. There is no basis in human reason for going beyond this moral order of the universe and for assuming, as a conclusion from effect to cause, some special being as the source of this effect. Consequently, the natural intelligence of man certainly does not come to this conclusion; only a philosophy that fails to understand itself deduces it.—"

As is characteristic of stubborn people, Fichte, in his "Appeal to the Public" and in his judicial vindication, spoke out even more sharply and harshly and in language that offends our deepest feelings. We who believe in a real God, a God who reveals Himself to our senses in infinite space and to our spirit in infinite thought; we who worship in nature a visible God and hear His invisible voice in our own souls; we are repelled by the harsh words with which Fichte declares our God to be a mere chimera and even treats Him with irony. It is doubtful, in fact, whether it is irony or simple madness when Fichte frees the dear Lord so absolutely from any sentient attribute that he even denies His existence, since existence is a sentient concept and is only possible as such! "The science of knowledge," he says, "knows no other mode of existence but the sentient, and since existence can be attributed only to the phenomena of experience, this predicate cannot be used to apply to God." Accordingly, Fichte's God has no existence; He does not exist; He manifests Himself only as pure action, as a sequence of events, as *ordo ordinans*,[135] as the law of the universe.

It is in such a way that idealism filtered deity through every possible abstraction until in the end not a vestige of it remained. From then on, instead of a king, as with you, instead of a god, as with us, law was sovereign.

But which is more absurd, a *loix athée*,[136] a law that has no god, or a *Dieu-loix*,[137] a god who is only a law?

Fichtean idealism is one of the most colossal errors ever contrived by the human mind. It is more godless and more detestable than the grossest materialism. What is called here in France the atheism of the materialists would be, as I could easily demonstrate, an edifying and devout doctrine in comparison with the consequences of Fichte's transcendental idealism. This much I know: both are repugnant to me. Both views are also anti-poetic. The French materialists have written just as bad verses as the German transcendental idealists. But Fichte's doctrine was not at all dangerous to the State and deserved still less to be persecuted as such. In order to be capable of being led astray by this heresy, one had need of a speculative acumen to be found only in very few people.

135. Regulating order.
136. Law of atheism.
137. A God-law.

This false doctrine was completely inaccessible to the great masses with their thousands of thick heads. Fichte's views about God should have been refuted, therefore, by the use of reason, but not by the use of the police. The accusation of atheism in philosophy was something so strange even in Germany that at first Fichte really did not understand what it meant. He said, and quite rightly, that the question as to whether a certain philosophy was atheistic or not sounded to a philosopher just as peculiar as the question whether a triangle was green or red would sound to a mathematician.

This accusation thus had its secret motives, and Fichte soon understood them. Since he was the most honorable person in the world, we can put absolute trust in a letter to Reinhold in which he discusses these secret motives, and since this letter, dated May 22, 1799, describes the entire period and succeeds in giving a clear picture of the man's whole distressing predicament, we shall quote a part of it:

"Weariness and disgust determine[138] my decision, which I have already told you about, to disappear completely for a few years. From the view I took of the matter at that time, I was even convinced that duty required this decision, for in the midst of the present turmoil I would not be listened to anyway and would only make the turmoil worse; but after a few years when the first reaction of astonishment had calmed down, I would speak with all the greater force.—I now think differently. I dare not hold my tongue; if I keep silent now, I might very likely never again have a chance to speak out. Since the alliance between Russia and Austria, I have long thought probable what is now for me a complete certainty after the most recent events and especially since the shocking murder of the ambassadors,[139] about which people here are jubilant, and about which S. and G.[140] exclaimed, 'That's right, these dogs must be killed!', namely, that from now on despotism will defend itself desperately, that with the aid of Paul

138. In the original the past tense was used here, as is necessary to fit properly with what follows. Heine's occasional deviations from Fichte's text are usually not significant, but this one is.
139. On April 28, 1799, the French ambassadors Roberjot, Bonnier, and Jean Debry were attacked by Austrian hussars. Debry escaped; the others were murdered.
140. Schiller and Goethe.

and Pitt[141] it will become consistent, that the basis of its plan is to wipe out freedom of thought, and that the Germans will not hinder the attainment of this object.

"Don't imagine, for example, that the court of Weimar believed that attendance at the university would be adversely affected by my presence; it knows the opposite only too well. It was *forced* to remove me as the result of a general plan, strongly supported by the Electorate of Saxony. Burscher[142] in Leipzig, privy to these secrets, bet a considerable sum as early as the end of last year that I would be an exile by the end of this year. Voigt[143] was long ago won over to the opposition through Burgsdorf. The department of science at Dresden has announced that no one who specializes in modern philosophy will be promoted or, if already promoted, will not be allowed to advance further. In the Free School at Leipzig even Rosenmüller's enlightened views were thought suspicious.[144] Luther's Cathechism has recently been reintroduced there, and the teachers have once more been confirmed according to the symbolical books.[145] This sort of thing will keep on and will spread.—In short, nothing is more certain[146] than the absolute certainty that unless the French gain the most tremendous ascendancy and unless they accomplish a change in Germany, at least in a considerable portion of it, in a few years no one in Germany who is known to have thought a free thought in the course of his life will any longer find a resting-place.—So for me it is more certain than absolute certainty that even if I now find a modest niche somewhere, within a year or in two years at the most, I would be chased out of it again, and it is dangerous to let oneself be chased from place to place. Rousseau's case is an historical example.

"Suppose I should remain completely silent and never write another word—will I be left in peace on this condition? I think not. And suppose I could hope for this peace from the courts,

141. Paul, the czar of Russia from 1796 to 1801, and William Pitt (1759–1806), the famous English statesman.

142. A theologian and philosopher, professor at the University of Leipzig.

143. Secretary of state in Weimar.

144. Johann Georg Rosenmüller (1736–1815), from 1785 on professor of theology in Leipzig, established a modern Lutheran liturgy.

145. I.e., the officially recognized Protestant doctrines.

146. Here Heine again changed Fichte's wording. The original reads *es ist mir gewisser als* (it is more certain than).

won't the *clergy*, wherever I go, stir up the masses against me and incite them to stone me and then—request the governments to banish me as a person who disturbs the peace? But *can* I be silent? No, I really can't, for I have reason to believe that if anything of the German spirit can still be saved, it can be saved by my speaking, and by my silence philosophy would be totally and prematurely ruined. Those I do not trust to allow me to exist in silence, I trust even less to permit me to speak.

"But I shall convince them of the harmlessness of my doctrine.— Dear Reinhold, how can you think so well of these people! The more my reputation is cleared, the more innocent I appear, the blacker do these people become and the more enormous does my real crime become. I never did believe they were persecuting my so-called *atheism;* what they are persecuting in me is a free-thinker who is beginning to make himself *intelligible* (Kant's obscurity was his good fortune) and a disreputable *democrat;* they are frightened as by a ghost at the *independence* which, as they vaguely suspect, my philosophy is arousing."

I call attention once more to the fact that this letter was not written yesterday, but bears the date of May 22, 1799. The political conditions of that time possess a very sad resemblance to present-day conditions in Germany, except that then the spirit of liberty flourished more among scholars, poets, and other men of letters, while today this spirit finds expression much less among such men, but rather among the great active mass of people, among artisans and tradespeople. At the time of the first revolution, while a leaden, most Teutonic lethargy oppressed the people and a brutal calm prevailed in all of Germany, our literary life revealed the wildest seething and ferment. The most isolated author, living in some remote little corner of Germany, participated in this movement; though not being accurately informed about political events, he sensed their social importance with an almost intuitive affinity and expressed it in his writings. This phenomenon reminds me of the big sea shells which are sometimes placed as ornaments on our fireplace mantels and which, however distant they may be from the sea, nonetheless suddenly begin to roar as soon as the hour of flood tide arrives and the waves break against the coast. When the tide of the Revolution began to rise here in Paris, that great human ocean, when its waves surged and roared here, German hearts across the Rhine also roared and raged.—But they were so isolated, surrounded as they were by nothing but unfeeling porcelain, tea cups and coffee pots and Chinese pagodas that nodded their heads mechanically as if they understood what it was all about. Alas, our poor predecessors in Germany had to atone very bitterly for their revolutionary sympathies. Junkers and clerics played their coarsest and meanest tricks on them. Some of them fled to Paris and disappeared or died here in poverty and misery. I recently saw a blind fellow countryman who has been in Paris since that time. I saw him at the Palais Royal, where he had been warming himself a bit in the sun. It was painful to see how pale and thin he was and how he groped his way along the sides of the houses. They told me he was the old Danish poet Heiberg.[147] I also saw not long ago the attic in which citizen Georg Forster died.[148] The friends of liberty who remained in Germany would have had a far worse fate if Napoleon and his Frenchmen had not soon conquered us. Napoleon certainly never had any idea that he himself had been the saviour of ideology. Without him our philosophers along with their ideas would have been exterminated by the gallows and the wheel. But the German friends of liberty, too republican in their sentiments to do homage to Napoleon, and too honorable to ally themselves with a foreign rule, from this time on veiled themselves in profound silence. They went about sorrowfully with broken hearts and sealed lips. When Napoleon fell, they smiled, though sadly, and were silent; they took scarcely any part in the patriotic enthusiasm which then, with the sanction of the highest authorities, burst forth jubilantly in Germany. They knew what they knew, and were silent. As these Republicans lead a very chaste and simple life, they usually live to be very old, and when the July Revolution broke out, many of them were still alive, and we were not a little surprised when the old fellows, whom we had always used to see walking around bent over and in almost imbecile silence, suddenly

147. Peter Andreas Heiberg (1758–1841), known chiefly for his comedies. Due to his liberal political opinions he was exiled from Denmark in 1799, and in 1800 he went to Paris, where he spent the rest of his life.
148. Johann Georg Forster (1754–1794) followed in the footsteps of his father to become a traveler and naturalist. His sympathy with the French Revolution led to his going to Paris in 1792 as deputy of the Jacobin Club in Mainz with the mission of effecting a union between France and the Rhineland left of the Rhine. He died in Paris two years later.

raised their heads, smiled affably at us young ones, shook hands with us, and told funny stories. I even heard one of them singing; he sang the *Marseillaise* for us in a café, and we learned the melody and the lovely words, and it wasn't long until we sang it better than the old man himself, for sometimes in the middle of the best stanza he would laugh like a fool or cry like a child. It is always a good thing when such old people remain alive to teach young ones the songs. We youngsters shall not forget them, and some of us will one day teach them to grandchildren not yet born. Many of us, however, will have rotted by that time, in prison at home or in an attic in a foreign country.

Let us talk about philosophy again. I have showed above how Fichte's philosophy, constructed of extremely tenuous abstractions, nonetheless manifested an iron inflexibility in its deductions, which ascended to the most audacious heights. But one fine morning we perceived a great change in this philosophy. It began to be florid, and it sniveled; it became gentle and modest. The idealistic Titan who had climbed to heaven on the ladder of ideas and had rummaged around with daring hand in its empty chambers became a creature bowed down with Christian humility who sighed a great deal about love. Such is Fichte's second period, which concerns us little here. His whole system of philosophy underwent the oddest modifications. During this time he wrote a book that you[149] recently translated, *The Destiny of Man.* A similar work, *The Way towards the Blessed Life,* also belongs to this period.

Naturally Fichte, obstinate man that he was, was never willing to admit his own great transformation. He maintained that his philosophy was still the same, except that the terminology had changed and improved; people had never understood him. He also maintained that nature philosophy, which was becoming fashionable in Germany at that time and was supplanting idealism, was, all of it, in principle his own system, and that his pupil, Mr. Joseph Schelling, who had renounced him and introduced this new philosophy, had merely revised the terminology and had amplified his, Fichte's, old theory with uninspiring additions.

We arrive here at a new phase of German thought. We have mentioned the names Joseph Schelling and nature philosophy, but

149. I.e., the French.

as the former is almost completely unknown here and even the term nature philosophy is not generally understood, I must explain the significance of both. It is, of course, impossible to do so exhaustively in this work; we shall devote a later book to this task. At present we shall simply refute certain errors that have crept in and devote some attention only to the social importance of this philosophy.

First of all I must mention that Fichte was not very far wrong in arguing that Mr. Joseph Schelling's doctrine was in reality his own, merely formulated differently and amplified. Just as did Mr. Joseph Schelling, Fichte also taught that there exists only one being, the Ego, the absolute, and he taught the identity of the ideal and the real. In the *Science of Knowledge,* as I have shown, Fichte attempted by means of an intellectual system of ideas to construct the real from the ideal. Mr. Joseph Schelling reversed the procedure; he tried to explain the ideal by the real. To express my meaning more clearly: proceeding from the axiom that thought and nature are one and the same, Fichte, by an operation of the intellect, arrived at the external world; from thought he created nature, from the ideal the real. For Mr. Schelling, however, though he started from the same axiom, the external world became pure ideas; for him nature became thought; the real became the ideal. The two tendencies, Fichte's and Schelling's, thus supplement each other to some extent. For according to the main axiom just referred to, philosophy can be divided into two parts, one of which would show how from the idea nature takes on phenomenal substance, and the other would show how nature resolves itself into pure ideas. Philosophy can therefore be divided into transcendental idealism and nature philosophy. Mr. Schelling actually acknowledged the validity of both tendencies; the latter he pursued in his *Ideas towards a Philosophy of Nature,* and the former in his *System of Transcendental Idealism.*

I mention these works, one of which appeared in 1797 and the other in 1800, only because those reciprocally complementary tendencies are expressed in their very titles and not, for instance, because they contain a complete system. No, such a system is not to be found in any of Mr. Schelling's works. Unlike Kant and Fichte, there is no main work of his that may be considered the focal point of his philosophy. It would be unjust to judge Mr.

Schelling by the scope of one book or by a strict interpretation of the letter. On the contrary, one must read his books in chronological order, follow in them the gradual development of his thought, and then take firm grasp of his fundamental idea. Indeed, it also often seems to me necessary, in reading his works, to distinguish where thought ceases and poetry begins. For Mr. Schelling is one of those beings on whom nature bestowed more inclination to poetry than poetic power and who, incapable of satisfying the daughters of Parnassus, fled to the forests of philosophy, where he entered into an utterly barren union with abstract hamadryads. The feeling of such persons is poetic, but the instrument, the word, is feeble; they strive in vain for an art form in which to communicate their ideas and their knowledge. Poetry is Mr. Schelling's strength and his weakness. This is what distinguishes him from Fichte, both to his advantage and to his disadvantage. Fichte is merely a philosopher; his power consists in dialectic, and his strength lies in demonstration. This, however, is Schelling's weak side; he lives among intuitive perceptions; he does not feel at home on the cold heights of logic; he likes to slip over into the flowery valleys of symbolism, and his philosophical strength lies in the art of synthesis. But this is an intellectual aptitude found as frequently among second-rate poets as among the best philosophers.

From this last indication it becomes clear that Mr. Schelling, in that part of philosophy which is purely transcendental idealism, remained, and had to remain, only a parrot of Fichte, but that in the philosophy of nature, where he had to do with flowers and stars, he could not help but blossom and shine brilliantly. Not only he himself, but also like-minded friends, pursued this direction by preference, and the tumult that accompanied it was, so to speak, only the reaction of poetasters against the former abstract philosophy of the intellect. Like schoolboys set free after groaning all day in classrooms under the burden of memorizing vocabulary and doing arithmetic, Mr. Schelling's pupils stormed out into nature, into the fragrant, sunny world of the real, shouting with joy, turning somersaults, and making a tremendous uproar.

The expression "Mr. Schelling's pupils" must not be taken in its usual sense. Mr. Schelling himself said he had intended to found a school only after the fashion of the ancient poets, a school of poets in which no one is bound to a specific doctrine nor by a specific discipline, but one in which each member obeys the spirit and reveals it in his own way. He might also have said that he was founding a school of prophets in which the inspired begin to prophesy according to their own desire and fancy and in whatever tongue they pleased. This, in fact, was actually done by the disciples whom the master's spirit had moved, the most shallow-brained began to prophesy, each in a different tongue, and a great day of Pentecost in philosophy ensued.

We see here in the case of philosophy how the most significant and sublime things can be used for pure masquerade and tomfoolery and how a rabble of cowardly knaves and melancholy clowns is capable of compromising a great idea. But this philosophy really does not deserve the ridicule brought upon it by Schelling's school of pupils or school of poets. For the fundamental idea of nature philosophy is indeed basically nothing but the idea of Spinoza, pantheism.

Spinoza's doctrine and nature philosophy, as set forth by Schelling during his better period, are essentially one and the same. After scornfully rejecting Locke's materialism and carrying Leibnitz' idealism to extremes and then finding it equally unfruitful, the Germans finally arrived at the third son of Descartes, Spinoza. Philosophy had once more completed a great circle, the same, it may be said, that it had already traversed in Greece two thousand years before. But a closer comparison of these two circles reveals an essential difference. The Greeks had just as daring sceptics as do we; the Eleatics denied the reality of the external world just as positively as our modern transcendental idealists. Plato rediscovered the world of thought in the world of phenomena just as did Mr. Schelling. But we have an advantage over the Greeks as well as over the Cartesian schools, namely, that we began our philosophical orbit with an investigation of the sources of human knowledge, with our Immanuel Kant's *Critique of Pure Reason*.

On mentioning Kant I might add to the above observations that the proof for the existence of God which Kant allowed to stand, namely, the so-called moral proof, was overthrown with great éclat by Mr. Schelling. I have already remarked, however, that this proof was not very sound and that Kant had perhaps let it stand just from sheer good nature. Mr. Schelling's God is the God-universe of Spinoza—at any rate, this is what he was in 1801, in the second volume of the *Journal of Speculative Physics*. Here God is the absolute identity of nature and thought, of matter and mind, and this absolute identity is not the cause of the universe, but is the universe itself, consequently the God-universe. In it there exist neither opposites nor divisions. Absolute identity is also absolute totality. A year later Mr. Schelling developed his God still further in a work entitled *Bruno, or Concerning the Divine or Natural Principle of Things*. This title recalls the noblest martyr of our doctrine, Giordano Bruno of Nola,[150] of glorious memory. The Italians maintain that Mr. Schelling borrowed his best ideas from old Bruno and accuse him of plagiarism. They are wrong, for there is no such thing as plagiarism in philosophy. In 1804 Mr. Schelling's God appeared at last in his complete form in a work called *Philosophy and Religion*. Here we find the doctrine of the absolute in its entirety, expressed in three formulas. The first is the categorical: The absolute is neither the ideal nor the real (neither mind nor matter), but is the identity of both. The second formula is the hypothetical: When a subject and an object are present, the absolute is the essential equality of both. The third formula is the disjunctive: There is only *one* being, but this unity of being can be regarded, at one and the same time, or alternately, as wholly ideal or as wholly real. The first formula is strictly negative, the second posits a condition even more difficult to understand than the hypothesis itself, and the third formula is exactly the same as Spinoza's: Absolute substance is cognizable either as thought or as spatial dimension. On the path of philosophy, therefore, Mr. Schelling could go no further than Spinoza, since the absolute can be comprehended only under the form of these two attributes, thought and spatial dimension. But at this point Mr. Schelling abandons the philosophical route and seeks by a kind of mystical intuition to arrive at the contemplation of the absolute itself; he seeks to contemplate it in its very center, in its essence, where it is neither ideal nor real, neither thought nor spatial dimension, neither subject nor object, neither mind nor matter, but—Heaven knows what!

Here philosophy stops with Schelling, and poetry—I mean folly—begins. But it is here that he finds the greatest support from a lot

150. Bruno (1548–1600) believed in a kind of pantheism, in opposition to the Catholic Church. He was imprisoned as a heretic for several years and was finally burned at the stake.

of scatterbrains whom it suits admirably to abandon calm reflection and to imitate, as it were, those dancing dervishes who, as our friend Jules David tells,[151] spin around in a circle until both objective and subjective worlds vanish and the two worlds blend into a colorless nothing that is neither real nor ideal, until they see things that are invisible, hear what is inaudible, until they hear colors and see tones, until the absolute reveals itself to them.

It is my opinion that with the attempt to perceive the absolute intellectually Mr. Schelling's philosophical career came to a close. A greater thinker now appeared who developed nature philosophy into a complete system, explained from its synthetic basis the whole world of phenomena, supplemented the great ideas of his predecessors by greater ones, subjected these ideas to all disciplines, and thus established them on a scientific basis. He was a pupil of Mr. Schelling's, but a pupil who gradually seized possession of all his master's influence in the realm of philosophy, and, eager for power, outstripped him, and finally thrust him into obscurity. This is the great Hegel, the greatest philosopher Germany has produced since Leibnitz. There is no doubt that he far surpasses Kant and Fichte. He is as penetrating as the former and as forceful as the latter, and possesses in addition a fundamental tranquility of mind, a harmony of thought, not to be found in Kant and Fichte, in both of whom a revolutionary spirit prevails. To compare this man with Mr. Joseph Schelling is simply impossible, for Hegel was a man of character. And though, like Schelling, he bestowed on the existing order in state and church some all too dubious vindications, he did so for a state which, in theory at least, does homage to the principle of progress, and for a church which regards the principle of free inquiry as its vital element. And he made no secret of this; he openly admitted all his intentions. Mr. Schelling, on the other hand, goes cringing about in the antechambers of practical and theoretical absolutism, and he lends a hand in the Jesuits' den, where fetters for the mind are forged; and all the while he wants to fool us into believing that he is still unalterably the same man of enlightenment he once was; he disavows his disavowal, and to the disgrace of apostasy he adds the cowardice of lying!

151. Probably Félicien César David, composer and Saint-Simonist, who lived in the Orient in 1833–34.

We must not conceal, either out of loyalty or prudence, and we do not wish to keep it a secret, that the man who proclaimed the religion of pantheism most daringly in Germany, who announced most loudly the sanctification of nature and the reinstatement of man in his God-given rights—this man has become apostate to his own doctrine; he has forsaken the altar which he himself consecrated; he has slunk back into the religious kennels of the past; he is now a good Catholic and preaches an extramundane, personal God "who committed the folly of creating the world." Let the orthodox ring their bells and sing *Kyrie eleison* over such a conversion—it still is no proof for their opinion; it proves only that man inclines toward Catholicism when he grows old and weary, when he has lost his physical and intellectual powers, when he can no longer either enjoy or reason. So many freethinkers have been converted on their deathbeds—but just don't boast about it. Such tales of conversion belong at best to pathology and would provide only poor testimony for your cause. After all, they prove only that it was impossible for you to convert those freethinkers as long as they were walking about with healthy senses under God's open heavens and were in complete possession of their reasoning faculty.

I believe it is Ballanche[152] who said it was a law of nature that initiators had to die as soon as they had completed the task of initiation. Alas, worthy Ballanche, this is only partly true, and I would prefer to maintain that when the task of initiation has been completed, the initiator dies—or becomes apostate. And so we can perhaps soften somewhat the severe judgment which thoughtful Germans pronounced on Mr. Schelling; we can perhaps transform into silent commiseration the grave and onerous contempt that is his burden and explain his desertion of his own doctrine merely as a consequence of the natural law that he who has devoted all his powers to the expression or the execution of an idea afterward collapses exhausted when he has expressed or executed this idea, collapses either into the arms of death or into the arms of his former opponents.

After such an explanation we understand perhaps even more

152. Pierre Simon Ballanche (1776–1847), a philosopher of history who tended toward a mystical type of socialism.

lurid phenomena of today which grieve us so profoundly. We understand perhaps why men who have sacrificed everything for their opinion, who have fought and suffered for it, finally, when it has won the victory, abandon that opinion and go over to the enemy camp. After such an explanation I might also point out that not only Mr. Joseph Schelling, but, to a certain extent, also Fichte and Kant, can be accused of desertion. Fichte died early enough, before his desertion of his own philosophy could become all too notorious. And Kant immediately became unfaithful to the *Critique of Pure Reason* by writing the *Critique of Practical Reason*. The initiator dies—or becomes apostate.

I don't know why this last sentence has such a depressingly paralyzing effect on my feelings that I am simply unable to communicate here the remaining bitter truths about Mr. Schelling as he is today. Instead let us praise that earlier Schelling, whose memory blooms unforgettably in the annals of German thought; for the earlier Schelling, like Kant and Fichte, represents one of the great phases of our philosophical revolution, which I have compared in these pages with the phases of the political revolution in France. Indeed, if one sees in Kant the terrorist Convention and in Fichte the Napoleonic Empire, in Mr. Schelling one sees the reaction of the Restoration which followed. But at first it was a restoration in the better sense. Mr. Schelling reinstated nature in its legitimate rights; he strove for a reconciliation between mind and nature; he tried to reunite them in the eternal world-soul. He restored that great nature philosophy which we find in the ancient Greek philosophers, which was first directed by Socrates more toward the human spirit itself, and which later blended with idealism. He restored that great nature philosophy which, sprouting up unobtrusively from the old pantheistic religion of the Germans, produced its fairest flowers during the age of Paracelsus, but was stifled by the introduction of Cartesianism. And, alas, he ended by restoring things which make it possible to compare him with the French Restoration in the bad sense. But then rational public opinion could no longer endure him, he was ignominiously driven from the throne of thought. Hegel, his major-domo, seized his crown and shaved his head, and since then the deposed Schelling has been living like a wretched monk in Munich, a city that shows even in its name its monkish character, and in Latin is called *monacho monachorum.*[153] I saw him there with his large, pale eyes and his dejected, stupefied face, wandering about irresolutely like a ghost, a pitiable picture of fallen grandeur. Hegel, however, had himself crowned in Berlin, unfortunately also anointed a little, and has ever since ruled supreme over German philosophy.

Our philosophical revolution is over. Hegel closed its great circle. Since then there has been only development and perfection of the doctrine of nature philosophy. As I have already said, this philosophy has penetrated into all branches of knowledge and has produced the most extraordinary and grandiose results. As I have also indicated, many undesirable effects inevitably appeared. The effects are so numerous that a whole book would be needed even to enumerate them. This is the really interesting and colorful part of our philosophical history. I am convinced, however, that it will be more beneficial for the French to learn nothing at all about this part, for such information could only contribute greater confusion in French minds; many propositions of nature philosophy, taken out of context, could cause considerable trouble among you. So much I know—if you had been familiar with German nature philosophy four years ago, you could never have carried out the July Revolution. For this act a concentration of ideas and of forces was necessary, a high-minded partiality, a complacent recklessness, such as only your old school of philosophy permitted. Preposterous philosophical ideas with which, in case of need, legitimacy and the Catholic doctrine of incarnation could be justified, would have dampened your enthusiasm and paralyzed your courage. Hence I regard it as significant for world history that your great eclectic,[154] who at that time wanted to teach you German philosophy, did not have the slightest understanding of it. His providential ignorance was salutary for France and for all mankind.

Alas, nature philosophy, which in many areas of knowledge, especially in the natural sciences, in the strict sense, produced the most glorious fruits, in other areas brought forth the most pernicious

153. "Munich of the monks." The German *München* is related to *der Mönch* (monk) and to an old parallel form *der Münch,* and all these words are derived from the Latin word for monk, *monachus.*
154. Victor Cousin. See above, p. 73, note 141.

weeds. While Oken,[155] a very brilliant thinker and one of Germany's greatest citizens, was discovering his new worlds of ideas and inspiring the youth of Germany with enthusiasm for the natural rights of man, for liberty and equality,—alas, at that very time Adam Müller[156] was lecturing on the stable-feeding[157] of nations according to the principles of nature philosophy; at that very time Mr. Görres[158] was preaching the obscurantism of the Middle Ages from the point of view of the natural sciences, maintaining that the state was only a tree and had to have in its organic structure a trunk, branches and leaves as well, all of which could be found so nicely in the corporate hierarchy of the Middle Ages; at that very time Mr. Steffens[159] was proclaiming the law of philosophy according to which the peasantry is distinguished from the nobility by the fact that the peasant is destined by nature to work without enjoying, whereas the nobleman is entitled to enjoy without working;—indeed, as I am told, a few months ago a dolt of a country squire in Westphalia, a fool by the name of Haxthausen, I believe, published a pamphlet in which he asked the Government of the King of Prussia to pay some attention to the consistent parallelism demonstrated by philosophy as existing in the organization of the world and to differentiate more strictly among the political estates; for just as there are in nature four elements, fire, air, water, and earth, so there are in society four analogous elements, namely, the nobility, the clergy, the middle class, and the peasants.

When such grievous follies were seen to sprout from philosophy and to grow into the most noxious flowers; when it was observed especially that German young people, absorbed in metaphysical abstractions, were oblivious to the most urgent questions of the time and became unfit for practical life, then indeed patriots and friends of liberty naturally felt a righteous indignation at philosophy,

---

155. Lorenz Oken (1779–1851), a nature philosopher, professor in Jena from 1807 on, for many years the editor of *Isis,* a liberal journal primarily devoted to the natural sciences.

156. A writer with a decidedly reactionary tendency (1779–1829). He presented the first extensive application of Romantic ideas to concrete political problems.

157. A note in the edition of Heine's works edited by Oskar Walzel (vol. VII, 498) suggests that Heine uses this unusual expression as an allusion to Müller's *Letters on Agronomy (Agronomische Briefe).*

158. See above, p. 19, note 55.

159. Henrich Steffens (1773–1845), born in Norway, a professor in Halle, Breslau, and Berlin, a disciple of Schelling's, conservative in his views.

and some went so far as to condemn it completely as an idle and useless tilting at windmills.

We shall not be so foolish as to refute these malcontents seriously. German philosophy is an important matter which concerns the whole human race, and only our latest descendants will be able to decide whether we should be blamed or praised for first developing our philosophy and afterward our revolution. In my opinion, a methodical people like us had to begin with the Reformation, only after that could it occupy itself with philosophy, and only after completion of the latter could it go on to political revolution. I find this sequence very rational. The heads that philosophy used for speculation can be cut off afterward by the revolution for any purpose it likes. But philosophy could never have used the heads cut off by a preceding revolution. Don't be uneasy, though, you German Republicans; the German revolution will not turn out to be any milder or gentler because it was preceded by Kant's *Critique*, Fichte's transcendental idealism, or even nature philosophy. Because of these doctrines revolutionary forces have developed that are only waiting for the day when they can break out and fill the world with terror and with admiration. Kantians will appear who have no more use for piety even in the world of appearances, who with sword and axe will mercilessly rummage around in the soil of our European culture in order to eradicate the last roots of the past. Armed Fichteans will enter on the scene who, in their fanaticism of will, can be restrained neither by fear nor by self-interest, for they live in the spirit and defy matter like the first Christians, who likewise could be subdued neither by bodily torture nor by bodily delights. In fact, in a time of social revolution such transcendental idealists would be even more obstinate than the early Christians, since the latter endured earthly martyrdom in order to attain salvation in heaven, while the transcendental idealist regards martyrdom itself as an empty appearance and is inaccessible within the entrenchment of his own thought. But nature philosophers would be more terrifying than anyone else, since they would actively take part in a German revolution and would identify themselves with the work of destruction. If the hand of the Kantian strikes a strong, unerring blow because his heart is not moved by any traditional reverence, if the Fichtean courageously defies every danger because for him danger simply doesn't exist in reality—the nature philosopher will be terrible because he allies himself with the primitive powers of nature, can conjure up the demonic forces of ancient German pantheism, and there awakens in him that lust for battle which we find among the ancient Germans and which fights not in order to destroy, nor in order to win, but simply in order to fight. Christianity—and this is its finest merit—subdued to a certain extent that brutal Germanic lust for battle, but could not destroy it, and if some day that restraining talisman, the Cross, falls to pieces, then the savagery of the old warriors will explode again, the mad berserker rage about which the Nordic poets have told so much. This talisman is decaying, and the day will come when it will sorrily disintegrate. The old stone gods will then arise from the forgotten ruins and wipe the dust of centuries from their eyes, and Thor will at last leap up with his giant hammer and smash the Gothic cathedrals. When you hear the crash and the clashing of arms, watch out, you neighbor children, you French, and don't meddle in what we are doing at home in Germany. It might cost you dearly. Take care not to fan the fire; take care not to put it out. You could easily burn your fingers in the flames. Don't smile at my advice, the advice of a dreamer who warns you against Kantians, Fichteans, and nature philosophers. Don't smile at the visionary who expects in the realm of reality the same revolution that has taken place in the realm of the intellect. The thought precedes the deed as lightning precedes thunder. German thunder is of course truly German; it is not very nimble but rumbles along rather slowly. It will come, though, and if some day you hear a crash such as has never been heard before in world history, you will know the German thunder has finally reached its mark. At this commotion the eagles will drop down dead from the skies, and the lions in the farthest desert of Africa will put their tails between their legs and hide themselves in their royal lairs. A play will be performed in Germany compared with which the French Revolution might seem merely an innocent idyll. Just now, to be sure, everything is rather quiet, and though here and there a few people create a little stir, don't think they are going to appear as the real actors in the piece. They are only the little curs running around in the empty arena, barking and snapping at each other, until the hour arrives when the troop of gladiators appears who are destined to fight in the struggle for life or death.

And the hour will come. As on the steps of an amphitheater, the nations will gather around Germany to witness the great contests. I advise you, you French, keep very quiet, and for Heaven's sake, don't applaud. We might easily misunderstand you and, in our rude fashion, might somewhat roughly shut you up. If in times past, in our servile, discontented state, we could sometimes overpower you, we could do so far more easily in the elation of our intoxication with liberty. You know yourselves what one is capable of in such a state—and you are no longer in that state. Beware then. I have your welfare at heart, and for this reason I tell you the bitter truth. You have more to fear from a free Germany than from the entire Holy Alliance together with all its Croats and Cossacks. For, in the first place, you are not loved in Germany, a thing which is almost incomprehensible, since you are really so lovable, and during your stay among us took such pains to please at least the better and more beautiful half of the German people. And even if this half loved you, it is just the half that does not bear arms and whose friendship is thus of little benefit to you. What you are actually accused of I could never understand. Once in a beer parlor in Göttingen a young German chauvinist[160] remarked that we ought to take revenge on the French for Konradin von Staufen whom they beheaded in Naples. You have probably forgotten that long since. But we forget nothing. So you see that if some day we take a notion to pick a quarrel with you, we won't lack for valid reasons. In any case, I advise you to be on your guard. Whatever happens in Germany, whether the Crown Prince of Prussia or Dr. Wirth[161] should come to power, keep yourselves armed; stay quietly at your posts, guns in your hands. I have your welfare at heart, and I was almost frightened when I heard recently that your Ministry intended to disarm France.

Since, despite your present romantic movement, you are born classicists, you are familiar with Olympus. Among the nude gods and goddesses amusing themselves while feasting on nectar and ambrosia, you may see one goddess who, though surrounded by such gaiety and pastime, nonetheless always wears a coat of mail, a helmet on her head, and keeps her spear in her hand.

She is the goddess of wisdom.

160. *Ein junger Altdeutscher.*
161. Johann Wirth, editor of the *Deutsche Tribüne*, a liberal journal, and active in political affairs.

Introduction to *Kahldorf Concerning the Nobility in Letters to Count M. von Moltke*

The Gallic cock has now crowed for the second time,[1] and in Germany, too, dawn is breaking. In remote monasteries, castles, Hansa towns, and similar last hiding places of the Middle Ages the uncanny shades and specters are now taking refuge. The sun's rays sparkle. We rub our eyes. The glorious sunlight presses into our hearts. The stir of life rustles around us. We are amazed, and we ask one another: "What did we do last night?"

Yes, we dreamed, in our German fashion; that is, we philosophized. True, not about matters which concerned us immediately or which had just happened; no, we philosophized about the reality of things in and of themselves, about the ultimate grounds of existence, and similar metaphysical and transcendental visions, while the bloody spectacle performed by our western neighbor sometimes disturbed us, nay, even irritated us, since not infrequently French bullets whistled their way straight into our philosophical systems and swept away whole shreds.

It is strange yet true that the practical activity of our neighbors on the other side of the Rhine has a unique elective affinity with our philosophical dreams in complacent Germany. By merely comparing the history of the French Revolution with that of

---

1. Reference to the second French revolution in July of 1830. Heine wrote this introduction in March of 1831, shortly before leaving Germany for Paris.

German philosophy one might be led to believe that the French, who had so much real business at hand, for which they had to stay awake, had asked us to sleep and dream for them and that our German philosophy is nothing but the dream of the French Revolution. Thus we have experienced a break with the status quo and tradition in the sphere of thought, just as the French have experienced theirs in the social sphere. Around the *Critique of Pure Reason* were assembled our philosophical Jacobins who would let nothing pass which had not stood the test of that *Critique;* Kant was our Robespierre. Then came Fichte, the Napoleon of philosophy, with his Ego, the highest Love and the highest Egoism, the omnipotence of thought, the sovereign will which rapidly improvised a universal empire, and which disappeared just as rapidly— the despotic, terrifyingly lonely idealism. Under its consistent footsteps the retiring flowers that had escaped the Kantian guillotine or had since sprouted unobserved sighed heavily; the oppressed earth spirits stirred; the ground shook; counter-revolution broke out; and under Schelling, the past with its traditional interests once more received recognition, and even indemnification, and during the new Restoration, in the Philosophy of Nature, the gray emigres— mysticism, pietism, Jesuitism, legitimacy, Romanticism, Germanism, complacency—who had constantly conspired against the supremacy of reason and the idea again raised havoc. Then came Hegel, the Orleans of Philosophy,[2] and established a new regime, or rather ordained one, an eclectic regime, in which, of course, he himself was of small importance, though he had been placed at its head, and in which he assigned fixed, constitutional posts to the old Kantian Jacobins, the Fichtean Bonapartists, the Schellingian peers, and his own creatures.

Thus, since we had successfully come full cycle in philosophy, it is natural that we now are proceeding into politics. Will we here follow the same course? Will we open our course with the system of the *Comité du salut public,*[3] or with the system of the *Ordre légal?*[4] These questions fill all hearts with trembling, and whoever

2. Reference to Louis Philippe, Duke of Orléans, the "Citizen King" of France, who assumed power following the July Revolution.
3. Committee of Public Safety, the ruling body during the Jacobins' rule of France.
4. Literally "legal order." Heine means by this the July monarchy.

has something precious to lose, be it only his own head, whispers timidly: "Will the German Revolution be a dry one, or a red and wet one?"

The aristocracy and the clergy constantly frighten us with specters of the time of the Terror; liberals and humanitarians on the other hand promise us the loveliest scenes of the Great Week and a most peaceful after-celebration. Both sides either deceive themselves, or wish to deceive others. Because the French Revolution of the nineties was so bloody and horrible, and that of last July was so humane and forebearing, we must not conclude that a German revolution will resemble either one or the other. Only when similar conditions prevail can we have similar results. The character of the French Revolution was determined at every moment by the moral condition of the people, and particularly their political education. Before the first eruption of the Revolution, a mature culture existed in France, but only among the upper classes, and here and there among the middle classes; the lower classes had been culturally neglected and kept from every noble aspiration by a narrow-minded despotism. So far as political education was concerned, it was lacking not only in the lower, but also in the upper strata of society. At that time one only heard about the petty maneuvers of rival corporations, mutual attempts to weaken one another, traditional routines, the art of equivocation, the influence of mistresses, and other such diplomatic miseries. Montesquieu had been able to arouse only a comparatively small number of minds. Since he wrote purely from a historical point of view, he had little influence on the masses of an enthusiastic nation which is most receptive to thoughts that are original and spring spontaneously from the heart, as they do in the works of Rousseau. However, when Rousseau, the Hamlet of France, perceived the angered spirit and saw through the deceitful character of the crowned poisoners, the hypocritical emptiness of their lackeys and flunkeys, the clumsy falsehoods of the court etiquette and the general rottenness, and cried out in sorrow, "The world is out of joint; woe is me, that I am supposed to set it right!" when Rousseau raised his voice in remonstrance and accusation, partly with feigned, partly with real desperation;— when Voltaire, the Lucian[5] of Christianity, destroyed with his

5. Late Greek satirist and sceptic of the second century.

ridicule the clerical fraud of Rome and the divine right of despotism
built upon it;—when Lafayette, the hero of two worlds and two
centuries,[6] returned from America with the Argonauts of freedom,
bringing with him the Golden Fleece, the idea of a free constitution;—when Necker calculated, and Sieyès defined, and Mirabeau
spoke,[7] and the thunders of the constituent assembly rolled over
the heads of the withering monarchy and its flourishing deficit, and
new economic and political ideas shot forth like sudden lightning;—
then for the first time the French were forced to learn the great
science of freedom—politics—and the study of the first rudiments
was expensive for them. It cost them their best blood.

It was the fault of the stupid, obscurantist despotism that the
French had to pay so high a tuition fee; for, as I have said, it had
sought to keep the people in mental immaturity; it had thwarted
all their efforts to acquire political education; it had transferred
the censorship of books to the Jesuits and the obscurantists of the
Sorbonne; and it had even suppressed, in the most ridiculous
fashion, the press, the mightiest instrument for the advancement
of popular knowledge. You have only to read the article on the
pre-Revolutionary censorship in Mercier's *Tableau de Paris*,[8] and
you will no longer be amazed at the crass political ignorance of
the French, which was responsible for the fact that they were
frequently more blinded than enlightened by the new political
ideas, more heated than warmed; that they gave credence to every
pamphleteer and journalist; and that they allowed themselves to
be seduced into the most extravagant actions by every self-deceived
visionary, and every intriguer suborned by Pitt.[9] For that is the
blessing bestowed by the freedom of the press, that it robs the bold
speech of the demagogue of all novel magic; it neutralizes the
passionate oration by an equally passionate counter-oration; it
strangles mendacious rumors in the cradle, which, whether planted
by accident or malice, multiply so fatally and shamelessly in the
dark, like those poisonous plants that thrive only in dismal forest

6. Lafayette participated in the American War of Independence as well as in
both French revolutions as leader of the National Guard.
7. Necker was the minister of finance under Louis XVI. Sieyès and Mirabeau
were both prominent representatives of the bourgeoisie during the first revolution.
8. Sebastian Mercier, dramatist and political writer, gave a comprehensive account
of pre-revolutionary French society in this twelve-volume work.
9. William Pitt, British minister and violent opponent of the French Revolution.

swamps, and in the shadows of ancient ruined castles and churches, but wither away miserably and pitifully in the bright light of the sun. Naturally, the bright sunlight of the freedom of the press is equally fatal to the slave who would rather receive his kicks from on high in the dark, and the despot, who would rather not see his lonely impotence exposed to the light. It is true that these people find censorship very comfortable. But it is no less true that censorship, while it may for the time being give an advantage to despotism, in the end destroys despotism along with the despot. Where once the guillotine of thought has done its work, there censorship of human beings is soon introduced. The slave who has been the executioner of thought will soon with the same equanimity erase his own masters from the book of life.

Alas, these executioners of thought make criminals of us; for the author, while he is writing, is as fretful and excited as a woman in child-birth, and under these circumstances, frequently commits infanticide of thought from the insane terror of the censor's sword of judgment. I myself have at this very moment suppressed new-born innocent reflections on the patience and equanimity with which my dear compatriots have for so many years suffered that thought-killing law, which, in France, Polignac had merely to promulgate to produce a revolution.[10] I am speaking of the famous ordinances, the most serious of which provided for a severe censorship of all newspapers and filled all noble hearts in Paris with dread. Even the most peaceful citizens seized arms. They barricaded the streets; they fought; they attacked; cannons thundered; bells pealed alarms; the leaden nightingales whistled. The young brood of the dead eagle, the students of the *École Polytechnique,* flew from their perches with lightning in their claws; the old pelicans of freedom rushed upon bayonets and with their own blood nourished the enthusiasm of the young. Lafayette mounted his charger, Lafayette the incomparable, whose equal Nature could not recreate, and hence in her economical fashion she sought to use him in two worlds and in two centuries. And after three heroic days, slavery lay undone, with its red-liveried gendarmes and its white lilies; and the holy tricolor, resplendent by the glory of

10. Prince Jules de Polignac, reactionary foreign minister under Charles X. He was one of the authors of the "Four Ordinances," which were among the immediate causes of the July Revolution.

victory, waved above the steeple of Our Dear Lady of Paris! There were no atrocities committed then, no wanton murders. Then the most Christian of guillotines was not erected; no gory jests were perpetrated, as for example occurred on the celebrated return from Versailles, when the bloody heads of MM. de Deshuttes and de Varicourt were borne aloft like standards,[11] and then washed and prettily dressed by a citizen hair-dresser at Sèvres.—No, since that day of horrible memory, the French press has made the people of Paris more receptive to finer sentiments and less sanguine jests. It has weeded out ignorance from their hearts and planted intelligence. And the fruit of that seed was the noble, legendary moderation and touching humanity of the Paris population during that great week. And indeed, if Polignac did not later lose his head physically, he owes his good fortune solely to the mild after-effects of that very freedom of the press, which, in his folly, he has sought to suppress.

Thus, the sandal-tree refreshes with its delicious fragrance the very foe who has heinously injured its bark.

I believe that in these cursory remarks I have sufficiently indicated that every question about the character that the German revolution might assume turns out to be a question about the cultural state and political education of the German people; that this education is wholly dependent on the freedom of the press; and that it is our most fervent wish that it may soon diffuse its light as far as possible, before the hour strikes when darkness may do more harm than passion, and opinions and views hitherto repressed or unuttered may all the more violently and horribly influence the blind populace and be used as battle cries by various parties.

In Germany, "civil equality" could now become the first battle cry, as it once was in France; a true friend of the fatherland should not hesitate if he wants to contribute to a balanced, even-handed, and peaceful discussion of the controversy *Concerning the Nobility*. For in short order disorderly disputants will be joining in with bodies of all too striking evidence, against which neither the chain-logic of the police, the sharpest arguments of the infantry and cavalry, nor even the *ultima ratio regis*—which can easily turn into

11. Both fell defending the royal chambers in Versailles in 1789.

the *ultimi ratio regis*[12]—will be able to accomplish a thing. In this gloomy respect I regard the publication of this work as a meritorious undertaking. I feel that the tone of moderation which dominates in it is suited to its implied purpose. The author is opposing, with the patience of a Buddha, a brochure entitled:

> *Concerning the Nobility and Its Relationship to the Middle Class*, by Count M. v. Moltke, Danish royal chamberlain and member of the Supreme Court at Gattorff. Hamburg: Perthes et Besser, 1830.

Yet in this brochure, as in the reply, the topic has hardly been exhausted, and the arguments hurled back and forth have only touched on the general, as it were, dogmatic part of the controversy. The well-born knight, mounted high atop his tournament steed, boldly asserts that medieval platitude which contends that noble breeding produced better blood than middle-class breeding; he defends privileges of birth, preference in lucrative diplomatic, military and court appointments, etc.; a noble should be rewarded for making the supreme effort of merely being born; and so forth. Against these views arises a combatant who knocks down piece by piece these bestial and preposterous assertions; and the battlefield is strewn with the glittering tatters of prejudice and the armorial rubble of old-aristocratic insolence. This middle-class knight fights likewise with a closed visor. The title page of his work reveals only his assumed name, which will perhaps become in the future a stalwart *nom de guerre*. I myself do not have much more to say about him except that his father was a sword-maker who made good blades.

I certainly do not need to assure the reader that I myself am not the author of this work, but only someone who is promoting its publication. For I could never have discussed noble pretensions and this lineage of lies with such equanimity. How furious I once became while strolling on the terrace of a castle one day, when a dainty little count, my best friend, tried to demonstrate the superior blood of the nobility! In the midst of our argument, his servant committed a small oversight, and the high-born lord slapped the

12. These two Latin phrases can be translated "the last business of the king" and "the business of the last king."

face of the low-born slave so that the ignoble blood spurted forth. Then the count threw him down the terrace as well. At that time I was ten years younger, and I immediately threw the noble count down the terrace too—he was my best friend, and he broke a leg. When I saw him again after his recovery—he was still limping a little—he had still not been cured of his pride of birth and declared anew that the nobility had been installed as the mediator between the people and its king, following the example of God, who had set the angels between Himself and man, and placed them close to His throne, like an aristocracy of heaven. "Glorious angel," I answered, "do take a few steps back and forth"—he did—and the comparison was lame.

Just as lame is a comparison which Count Moltke communicates in the same connection. In order to show his method by way of an example I will use his own words: "The attempt to destroy the nobility, in whom fleeting esteem becomes embodied in a permanent figure, would isolate man, would place him on precarious heights, where the necessary links to the subordinate masses are lacking. It would surround him with instruments of arbitrariness, and thereby, as one so often witnesses in the Orient, the existence of the ruler would be endangered. Burke[13] called the nobility the Corinthian capital of well-ordered states; and that this is no mere figure of speech is proven by the sublime spirit of this extraordinary man, whose entire life has been dedicated to the service of a judicious freedom."

The same example may be used to show how the noble Count is deceived by pseudo-knowledge. Burke, namely, in no way merits the accolades which are showered upon him; for he lacks that consistency which the English consider the primary virtue of a statesman. Burke possessed only rhetorical talent, and with it he opposed in the second half of his life the liberal principles he espoused in the first. Whether he wanted to ingratiate himself with the eminent by changing his views; whether Sheridan's liberal triumph in St. Stephen[14] caused Burke, out of spite and envy, to oppose him by defending that medieval past that offered such a

13. Edmund Burke, English writer and politician, who attacked the French Revolution.
14. Sheridan was the leader of the liberal opposition in English Parliament, which met at that time in St. Stephen's Chapel.

fertile field for romantic descriptions and rhetorical figures; whether he was a rogue or a fool—all this I do not know. But I think that it is always suspicious when a man changes his views for the favor of the ruling powers, and that he then remains a dubious source of authority. Someone who is not in this position once said: "The nobles are not the supports, but the caryatids of the throne." I think that this comparison is more accurate than the one about the capital of a Corinthian column. Indeed, we wish to reject the latter view as strongly as possible; otherwise a few well-known capitalists could get the capital idea of elevating themselves, instead of the nobility, to the Corinthian capital of the column of state. And that would be the most repugnant sight of all.

I am touching on matters here, however, which I wanted to illuminate in a later work; perhaps the specific, practical part of the controversy concerning the nobility will also be taken up there in more detail. For, as I have already indicated above, the present work concerns itself only with questions of principle; it debates legalities and merely demonstrates that the nobility contradicts reason, the age, and itself. The specific, practical part of this issue, however, deals with the successful arrogations and factual usurpations of the nobility by means of which it threatens so utterly the well-being of nations, undermining them more and more with every passing day. Indeed, it seems to me that the nobility itself does not believe its own pretensions, that it only utters this drivel as a decoy for middle-class polemics to take up so that their attention is diverted from the main issue. For the issue is not the institution of the nobility as such, not the specific privileges, not the compulsory labor and services, the legal advantages and judicial prerogatives, not all of these customary, material freedoms. The main issue is rather the invisible alliances among those who are able to demonstrate so and so many ancestors; these people have surreptitiously reached an agreement to seize the controlling power of all nations by repelling in unison the middle-class plebians and usurping the higher military commissions and all diplomatic posts; by coercing respect from the commoners with subservient soldiers; and by forcing the peoples, through diplomatic agitation, to fight against each other when they would rather shake off the fetters of the aristocracy or unite in brotherhood for this purpose.

Since the beginning of the French Revolution the nobility has been at war with the people, fighting openly or furtively against the principles of freedom and equality and its representatives, the French. The English nobility, which was the most powerful due to favorable laws and property, became the standard bearer of European aristocracy, and John Bull payed for this honor with many a fine guinea and wound up conquering himself into bankruptcy. During the peace which followed that pitiful victory Austria carried the noble banner and looked after the interests of the nobility; every cowardly agreement against liberalism was adorned with its well-known sealing wax. The peoples themselves, like their unfortunate leaders, were kept under strict surveillance; Europe was a Saint Helena, and Metternich was its Hudson Lowe.[15] But they could only take revenge on the moribund corpse of the Revolution; only the Revolution that had descended to man, which, with boots and spurs and sullied by the blood of the battlefield, climbed into bed with a blond empress and soiled the white sheets of the Hapsburgs[16]—only this Revolution could die from its own cancerous bowels. The spirit of the Revolution, however, is immortal and does not lie under the weeping willows of Longwood.[17] And in the childbed of late July the Revolution was reborn, not as a single being, but as an entire nation, and in this labor process it mocked its jailor who let his ring of keys fall from his hand in shock. What an embarrassment for the nobility! In the years of peace it had recuperated somewhat from its earlier exertions, and since then it had fortified itself by drinking a daily portion of donkey's milk from the pope's donkey; but it still lacked sufficient strength for a new battle. The English Bull is the last one who can rear its head at the enemy, as it did previously; for it is the most exhausted of all. The repeated changes of ministers has sapped all its strength. The radical cure, if not the hunger cure, has been prescribed, and on top of this the Irish infection is scheduled to be amputated as well. Austria likewise is not in a heroic enough mood to undertake the role of the Agamemnon of the nobility against France; Staberle[18] does not like to don his war uniform and knows

---

15. Sir Hudson Lowe was governor of the island of St. Helena, where Napoleon was kept in forced exile from 1815–1821.
16. Allusion to Princess Marie-Luise, whom Napoleon married in 1809.
17. Napoleon's grave on St. Helena.
18. Mocking reference to Austria.

too well that his umbrellas are no protection against showers of bullets. What is more, the Hungarians are frightening him with their grim mustaches, and in Italy he is compelled to place a sentry in front of every enthusiastic lemon tree. At home he has to engender archduchesses in order, if need be, to appease the revolutionary monster in this fashion.

But in France the sun of freedom blazes ever more powerfully and illuminates the entire world with its rays.—Daily the idea presses forward, the idea of a citizen king without courtly airs, without pages, without courtesans and matchmakers, without diamond gratuities and all other attendant splendor.—The *Chambre des pairs* is already considered a hospital for the chronic cases of the old regime, who are only tolerated out of pity and will be likewise removed in due time.—Strange turn of events! In its time of need the nobility is turning to the very state which a short time ago it regarded with hatred as its worst enemy: it is turning to Russia. The great Czar has now been chosen standard bearer by that very aristocracy, and he is forced to be their champion. For although the Russian state rests on the antifeudal principle of civil equality, determined not by birth but by the acquired public office, nevertheless absolute Czardom is irreconcilable with the idea of a constitutional freedom that would protect the meanest subject against a beneficent royal caprice. Because of this principle of civil equality Emperor Nicolas I may have been hated by the feudal order and, with all his power, may have been considered—as the open enemy of England and the furtive enemy of Austria—the factual representative of the liberals. But since the end of July he has been their greatest opponent, now that their victorious ideas of constitutional freedom threaten his absolutism. And in that very role as autocrat the European aristocracy has been able to incite him to fight against a free and open France. The English Bull has worn down its horns in just such a fight, and now the Russian Wolf is supposed to take his turn. The high *noblesse* of Europe knows just how to use the horror of the Muscovite woods for their own purposes, and it is not unflattering to the rowdy guest that he should defend the honor of the ancient divine right by God's grace against the calumniators of princes and the deniers of nobility. With obvious pleasure he allows them to drape over his shoulders the moth-eaten purple robe with all its elaborate embroidery from the Byzantine legacy; he feels honored with the worn-out Holy-Roman-Empire trousers from the former German Emperor; and he places upon his head the old-Franconian diamond-studded cap of Carolus Magnus.[19]—

The Wolf has put on the wardrobe of the old grandmother and is ripping you, Red Riding Hood of freedom, to shreds.

As I write these lines it is as if the blood from Warsaw spurted all the way onto my paper,[20] and I can almost hear the jubilation of Berlin officers and diplomats. Do they rejoice too soon? I don't know; but I and all of us are very concerned by the Russian Wolf, and I fear that we German Red Riding Hoods will soon feel its strange long hands and big mouth as well. At the same time we are supposed to be on the alert for fighting against France. Good Lord! Against France? Yes, hurrah! We will fight the French and the Berlin ukasists and knoutologs claim that we are still the same saviours of God, King, and Fatherland as in 1813 and that Körner's lyre and sword should again be our guide.[21] Fouqué will compose a few battle ditties; Görres will be brought back from the Jesuits to continue the *Rhineland Mercury;*[22] and anybody who volunteers for this holy war will get an oak leaf on his cap and will be addressed with "Sir" and will afterwards receive free theater passes or will at least be considered a child and only have to pay half price—and for the patriotic extra effort, as an added bonus, the entire nation will be promised a constitution.

Free theater passes are certainly a wonderful thing to have; but a constitution wouldn't be so bad either. Yes, in due time, we may even develop a hankering for it. Not that we distrust the absolute kindness or the kindly absolutism of our monarchs. On the contrary, we know that they are nothing if not charming people; and if there is one among them who dishonors the office, as for example His Majesty King Don Miguel,[23] he is only an exception, and if his all-highest colleagues do not put an end to that sort of bloody scandal, as they could very easily, it is simply that they may, by comparison

---

19. Charlemagne.
20. Reference to the bloody suppression of the Polish uprising of 1830–1831.
21. See p. 21, note 59.
22. See p. 38, note 88.
23. Pretender to and usurper of the throne of Portugal, he was eventually overthrown.

with that crowned wretch, appear all the more humane and noble and be all the more beloved by their subjects. But a good constitution has its points, and the people are to be forgiven if they ask for something in writing even from the best of monarchs about such matters as life and death. A reasonable father behaves quite reasonably when he erects a few salutary barriers in front of the abysses of sovereign power, lest his children meet with some misadventure when, mounted on the high horses of their pride, and accompanied by their boastful Junker companions, they gallop somewhat recklessly. I know the son of a royal house[24] who, in a bad riding school, dared to learn in advance the most impressive leaps. For such princes one must erect barriers that are twice as high; they must be equipped with golden spurs and given a tamer steed and more modest middle-class companionship. I know a hunting tale—by Saint Hubert!—and I also know someone who would give a thousand talers in Prussian currency if it were a lie.

Alas! our whole history today is nothing but a hunting tale. It is now the time of the grand hunt against liberal ideas, and the high nobility are more zealous than ever, and their uniformed huntsmen shoot at every honest heart in which liberal ideas have found refuge; and there is no lack of learned hounds who drag around the bleeding word as they would rich booty. Berlin is fattening the best leash of hounds, and I can already hear the pack howling at this book.

March 8, 1831   HEINRICH HEINE

24. Heine refers here to Friedrich Wilhelm IV of Prussia.

Various Conceptions of History

The book of history lends itself to various interpretations. Two entirely divergent views concerning it stand out in bold relief. The first regards the whole course of world events merely as a depressing cycle. It views the life of nations—no less than the lives of individuals—and all of organic nature in general—as a system of growth, flowering, withering, and death—spring, summer, autumn, and winter. "There is nothing new under the sun," is its motto; and even the motto is not new, for two thousand years ago the King of the East spoke it, and sighed. The proponents of this view shrug their shoulders at civilization, which, they claim, will eventually relapse into barbarism. They shake their heads at our battles for freedom, which, in their eyes, only give rise to new tyrants; they smile at all aspirations which stem from political enthusiasm to make a better and happier world, and which eventually cool and die out. They regard the history of mankind as little chronicles of hopes, tribulations, misfortunes, sorrows and joys, errors and disenchantments, which fill the lives of men and constitute their whole history. In Germany, the wiseacres of the historical school and the poets of the art-epoch of Wolfgang Goethe incline to this viewpoint. These were in the habit of idealizing in the most saccharine fashion a sentimental indifference to all political affairs of the fatherland. Sufficiently well-known is the fact that a certain government of North Germany[1] has understood the true value of that viewpoint. It commissions persons to travel abroad, so that amid the elegiac ruins of Italy they may cultivate a convenient

1. Prussia.

and soothing fatalism, and thereafter in company and with the assistance of preachers of Christian servility and by means of well-calculated journalistic coups, they may dampen the three-day fever for freedom in the German people.[2] Let him who cannot rise by his own strength of mind, creep on the ground; but the future will surely show that government how far one may go with these creepers and ranklers.

Opposed to this quite fatal and fatalistic outlook is one which is much brighter, and in greater harmony with the idea of providence. According to this notion, all earthly things are ripening to a beautiful perfection. The great heroes and heroic epochs are only rungs in a ladder leading to a higher, god-like condition of the human race, whose moral and political struggles will eventuate in the holiest peace, in the purest brotherhood, and the most everlasting happiness. The Golden Age, it is claimed, lies not in the past, but in the future. We were not driven from Paradise with a flaming sword; rather, it behooves us to conquer it with our flaming hearts, with love. The fruit of the tree of knowledge is not death, but everlasting life. The word "civilization" was for a long time the motto of the adherents of this doctrine. In Germany it was preeminently the humanistic school that paid homage to it. It is well known with what determination the so-called philosophical school labored toward this end. It was especially conducive to an inquiry into political problems, and as the ripest fulfillment of this outlook it preached an ideal form of government, founded exclusively on reason, which would eventually ennoble and make blessed all of mankind. I have no need to name the inspired knights of this doctrine. Their highest aspirations are certainly more gratifying than the petty sinuousness of the lowly ranklers. If we ever come to battle with them, let it be with our worthiest swords of honor; but we shall finish off the creeping slaves with the more fitting knout.

Neither view, as I have intimated, harmonizes fully with our own vivid sense of life. On the one hand, we do not wish to be inspired uselessly and stake the best we possess on a futile past. On the other hand, we also demand that the living present be

2. Reference to the Prussian historian Leopold von Ranke, who is an unnamed target of Heine's critique in several places in this short piece.

valued as it deserves, and not serve merely as a means to some distant end. As a matter of fact, we consider ourselves more important than merely means to an end. We believe that means and ends are only conventional concepts, which brooding man has read into Nature and History, and of which the Creator knows nothing. For every creation is self-purposed, and every event is self-conditioned, and everything—like the whole world itself—is here and happens for its own sake. Life is neither means nor end. Life is a right. Life desires to validate this right against the claims of petrifying death, against the past, and this act of validating life is the Revolution. The elegiac indifference of historians and poets must not paralyze our energies when we are engaged in this enterprise. Nor must the romantic visions of those who promise us happiness in the future seduce us into jeopardizing the interests of the present, the immediate struggle for the rights of man, the right of life itself.

"*Le pain est le droit du peuple,*" said Saint-Just.[3] And that is the greatest word spoken in the entire Revolution.

3. See p. 180, note 80.

Ludwig Börne: A Memorial

SECOND BOOK

Helgoland, July 1, 1830

—I am weary of this guerilla warfare and long for peace; at least for a state of affairs in which I can surrender myself freely to my natural inclinations, my dreamy way of life, my fantastic reveries and ruminations. What an irony of fate, that I, who am so fond of reclining on the soft cushions of sentimental contemplation, should be marked out to scourge my fellow Germans out of their complacency, and move them to action! I, who most of all like to pass my time watching trailing clouds, solving metrical word sorcery, eavesdropping on the secrets of the elemental spirits, and losing myself in the wonder-realms of old tales! . . . I had to edit *Political Annals*, advance the interests of the day, arouse revolutionary action, stir up the passions, and go on pulling the nose of poor honest Hans, to shake him from his sound, giant sleep. . . . Of course, all I have been able to extract from this snoring giant is a gentle sneeze, and I have been very far from waking him. . . . Even if I rudely snatched the pillow from under his head, he would restore it again with his sleepy hand. . . . Once in despair I was about to set fire to his nightcap, but it was so damp with the sweat of his thoughts, that it only smoked a little . . . . and Hans smiled in his sleep . . . . I am tired and long for rest. I shall get myself a German nightcap too, and pull it over my ears. If only I knew where to lay my head! It is impossible in Germany. Every moment a policeman would come and shake me to find out if I were really asleep, and this very idea completely ruins my peace of mind. . . .

But really, where should I go? South again? To the land where the lemons and the golden oranges bloom? Alas! In front of every lemon tree stands an Austrian sentinel thundering his frightful "Who goes there?" Like the lemons, the golden oranges are now very sour. Or should I go north? North-east perhaps? Ah! the polar bears are now more dangerous than ever, since they have become civilized and wear kid gloves. Or should I go once more to infernal England, where I would not even wish to hang in effigy, much less live in person! ... One should really be paid to live there, but instead a stay in England costs twice as much as anywhere else. I shall never return to this despicable land, where machines behave like men and men like machines. The whirring and silence is so very annoying. When I was presented to the local governor and this thoroughly English Englishman stood motionless before me for several minutes without uttering a word, I inadvertently had the thought of looking at his back to determine whether one hadn't forgotten to wind up the machine. That the island of Helgoland stands under British rule has been a bane to me for quite a while. Sometimes I imagine that I smell the boredom which the sons of Albion exude from every pore. In all seriousness, every Englishman emits a certain gas, the deadly stench of boredom, and I have observed it with my own eyes, not in England, where the atmosphere is saturated with it, but in southern lands, where the travelling British wander around in isolation. The gray aureole of boredom which encircles their heads is clearly visible against the sunny blue skies. The English of course believe that their dense boredom is the product of their native land, and to escape from it they travel through all countries, boring themselves everywhere only to return home with the diary of an *ennuyé*. They are like the soldier asleep on a bench whose comrade rubbed excrement under his nose; when he awoke he noticed that it smelled bad in the guardroom. He went out, but quickly returned, claiming that it smelled bad outside too, the whole world stinks.

One of my friends who recently returned from France asserted that the English traverse the continent because of their despair of the horrid cuisine in their homeland; at the French *tables d'hôte* one can see fat Englishmen who do nothing but gulp down *vol-au-vents*, *crème*, *suprêmes*, *ragoûts*, *gelées*, and similar heavenly foods. And they do so with that colossal appetite which at home has practiced on masses of roast beef and Yorkshire pudding and which in France threatens to ruin the native innkeepers. Could it be that the secret reason for the English travelling involves the exploitation of the *tables d'hôte?* While we laugh about their superficiality in sightseeing and gallery visits, they are perhaps really mystifying us, and their ridiculed curiosity is nothing but a cunning decoy for their gastronomical intentions.

But however excellent French cuisine may be, in France itself it is reported to have deteriorated markedly, and there is no end in sight for this great decline. The Jesuits flourish there, singing songs of triumph. The present rulers are the same fools whose heads were lopped off fifty years ago. To what avail! They have climbed out of their graves, and their present regime is even more foolish that the earlier one. For when they were allowed to ascend from the underworld and glimpse the light of day, a few of them hastily grabbed the first head which they could lay their hands on, and several dreadful blunders resulted. Sometimes the heads don't match the torso and the heart which it haunts. There are some who sound like reason itself from the podium, so that we admire their intelligence, yet in the next moment they let their incorrigible senseless hearts seduce them into the most stupid actions. . . . There is a horrible contradiction between the thoughts and the feelings, the principles and the passions, the speeches and the actions of these *revenants!*

Or should I go to America, that monstrous prison of freedom, where the invisible chains would oppress me even more heavily than the visible ones at home, and where the most repulsive of all tyrants, the populace, hold vulgar sway! You know well what I think of that accursed land, which I once loved, before I knew it well. . . . And yet I must publicly laud it, merely out of professional duty. . . . You dear German peasants! Go to America! There are no princes or nobles there; all men are equal—equal dolts . . . with the exception, naturally, of a few million, who have black or brown skin, and who are treated like dogs! Actual slavery, which has been abolished in most of the North American states, does not revolt me as much as the brutality with which the free blacks and the mulattoes are treated. Whoever is even in the slightest degree descended from Negroes, even if this is not betrayed in his color, but only in his facial features, is forced to suffer the most frightful humiliations, which we in Europe would scarcely believe. At the same time Americans make such a to-do about their Christianity and are zealous church-goers. They have learned this hypocrisy from the English, who incidentally have bequeathed to them their worst characteristics. Worldly pursuits are their true religion, and money is their God, their only Almighty God. Of course, there may be many noble souls who in secret deprecate this universal self-seeking and injustice. But if they fight against it, they expose themselves to martyrdom, the like of which is inconceivable in Europe. I believe that it was in New York, where a Protestant minister became so upset about the mistreatment of the colored people that he, in defiance of this horrid prejudice, married his daughter to a Negro. As soon as this truly Christian deed became known, the people stormed the minister's house, and he was only able to escape death by flight; the house was demolished, and the minister's daughter, poor victim of the affair, was grabbed by the mob and had to endure its wrath. She was flinshed,[1] that is, she was stripped naked, coated with tar, rolled around in an opened feather-bed, and in this sticky feather covering dragged through the entire city in ridicule. . . .

O Freedom! You are a bad dream!

Helgoland, July 8

—Since yesterday was Sunday, and leaden boredom weighed down on this whole island and almost crushed my brain, in despair I took hold of the Bible . . . and I confess that, despite the fact that I am a Hellene in secret, the book not only diverted me, but actually edified me. What a book! Large and wide as the world, striking its deep roots into the abysses of creation and towering high into the blue secrets of heaven! . . . Sunrise and sunset, promise and fulfillment, birth and death—the whole drama of mankind, all of it is found in this book. . . . It is the book of books, Biblia. The Jews can console themselves because they lost Jerusalem and the Temple and the arc of the covenant and Solomon's golden utensils and jewels . . . such losses are really insignificant in comparison to the Bible, the indestructible treasure that they rescued. Unless I am

---

1. Heine presumably means "lynched."

mistaken, it was Mohammed who called the Jews the "People of the Book," a name which in the East has remained with them to this day, and is profoundly significant. A book is their fatherland, their possession, their ruler, their fortune and misfortune. They live within its peaceful precincts. Here they exercise their inalienable civil rights. From here they cannot be driven out. Here they cannot be despised. Here they are strong and admirable. Immersed in the reading of this book, they paid little heed to the changes which took place in the real world outside them. Nations rose and fell; states flourished and decayed; revolutions shook the land . . . but the Jews were bowed over their book and scarcely noticed the turmoil of the times which swept over their heads!

As the prophet of the East called them the "People of the Book," so the prophet of the West,[2] in his *Philosophy of History*, characterized them as the "People of the Spirit." Already in their earliest beginnings—as we observe in the Pentateuch—they manifest a predilection for the abstract, and their whole religion is nothing but an act of dialectics, by means of which matter and spirit are sundered, and the absolute is acknowledged only in the unique form of Spirit. What terribly isolated role they were forced to play among the nations of antiquity, which, devoting themselves to the most exuberant worship of nature, understood spirit rather as material phenomena, as image and symbol! What a striking antithesis they represented to multicolored Egypt, teaming with hieroglyphics; to Phoenicia, the great pleasure-temple of Astarte, or even to that beautiful sinner lovely fragrant Babylonia—and, finally, to Greece, burgeoning home of art!

It is a strange spectacle how a people gradually frees itself entirely from the material and becomes completely spiritual. Moses gave the spiritual its material bulwarks against the physical invasion by the neighboring tribes. All around the field in which spirit had been sown he planted the rigid ceremonial law and an egotistical nationalism as a protective hedge. When the holy spirit-plant had struck root so deeply and shot up so high that it could no longer be rooted out, Jesus Christ came and demolished the ceremonial law, which had no further meaning or use. He even passed final sentence of death on Jewish nationalism. . . . He called all nations

2. Hegel.

of the world to share in the Kingdom of God, which had once belonged only to the chosen people, and extended to all mankind Jewish civil rights. . . . That was the great problem of emancipation, which, however, was solved much more magnanimously than is being done at the present in Saxony or Hanover. . . . Naturally, the Saviour who had freed his brethren from the ceremonial law and nationalism, and had founded cosmopolitanism, fell prey to his own humanitarianism, and the magistrates of Jerusalem had him crucified and the populace mocked him. . . .

But only the body was mocked and crucified. The spirit was glorified, and the martyrdom of the triumphant one, who achieved world hegemony for the spirit, became a symbol of this triumph, and all mankind has since striven, in imitation of Christ, to achieve this physical extinction and this transcendental dissolution in the absolute spirit. . . .

When will harmony again be restored? When will the world recover from this one-sided striving for spiritualization, this insane error which sickens both body and soul? There is a tried remedy to be found in political movements and in art. Napoleon and Goethe have done excellent work. The former compelled nations to engage in wholesome physical activity; the latter made us once more receptive to Greek art and created such solid works that we cling to as if they were marble deities, lest we drown in the misty seas of the absolute spirit. . . .

Helgoland, July 18

I have read through the entire Book of Moses in the Old Testament. The sacred world of antiquity transversed my spirit like a long caravan. The camels stand out. On their high backs sit the mysterious roses of Canaan. Pious shepherds, oxen and cows driven onward. They cross barren mountains, scorching stretches of desert where only here and there a group of palm trees appears, fanning a refreshing breeze. The servants dig wells. Sweet, calm, sunny Orient! How lovely it is to repose under your tent! O Laban, if I could only tend your flocks! I would gladly serve you seven years for Rachel, and another seven years for Leah, whom you will throw into the bargain! I hear how they bleat, these sheep of Jacob, and I see how he places the peeled rods before them when they go to drink during the mating season. The speckled ones now belong to us. Meanwhile Reuben returns home and brings his mother a bouquet of dudaims which he plucked in the fields. Rachel requests the dudaims, and Leah gives them to her on the condition that Jacob sleep with her the next night. What are dudaims? The commentators have racked their brains in vain about them. Luther did not know what to do either and wound up calling these flowers simply dudaims. Perhaps they are Swabian wallflowers. The love story about Dinah and young Shechem moved me very much. But her brothers Simeon and Levy, did not look at the matter so sentimentally. It is abominable that they strangled the unfortunate Shechem and all his relatives in such an underhanded fashion; even though the poor lover had pledged to marry their sister, to give them their lands and their possessions, to join together with them in one happy family, and even though he had already had himself and his entire people circumcized for this purpose. The two fellows should have been delighted that their sister had found such an excellent match; to acquire such in-laws was of great benefit to their tribe, and they would have gained, besides the hefty dowry, a good piece of land which was also badly needed. . . . One can't behave more decently than this love-struck prince Shechem, who in the last analysis had only anticipated the marriage rights out of love. . . . But that is just it, he compromised their sister, and for this crime the honor-conscious brothers knew no other atonement besides death . . . and when the father makes them answer for their bloody deed, mentioning the advantages which would have resulted from the marriage with Shechem, they answer: should we really be making business deals with our sister's virginity?

Stubborn, cruel hearts, these brothers. But under the hard rock lies the tenderly fragrant feeling for morality. Strange, this feeling for morality, as it expresses itself at other times in the lives of the patriarchs, is not the result of a positive religion or of a political legislation—no, at that time the ancestors of the Jews had neither a positive religion nor a political law; both arose only in a later era. I believe therefore that I can claim an independence of morality from dogma and legislation. It is a pure product of a healthy human feeling, and true morality, the reason of the heart, will exist eternally, even if church and state perish.

I wish that we had another word to designate what we now call morality. Otherwise we could be misled into thinking that morality is a product of customs. The romance language nations are in the same predicament since their *morale* is derived from *mores*. But true morality is independent of not only dogma and legislation, but also the customs of a people. The latter are results of climate or history, and out of such factors arise legislation and dogmatics. There are thus Indian, Chinese, and Christian customs, but there is only one, namely a human, morality. Perhaps this cannot be expressed conceptually, and the law of morality, which we call morals, is only a dialectical game. Morality is made manifest through actions and only in their motives; there is no moral significance in their form and shading. On the title page of Golowin's *Travels to Japan* one finds as a motto the excellent words which the Russian traveller heard from a noble Japanese: "The customs of people are various, but good deeds are everywhere recognized as such."

As long as I have been able to think, I have mused about this subject, morality. The problem concerning the nature of good and evil which has plagued all the great thinkers for a millennium and a half has for me been valid only as the question of morality—

I sometimes jump from the Old Testament to the New, and here too the omnipotence of this great book fills me with awe. On what sacred soil your foot treads here! While reading one should remove one's shoes, as one does in the proximity of shrines.

The most remarkable words in the New Testament for me are found in the Gospel of St. John, chapter 16, verses 12–13. "I have yet many things to say unto you, but you cannot bear them now. Howbeit when he, the Spirit of truth, is come, he will guide you into all truth: for he shall not speak of himself; but whatsoever he shall hear, that shall he speak: and he will shew you things to come." The last word has thus not been said, and here is perhaps the ring to which a new revelation can be joined. It begins with the redemption from the word; it puts an end to martyrdom and founds an empire of eternal joy: the millennium. All promises finally find the most abundant fulfillment.

A certain mystical ambiguity abounds in the New Testament. The following words are a clever digression, not a system: "Render unto Caesar the things which are Caesar's; and unto God the things that are God's." Likewise when Christ is asked: "Art thou the King of the Jews?" his answer is evasive. The same thing for the question whether he is God's son. Mohammed appears much more open and concrete. When he was asked a similar question, namely, if he was God's son, he answered: "God has no children." What a great drama the Passion is! And how profoundly it is motivated by the prophecies of the Old Testament! The Passion could not be avoided, it was the final stamp of authority. Like the miracles, the Passion served as an advertisement. . . . If a saviour were to appear now, he wouldn't need to let himself be crucified to get his teaching into print with the requisite notoriety. . . . He could simply have it printed and take out an ad for the pamphlet in the *General Newspaper* at six kreuzers per line for the advertising fee.

What a beautiful figure is this Man-God! How narrow in comparison appears the hero of the Old Testament! Moses loves his people with touching sincerity; like a mother, he is solicitous for the future of his nation. Christ loves humanity; that sun inflamed the whole world all around with the warming rays of his love. What soothing balm are his words for all the wounds of this world! What a refreshing spring for all sufferers was the blood which flowed on Golgotha! . . . The white, marble Greek gods were bespattered with this blood, and sickened with horror, and could never more recover. Of course most of them had already been carrying the consuming disease within them for a long time, and terror only hastened their death. The first to die was Pan. Do you know the legend which Plutarch tells? This sea-tale of antiquity is truly remarkable.— It goes as follows:

One evening, during the reign of Tiberius, a ship passed close to the island of Parae, which lies off the coast of Aetolia. The crew had not gone to sleep yet, and many of them were sitting, drinking after the evening meal. Suddenly from the shore they heard a voice calling "Thamus!" (for this was the name of the steersman) so loudly that all were startled. At the first and second cry Thamus remained silent. But the third time he replied. Then more loudly the voice said to him these words: "When you reach the heights of Palodes, proclaim that the great god Pan has died!" When he then reached the heights, Thamus fulfilled the mission and from the stern of his boat he called toward the land, "The great god

Pan is dead!" Whereupon he heard the strangest sounds of lamentation, a mingling of groaning and cries of astonishment—as if coming from many throats simultaneously. The witnesses recounted this incident in Rome, where the most singular opinions were expressed as to this affair. Tiberius had the matter investigated further and did not doubt its authenticity.

Helgoland, July 29

I have been reading in the Old Testament again. What a great book! Even more noteworthy than its contents is its presentation, where every word is as natural as a tree, a flower, the sea, the stars—as man himself. It sprouts, it flows, it sparkles, it smiles—we know not how or why; but it all seems quite natural. This is truly the word of God; other books are merely products of man's wit. In Homer, that other great book, the presentation is a product of art, and though the material itself, as is the case with the Bible, is taken from reality, it is cast into poetic form, transfused, as it were, within the crucible of the human mind. It has been refined by means of the spiritual process which we call art. In the Bible no trace of art is evident. Its style is that of a notebook in which the absolute spirit, seemingly without the assistance of any individual human being, has jotted down the events of the day, almost with the same factual accuracy with which we write our laundry list. One cannot pass judgment on that style. One can only observe its effect on our minds. The Greek grammarians were more than a little perplexed when they were supposed to define some striking beauties of the Bible in the terms of traditional aesthetic principles. Longinus speaks of sublimity. Recent aestheticians speak of naivete. Alas! As I have already said, there are no criteria for judging this book . . . the Bible is the word of God.

In only one other writer do I find anything that recalls this unmediated style of the Bible. That is Shakespeare. With him, too, the word sometimes appears in that imposing nakedness which awes and moves us. In the works of Shakespeare we sometimes see the living truth without the covering of art. But this occurs only in rare instances. The genius of art, conscious perhaps of its impotence, for a very brief space transferred its office to Nature, and then once more asserts its supremacy all the more zealously in the plastic shaping and the artful entanglement of the drama. Shakespeare is at once Jew and Greek; or rather, both elements, spiritualism and art, prevail and are reconciled in him, and unfold in higher unity.

Is such a harmonious fusion of both these elements perhaps the task of all of European civilization? We are still very far removed from such a goal. Goethe the Greek (and within the whole poetic party) has in recent times expressed his antipathy to Jerusalem in an almost passionate manner. The counter-party which has no renowned name at its head, but only a few loud-mouths like the Jew Pustkuchen, the Jew Wolfgang Menzel, and the Jew Hengstenberg[3]—these have cawed their pharisaical screeches against Athens and the great heathen even more loudly.

My neighbor at the inn, a legal counsel from Königsberg who is vacationing here, thinks I am a pietist because I always have the Bible in my hands when he visits. He therefore enjoys teasing me a bit, and a caustic Prussian smile flickers across his lean, bachelor face when he begins to speak to me about religion. Yesterday we debated the trinity. With the Father everything is fine; He is, after all, the creator of the world, and everything has to have an origin. There is already a hitch with belief in the Son, whom the clever fellow is inclined to deny, but in the end, with almost ironic cheerfulness, accepts. However, the third person in the trinity, the Holy Ghost, met the most unconditional of objections. He could not comprehend in the least what the Holy Ghost is, and suddenly he cried out jokingly: "In the end you probably have the same thing with the Holy Ghost that you have with the third horse when traveling with post-horses; you always have to pay for it, but you never get to see it, this third horse."

The person who is staying in the room below me is neither pietist nor rationalist, but a Dutchman who is as indolent and limp as the cheese which he sells. Nothing fazes him; he is the picture of sober tranquility, and even when he talks to the innkeeper's wife about his favorite topic, salting fish, his voice never changes from the dullest monotone. Because of the thin floorboards I am

---

3. Three particularly harsh critics of Goethe, all of whom were Protestant. They were "Jewish" only in the unusual sense in which Heine employs the word here. See p. 26, note 66, and p. 32, note 75.

unfortunately forced to hear such conversations, and while I spoke with the Prussian about the trinity, below me the Dutchman explained how you distinguish among codfish, salt-cod, and dried-cod; in essence it's one and the same thing.

The innkeeper is a splendid sailor, famous on the entire island for his intrepidity in storm and danger, but at the same time cheerful and gentle as a child. He has just returned from a long voyage, and with playful seriousness he told me about a phenomenon which he encountered yesterday, July 28, on the high seas. It sounds odd: the innkeeeper claimed that the entire sea smelled like freshly baked cakes, and the warm and delicate aroma from them worked so seductively on him that his heart was extraordinarily moved. You see, that is the counterpart to the alluring mirage which appears to the thirsting wanderer in the Arabian desert as a clear, refreshing pool of water. A baked *fata morgana*.

Helgoland, August 1

—You have no idea how much I am enjoying this *dolce far niente*. I haven't taken along a single book which deals with current affairs. My entire library consists of Paul Warnefried's[4] *History of the Langobards*, the Bible, Homer, and a few musty old volumes on witchcraft. I would like to write an interesting little book on the latter topic. To this end I have recently been investigating the last traces of paganism in the so-called modern era. It is highly remarkable how long and under which guises the lovely beings of Greek fables have endured in Europe.—And in essence they are still with us to this very day, with us poets that is. Since the victory of the Christian church the poets have formed a sacred society where the joys of ancient idolatry, the exulting belief in the gods is handed down from one generation to the next through the tradition of holy songs . . . But alas! the *ecclesia pressa*, which esteems Homer as its highest prophet, is subject with each day to increased oppression; the zeal of the black familiars is fueled in an ever more auspicious fashion. Are we threatened with a new inquisition?

4. Paulus Diaconus, author of the *History of the Langobards,* composed toward the end of the eighth century.

Fear and hope alternate in my spirit, and I am very uncertain in my mind.

—I have made my peace with the ocean once more (you know we were *en délicatesse*) and we sit together again in the evening and have secret *tête-à-têtes.* Yes, I will shelve politics and philosophy and surrender myself to the contemplation of nature and art. For all this torment and bother are useless, and although I torture myself for the sake of the general welfare, it scarcely profits from it. The world is stuck, if not in a fixed and motionless state, then in the most meaningless rotation. Once, when I was young and inexperienced, I thought that great causes ultimately triumph even though individual soldiers in humanity's wars of liberation go down to defeat. . . . And I refresh myself with those beautiful verses by Byron:

"These are but the receding waves repulsed and broken for a moment on the shore, while the great tide is still rolling on and gaining ground with every breaker."

Alas! Observing this natural phenomenon for a longer time, one notices that the sea, though it pushes forward, retreats to its former bed after a certain period; later it advances anew, trying with the same vehemence to secure the abandoned terrain, and finally despondently withdraws as before; and it repeats this game constantly, yet never moves forward. . . . Humanity too moves according to the laws of ebb and flow, and the moon perhaps exercises its sidereal influence on the intellectual world as well.—

There is a fresh light today, and despite all the melancholy doubts by which my soul is tormented and assailed, strange presentiments come over to me. . . . Something extraordinary is happening in the world. . . . The sea smells like cake, and the monks in the clouds looked so sad, so troubled last night. . . .

I walked alone by the sea in the twilight. All around me was solemn silence. The high vault of heaven was like a dome of a Gothic cathedral. The stars hung there like countless lamps, but they burned low and flickered. The waves of the sea roared like a hydraulic organ, stormy chorals, full of torment and despair, but triumphant at the same time. Above me was an airy train of white clouds that looked like monks, moving along with bowed heads and sorrowful mien, a sad procession. . . . It seemed almost as if they were following a hearse. . . . "Who is being buried? Who had died?" I said to myself. "Is the great god Pan dead?"

Helgoland, August 6

While his army was fighting the Lombards, the King of the Heruleans sat quietly in his tent playing chess. He threatened with death anyone who would bring him news of defeat. The scout, who was watching the battle from a tree, kept crying, "We are winning! We are winning!" Until at last he groaned aloud: "Unhappy king! Unhappy people of Herulean!" Then the King knew that the battle was lost, but too late. For in that same moment the Lombards rushed into the tent and stabbed him. . . .

I had just been reading this story in Paul Warnefried, when my thick mail delivery came from the mainland with the warm, burning hot news. There were sunbeams wrapped up in the printed paper; and they kindled my soul to a wild flame. It seemed as if I could set fire to the whole ocean up to the North Pole with the flames of my enthusiasm and the mad exultation which blazed within me. Now I know why all the sea smelled like cake. The Seine had spread the good news immediately into the whole sea, and in their crystal palaces the lovely water nymphs, who had ever looked with favor on heroism, had immediately given a *thé-dansant* to celebrate the great event. That is why the whole sea smelled like cake. I ran madly around the house and first kissed my fat landlady and then her old friendly sea-dog. I also embraced the Prussian court-magistrate, from whose lips the frosty smile of disbelief had not altogether disappeared. I even clasped the Dutchman to my heart . . . but his indifferent fat face remained cool and tranquil; and I believe if the July sun in person had fallen on his neck, Mynheer would merely have broken into a mild sweat, but under no circumstances would he have burst into flames. This sobriety in the midst of general exaltation is disgusting. Just as the Spartans kept their children from drunkenness by showing them an intoxicated Helot as a warning, so we should supply our educational institutions with a Dutchman so that his unsympathetic, smug fishlike nature might instill our children with a repugnance for sobriety. This Dutch sobriety is truly a much more fatal vice than the drunkenness of a Helot. I feel like giving Mynheer a thorough thrashing. . . .

But no. No excesses! The Parisians have given us such a brilliant example of moderation. You truly deserve to be free, you French, for you carry freedom in your hearts. In this you differ from your poor fathers who rose up against centuries of slavery, committing along with their heroic deeds such insane atrocities that the genius of humanity covered its face in shame. This time the hands of the people have only been bloodied in the tumultuous battle of just self-defense, not after the fray. The people even dressed the wounds of their enemies, and when the deed was done, they continued peacefully with their daily chores without demanding even a tip for their enormous effort!

> "Fear not the slave, when he is free,
> Nor dread the man of liberty."

You can see how giddy I am, how frenzied, how general. . . . I am quoting Schiller's "Glocke."

And the old boy whose incorrigible foolishness had spilled so much blood of the citizenry was treated by the Parisians with touching moderation. He actually sat playing chess, as the king of the Heruli did, when his conquerors stormed into his tent. He signed his abdication with a trembling hand. He had not wanted to hear the truth. He only had a ready ear for the lies of his courtiers, who kept shouting: "We are winning! We are winning!" This total conviction of the royal fool is incomprehensible. . . . He looked up in amazement when, like the sentry during the battle with the Langobards, the *Journal des Débats* suddenly cried out: *"Malheureux roi! Malheureuse France!"*

With him, with Charles X, Charlemagne's empire finally comes to an end, just as the empire of Romulus ended with Romulus Augustulus. Just as once a new Rome began, so now a new France begins.

Everything is still like a dream to me; in particular the name Lafayette sounds like a legend from my earliest childhood. Is he really now sitting on his horse once again, commanding the national guard? I am almost afraid it isn't true because it's in print. I want to go to Paris myself to convince myself with my own blessed eyes.

... It must be splendid to see him riding through the streets there, this citizen of two worlds, this godlike old man whose silver locks flow down over his sacred shoulders. ... With his old kindly eyes he greets the grandsons of the men who once fought with him for freedom and equality. ... It was sixty years ago when he returned from America with the Declaration of the Rights of Man, the ten commandments of the new world faith, which were revealed to him there amid the thunder and flashes of cannons. ... Now the tricolor again waves from the towers of Paris and the *Marseillaise* rings out!

Lafayette, the tricolor, the *Marseillaise*. ... I am again giddy. Bold hopes shoot passionately upward, like trees with golden fruits and wild rising branches which extend their foliage up into the clouds. ... But in rapid flight the clouds uproot these gigantic trees and race away with them. The sky hangs full of violins, and now I smell it, the sea has the scent of freshly baked cakes. There is a continuous playing of violins up above in heavenly blue jubilation, and from the emerald waves it sounds like the merry tittering of young girls. But under the earth there is a cracking and pounding; the earth opens; the old gods stick their heads out and ask with precipitous astonishment: "What is the meaning of this exaltation which penetrates to the very core of the earth? What is new? Do we dare to surface again?" No, you should remain down below in your misty home; soon a new deceased comrade will descend to you there. ... —"What is his name?" You know him well; it is he who once hurled you down into the realm of eternal night. ...

Pan is dead!

Helgoland, August 10

Lafayette, the tricolor, the *Marseillaise!* ... My longing for peace is gone. I know now what I want to do, what I should do, what I must do. ... I am the son of the Revolution and I take up the charmed weapons upon which my mother has pronounced her magic blessing. ... Flowers! Flowers! I will crown my head with flowers in this fight to the death. And my lyre, give me my lyre too, that I may sing a battle-hymn. ... Words like flaming stars that have shot from on high to burn palaces and illumine hovels!

. . . Words like bright javelins, that will go whizzing up into the seventh heaven and strike the pious hypocrites who have crept into the Holy of Holies. I am all joy and song, all sword and flame! Perhaps I am quite mad. . . . One of those wild sunbeams wrapped in printed paper has flown into my brain, and all my thoughts are in a blaze. In vain I dip my head in the sea. No water can douse this Greek flame. But it is no different with the rest. The other sea-shore visitors have also been hit by the Parisian sunstroke, especially the Berliners, who have flocked here in great numbers this year, and cross over from one island to the other, so that one may well say that the whole North Sea has been deluged by Berliners. Even the poor Helgolanders are jubilant, although they understand the events only by instinct. The fisherman who ferried me yesterday to the little island where I bathed, laughed and shouted: "The poor people have won!" Yes, instinctively, the people understand these events much better perhaps than we with all our learning. Thus Frau von Varnhagen once told me a story of how they were waiting for news of the battle of Leipzig, when suddenly the maid rushed into the room, crying with terror, "The nobles have won."

This time, however, the poor have won the battle. "But it does them no good, even if they have done away with the right of succession!" These words were spoken by the East Prussian legal councilor in a tone which greatly affected me. I don't know why these words, which I don't understand, remain so uneasily in my memory. What did the dull fellow mean by that?

This morning a package of newspapers was again delivered. I devour them like manna. Child that I am, the touching details occupy me much more than the significant whole. O, if I could only see the dog Medor. He interests me much more than the others who with their quick leaps retrieved the crown for Philipp of Orleans. The dog Medor retrieved rifle and cartridge box for his master, and when his master fell in battle and was buried together with his co-heroes in the courtyard of the Louvre, the poor dog stayed there, like a statue of loyalty, sitting motionless on his grave, day and night; he ate very little of the food which he was offered and buried the largest part of it in the earth, perhaps as nourishment for his interred master.

I cannot sleep any longer. My overexcited imagination is beset by the most bizarre nocturnal visions. Waking dreams come stumbling one after another and become strangely confused and appear as in a Chinese shadow-play, now dwarf-like, now enormously elongated, so that I am almost driven mad. In this condition it often seems to me that my own limbs have likewise expanded to colossal size, and with giant strides I am running back and forth between Germany and France. Yes, I remember, last night I ran in this fashion through all the German provinces and counties, and knocked on the doors of all my friends and roused them from their sleep. . . . They glared at me with astonished, glassy eyes, so that I myself was frightened and could not say right off what I was doing or why I had awakened them! I poked the ribs of many fat philistines who snored frightfully, and all they did was yawn and say, "What time is it?" Dear friends, in Paris the cock has crowed. That is all I know. On the way to Munich, behind Augsburg, I met a throng of Gothic cathedrals apparently in flight, and they waddled terror-stricken. Tired of so much running around, I took to wings, and flew from star to star. These are not populated worlds, as some dream, but merely radiant orbs of stone, desolate and barren. They do not fall down, because they do not know where to fall. And so they soar on high, up and down, in great perplexity. I arrived in heaven. All doors were ajar. Long, lofty, echoing halls, with old-fashioned gilding—quite empty. Only here and there in a velvet armchair sat an ancient, powdered attendant, in faded scarlet livery, dozing lightly. In some chambers the doors had been lifted from their hinges; in other places the doors were locked fast and sealed three times with large, round official seals, like the houses of bankrupts or deceased persons. Finally I came to a room in which an old thin man sat at a writing desk, rummaging among thick stacks of papers. He was dressed in black, had white hair, a wrinkled businessman's face, and he asked in a muffled voice, "What do you want?" In my naivete I took him for the good Lord, and I spoke to him quite confidentially, "Ah, dear Lord God, I would like to learn how to thunder. I already know how to strike with lightning. . . . Please, teach me how to thunder!" "Not so loud," the thin old man replied vehemently, and he turned his back on me and once more rummaged among his papers. "That is the Keeper of Records," one of the scarlet-liveried servants whispered as he rose from his reclining chair and rubbed his eyes and yawned. . . .

Pan is dead!

Cuxhafen, August 19

Unpleasant crossing in an open boat, against wind and weather; so that I, as always in such cases, suffered from seasickness. The sea, too, like other people, rewards my love with discomfort and afflictions. It goes well at first; I enjoy the playful swaying. But gradually I begin to get dizzy and all kinds of fantastic faces spin around me. From the dark sea eddies old demons rise, hideously naked to their hips, and they howl almost incomprehensible verses, while spraying me in the face with the white foam of the waves. Up above the clouds form even more grotesque caricatures; they hang down so low that they almost touch my head and with their stupid little falsettos whistle the most uncanny foolishness into my ear. Without being dangerous such a seasickness nonetheless causes the most horrible discomforts, which practically drive one insane. I finally imagined I was a whale carrying in my belly the prophet Jonah.

And the prophet Jonah raged and carried on in my belly, constantly shouting:

"O Nineveh! O Nineveh! You shall be overthrown! In your palaces beggars shall louse themselves, and in your temples the Babylonian *cuirassiers* shall feed their mares. But you, you priests of Baal, you shall be taken by the ears, and your ears shall be nailed fast to the gates of the temple! Yea, on the doors of your shops you shall be nailed by your ears, you bakers of the body of the Lord! For you have given false weights; you have sold the people light and dishonest breads. O you tonsured deceivers! When the people were starving, you offered them a thin homeopathic pseudo-nourishment, and when they were thirsty, you yourselves drank instead of them; at most you offered the filled chalice to the kings. But you, you Assyrian philistines and ruffians, you shall receive blows with sticks and rods; you shall be kicked and have your ears boxed; and I can predict it with precision; for in the first place I shall do everything possible to bring it about, and second I am the prophet, the prophet Jonah, the son of Amitai. . . . O Nineveh, O Nineveh, you shall be overthrown!"

My belly orator preached approximately in this manner, and he appeared to gesticulate and to wrap himself in my bowels so thoroughly that everything turned and whirled in my stomach . . . until I couldn't stand it any longer and spit out the prophet Jonah.

In this manner I was relieved and finally recovered completely when I landed and received a good cup of tea in the inn.

Here it is swarming with Hamburgers and their wives who use the seabath. Ships' captains from all countries waiting for a favorable wind also stroll about here on the high dams, or they lie in the pubs and drink very strong grog and cheer the three days of July. The French are given their well-earned *vivat* in all languages, and the Briton, otherwise so laconic, lauds them just as loquaciously as the garrulous Portuguese who regrets being unable to bring his shipment of oranges directly to Paris to refresh the people from the heat of battle. Even in Hamburg, I am told, in that very Hamburg where hatred of the French has its deepest roots, there now reigns nothing but enthusiasm for France. . . . Everything is forgotten; Davoust, the robbed bank,[5] the fusiladed citizens, the old German coats, the bad verses of liberation, father Blücher, "Hail thee in Victory Wreath," everything is forgotten. . . . In Hamburg the tricolor flutters in the breeze; the *Marseillaise* rings out everywhere; even the ladies appear in the theater with tricolored cockades on their bosoms, and they laugh with their blue eyes, their tiny red mouths, and their white little noses. . . . Even the rich bankers, who are losing a great deal of money in securities as a result of the revolution, partake generously in the general celebration, and every time a broker announces that the exchange has fallen even further, they look even more pleased and answer: "That's all right, it doesn't matter, it doesn't matter."—

Yes, everywhere, in all countries men will quickly grasp the meaning of these three July days and recognize in them the victory of their own interests, and celebrate. The great deed of the French speaks so clearly to all the nations and to all minds—the lowest as well as the highest—that even on the steppes the souls of the Bashkirs will be as deeply moved as on the heights of Andalusia. . . . I can already see how the macaroni sticks in the throat of the Nepalese and the potato in the throat of the Irishman when the news reaches them. . . . Pulcinella[6] is capable of taking up the

5. In 1812, when Napoleon's army was retreating from its defeat in Russia, Marshall Davoust occupied Hamburg and demanded a war contribution of 48 million marks. When this was not paid, he confiscated the funds of the Hamburg Bank.
6. Italy.

sword, and Paddy⁷ will perhaps do something crazy, which will
wipe the smile off the faces of the English.

And Germany? I do not know. Will we at last make good use
of our oak forests, that is, build barricades for the liberation of
the world? Will we, whom Nature has endowed with so much
profundity, so much power, and so much courage, at last use our
godly gifts and grasp the word of the great Teacher—the doctrine
of the rights of humanity, and proclaim and bring it into fulfillment?

It is now six years since I wandered through my fatherland on
foot, and coming to the Wartburg, visited the cell which housed
Dr. Luther. A good man, whom I will allow none to censure. He
fulfilled a gigantic task, and we will always kiss his hands in
gratitude for what he did. We will not take it amiss if he did not
treat some of our friends too politely when they wanted to go
somewhat farther in their exegesis of the divine word than he
himself did, when they also proposed the equality of man here on
earth. . . . Such a proposal was, of course, untimely then. And
Master Hemling, who cut off your head, poor Thomas Münzer,⁸
was in a certain respect perhaps justified in this matter, for the
sword was in his hands and his arm was strong!

On the Wartburg I visited the armory where the old armor hung,
the ancient spiked helmets, round shields, halberds, broadswords,
the iron wardrobe of the Middle Ages. I wandered pensively
through the hall with a university friend, a young aristocratic
gentleman, whose father was at that time one of the most powerful
quarter-princes in our country and held sway over the whole
shivering little slice of territory. His ancestors too had been mighty
barons, and the young man reveled in heraldic memories at the
sight of all this armor and these weapons, which, as an attached
notice indicated, belonged to this or that knight of his family.
When he took down an old ancestral longsword from its hook and
out of curiosity tried to swing it, he had to admit that it was too
heavy for him, and discouraged he let his arm sink. When I saw
that—when I saw that the arm of the grandson was too weak to

7. Ireland.
8. Münzer was a radical supporter of the peasants who came into conflict with
the more moderate Luther. He was executed on May 30, 1525. By Master Hemling
Heine presumably means an executioner.

hold his ancestors' sword—I thought to myself, "Germany can be free."

(Nine Years Later)

Between my first and second meeting with Ludwig Börne lies that very July Revolution that, so to speak, burst our era asunder in two halves. The previous letters are able to bear witness to my mood when the great event occurred, and in the present memorial they should serve as a mediating bridge between the first and the third book. Otherwise the transition would be too abrupt. I had second thoughts about including a greater number of these letters, since in the ones which immediately followed the intoxication for freedom staggered all too violently over all police regulations, while later all too sober observations occur, and my disappointed heart loses itself in despondent, dejected, and despairing thoughts. Even during the first days after my arrival in the capital city of the Revolution I noticed that things in reality were painted with entirely different colors than the ones which the illumination of my enthusiasm had imparted to them from afar. The silver hair that I had seen fluttering so majestically around the shoulders of Lafayette, the hero of two worlds, transformed itself on closer inspection into a brown wig covering miserably a narrow skull. And even the dog Medor, whom I visited in the courtyard of the Louvre, was letting himself be fed peacefully, encamped amidst tricolored flags and trophies: he was not the right dog, but just a common cur who claimed for himself others' honors, as often happens with the French; and like so many others he exploited the fame of the July Revolution. . . . He was pampered, promoted, and perhaps elevated to the highest positions of honor, while the real Medor had stolen away modestly a few days after the victory, like the real people who had made the Revolution. . . .

Poor people! Poor dog!

It is an old story by now. Not for themselves—from time immemorial—not for themselves did the people bleed and suffer, but for others. In July 1830 they fought to victory for that bourgeoisie which is worth just as little as the *noblesse* whose place it took, with the same egoism. . . . The people have won nothing with their victory except regret and greater depravity. But you can be certain that when the signal bells sound again and the people grab their rifles, this time they will fight for themselves and demand their well-deserved reward. This time the true, genuine Medor will be honored and fed. . . . God knows where he now wanders around, despised, ridiculed, and starving. . . .

But be still my heart, you are betraying yourself too much. . . .

Letters on Germany

I

... You, Sir, not long ago, in the *Revue des Deux Mondes,* on the occasion of a critique of your Frankfurt countrywoman Bettina Arnim, alluded to the authoress of *Corinna*[1] with an enthusiasm that was certainly the result of sincere feelings; for you wanted to show how far she surpassed contemporary woman writers, namely, the *mères d'eglise* and the *mères des compagnons.* I do not share your opinion in this respect, but I do not wish to refute your views here, and I shall respect them everywhere where they do not contribute to spreading erroneous views about Germany, its affairs, and their representatives. It was only with this intent that I opposed twelve years ago the book *De l'Allemagne* by Madame de Staël, in a book of my own that bore the same title. To this book I am now appending a series of letters, the first of which is dedicated to you.

Yes, a woman is a dangerous thing. I can sing a song about that. Others have also had this bitter experience, and only yesterday a friend told me a horrible story in this regard. He had spoken to a young German painter in the church of Saint Méry, and the latter said to him mysteriously: "You have attacked Madame la Comtesse de —— in a German article. She heard about it, and you are as good as dead if it should happen again. *Elle a quatre hommes, qui ne demandent pas mieux que d'obéir à ses ordres.*" Isn't that terrifying? Doesn't that sound like a nighttime horror story by Ann

1. Madame de Staël.

Radcliffe?[2] Isn't this woman a kind of *Tour de Nesle*?[3] She needs only to nod her head, and four assassins will pounce on you and finish you off, if not physically, then certainly morally. But how did this lady acquire such sinister power? Is she so beautiful, so rich, so noble, so virtuous, and so talented that she can exercise such an unconditional influence on her slaves, and these obey her blindly? No, she does not possess these gifts of nature and fortune to any too great extent. I don't want to say that she is ugly; no woman is ugly. But I can justly assert that if beautiful Helen had looked like this lady, then the entire Trojan War would not have occurred, Priam's citadel would never have been burned, and Homer would have never sang the wrath of Pelides Achilles. She is also not particularly noble, and the egg out of which she crept was neither fathered by a god nor hatched by the daughter of a king; she cannot be compared with Helen with respect to her birth either; she comes from a middle-class merchant family in Frankfurt. Her treasures are also not as great as those which the queen of Sparta brought with her when Paris, who played the zither so beautifully (the piano had not yet been invented then), abducted her; on the contrary, the lady's *fournisseurs* sigh; she allegedly still owes money for her last *ratelier*. Only with regard to virtue can she be compared with the famous Madame Menelaus.

Yes, women are dangerous; but I must really remark that the beautiful ones are not nearly so dangerous as the ugly ones. For the former are accustomed to being courted, while the latter court every man and in this manner acquire a powerful following. This is especially true in literature. I have to mention here immediately that the French women writers who are now most prominent are all very pretty. There is George Sand, the author of *Essai sur le développement du dogma catolique*, Delphine Girardin, Madame Merlin, Louise Collet—all ladies who put to shame all those nasty jokes about the gracelessness of the *bas bleux* and to whom, when we read their works at night in bed, we would like to deliver personally our respects. How beautiful is George Sand and how small a danger, even for those evil cats who caress her with one paw and scratch her with the other, even for the dogs who madly

2. English writer of supernatural suspense stories.
3. Old Parisian building and the title of a drama by Alexander Dumas.

bark at her; she looks down at them from on high with kindness, like the moon. Princess Belgiojoso, this beauty longing for truth, can also be injured without punishment; anyone can sling filth on a madonna by Raffael; she will not defend herself. Madame Merlin, who always speaks well not only of her enemies, but even of her friends, can likewise be insulted without danger; accustomed to homage, she is almost totally unfamiliar with the language of rudeness, and she stares at you in astonishment. The beautiful muse Delphine reaches for her lyre when you insult her, and her anger is poured out in a sparkling stream of alexandrines. If you say something derogatory about Madame Collet, then she will reach for a kitchen knife and will try to stab you with it. That isn't dangerous either. But don't insult Comtesse —— ! You're as good as dead. Four masked men will pounce on you—four *souteneurs littéraires*—that is the *Tour de Nesle*—you will be stabbed, strangled, and drowned—the next morning your corpse will be found in the *entrefilets* in *La Presse*.

I return to Madame de Staël, who was not beautiful and who caused the great Emperor Napoleon much trouble. She did not limit herself to writing books against him, but sought also to attack him with non-literary means; for some time she was the soul of diplomatic intrigues that preceded the coalition against Napoleon. She also knew how to throw assassins at the throat of her enemy, only these were not *valets*, like the champions of the lady I have just mentioned, but kings. Napoleon was defeated and Madame de Staël marched victoriously into Paris with her book *De l'Allemagne* and a few hundred thousand Germans, whom she brought along, so to speak, as living illustrations for her book. From this evidence the people could then convince themselves how faithfully she had portrayed us Germans and our virtues. What a splendid frontpiece Blücher[4] was, this gentle soul, this honest character who stank from tobacco and cheated while gambling and who once declared in a daily communiqué that he would have Napoleon flogged if he caught him. She also brought along our own A. W. von Schlegel,[5] this paradigm of German naiveté and chivalrous heroism. She also brought along Zacharias Werner[6] to the great

4. See p. 119, note 194.
5. See Heine's treatment of Schlegel in "The Romantic School," esp. pp. 46–59.
6. See pp. 105–7.

delight of the courtesans of the *palais royal,* who marched behind him in an orderly procession; at that time the *galerie de bois* still existed. That was the victorious era of Romanticism, and Chateaubriand came with an enormous bottle full of water from the Jordan and baptized again a France which had become heathen so that it renounced Satan and his glories and received compensation in the kingdom of heaven for the territorial conquests it had lost on earth.[7] Since that time the French have become Christians and Romantics and counts. That didn't concern me in the least, and a nation certainly has the right to become as boring and lukewarm as it wants, even more so since it was previously the most brilliant and heroic that had ever fortified and battled here on earth. But still I am somewhat interested in this transformation; for when the French renounced Satan and his glories, they also abandoned the Rhenish provinces, and I became by this event a Prussian. Yes, as horrible as the word sounds, I am one, I am a Prussian by the right of acquisition. Only with difficulty, when I couldn't stand it any longer, did I succeed in breaking the spell, and since that time I have lived as a Prussian *libéré* here in Paris where immediately after my arrival one of my most important occupations was to declare war against the prevailing book by Madame de Staël.

I did this in a series of articles that I soon thereafter published as a complete book under the title *De l'Allemagne.*[8] With this title I did not intend to enter into a literary competition with the book by that renowned woman. I am one of the greatest admirers of her intellectual abilities; she has genius; but unfortunately this genius has a sex, and what is more, it is feminine. It was my duty as a man to oppose that brilliant *cancan,* which had an even more dangerous effect since she brought forward in her information about Germany a mass of things that were unknown in France and that fascinated the spirits because of the charm of novelty. I did not dwell on individual errors and falsifications; I confined myself to showing the French what was the real meaning of that Romantic School which Madame de Staël exalted and celebrated so much. I showed that it consisted of only a handful of worms whom the holy fisherman in Rome knew how to use very well for luring

7. French Romantic writer who had traveled to Palestine in 1806–1807.
8. Essentially the first two essays in this volume.

innocent souls. Since that time many Frenchmen have also had the scales fall from their eyes, and even very Christian dispositions have understood how right I was in showing them in a German mirror the intrigues which creep around in France as well and now raise their shorn heads more boldly than ever.

Then I also wanted to give true information about German philosophy, and I believe I did this. I have candidly blurted out the school secret only known to the pupils of the highest class, and here in this country this revelation caused more than a little stir. I remember how Pierre Leroux met me and confessed frankly that he had always believed that German philosophy was a kind of mystical fog, and that German philosophers were a species of pious visionaries who only breathed the fear of God. Of course, I was not able to give the French an extensive description of our different systems—I also was too fond of them to bore them with this—but I did betray to them the very last thought which lies at the basis of all of these systems, and it is precisely the opposite of everything that we have previously called the fear of God. Philosophy in Germany has waged the same war against Christianity that it once waged in the Greek world against the older mythology, and here it has won the victory again. In theory contemporary religion has also been knocked on the head; it is dead as an idea and only lives a mechanical existence, like a fly whose head has been cut off and which appears not to have noticed, flying around as always in good spirits. How many centuries the great fly, Catholicism, still has in its belly (to borrow a phrase from Cousin) I don't know, but one doesn't even speak about it anymore. The real issue concerns much more our poor Protestantism, which has granted every possible concession in order to prolong its life, but which must nonetheless die: it did not help that it purified its God of all anthropomorphism, that it pumped out of him by phlebotomy the last drop of sensual blood, or that if filtered him, as it were, to a pure spirit consisting of nothing but love, justice, wisdom, and virtue.—Nothing helped, and a German Porphyrian named Feuerbach (in French *fleuve de flamme*) mocks not just a little this characterization of "God-as-pure-spirit," whose love merits no special praise since he after all has no human bile; whose justice likewise does not cost him much since he has no stomach that much be fed *per fas et nefas;*[9] whose wisdom does not count for much since his thought is never hindered by a cold; and who would in general have difficulty *not* being virtuous since he has no body! Yes, not only the Protestant nationalists, but even the deists have been defeated in Germany since philosophy has directed all its catapults against the concept of "God," as I have shown in my book *De l'Allemagne.*

I have annoyed many sides by tearing away the facade from the German heaven and showing everyone that all deities of the old faith have disappeared from there, and that only an old maid sits there with leaden hands and a sorrowful heart: Necessity.—Alas! I have only made an early announcement of what everyone will learn sooner or later, and what sounded so strange then is now preached from the rooftops on the other side of the Rhine. And in what a fantastic tone the anti-religious sermons are sometimes preached! We now have monks of atheism who would burn Monsieur Voltaire alive because he was a hardened deist. I have to confess that this music is not pleasing to me, but it also doesn't frighten me; for I stood behind the maestro[10] when he composed it, to be sure in indistinct and convoluted signs so that not everyone would decipher it.—I sometimes saw how he gazed around anxiously out of fear that he was understood. He was very fond of me, for he was sure that I wouldn't betray him; at that time I even thought that he was servile. Once when I was annoyed with the phrase: "Everything that is, is reasonable," he laughed strangely and remarked: "It could just as well read: 'Everything that is reasonable, must be.'" He glanced around hastily, but soon calmed himself, for only Heinrich Beer had heard what he said. I only understood such expressions later. Thus I also only understood later why he asserted in his philosophy of history that Christianity already represents progress because it teaches about one God who died while pagan gods knew nothing at all about death. What progress it would therefore be if God had never existed at all! We were standing once in the evening at a window, and I raved about the stars, the residence of the deceased souls. But the master mumbled to himself: "The stars are only a shining leprosy in the

9. "By everything proper or improper."
10. Hegel.

sky." "My God," I cried, "then there isn't a happy place above to reward virtue after death?" He looked at me derisively: "Then you also want another compensation for performing your obligations in life, for caring for your sick mother, for not letting your brother starve, and for not poisoning your enemies."

With the overthrow of the old doctrines of faith the older morality has also been uprooted. Still the Germans will cling to the latter for a long time. They are like certain ladies who were virtuous until they reached forty and afterwards did not think it any longer worthwhile to practice that beautiful vice, even though their principles had become more lax. The destruction of faith in heaven has not only a moral, but also a political significance: the masses no longer bear their worldly misery with Christian patience; they yearn for happiness on earth. Communism is a natural consequence of this altered world view, and it is spreading itself over all of Germany. It is just as natural a phenomenon that the proletarians in their struggle against the existing order have as leaders the most advanced minds, the philosophers of the great school; these proceed from doctrine to deed, the final purpose of all thought, and formulate the program. How does it read? I have dreamed it long ago and announced it in these words: "We do not want to be sansculottes, nor simple citizens, nor venal presidents; we want to found a democracy of gods, equal in majesty, in sanctity, and in bliss. You demand simple dress, austere morals, and unspiced pleasures, but we demand nectar and ambrosia, crimson robes, costly perfumes, luxury and splendor, the dancing of laughing nymphs, music and comedies."[11] These words are found in my book *De l'Allemagne* in which I distinctly predicted that the Germans' political revolution would proceed from that very philosophy whose system is so often decried as idle scholasticism. It was easy to prophesy. For I had seen how the dragon's teeth were sown, out of which are growing today the armored men who will fill the world with their clattering of weapons, but who will unfortunately also be at each others' throats!

Since that frequently mentioned book appeared, I have published nothing about German for the public. If I break my long silence today, then it happens less to satisfy the needs of my own heart

11. See p. 180.

than, rather, to accommodate the wishes of my friends. They are sometimes much more indignant than I am about the stunning ignorance which prevails with respect to German intellectual life here in France, an ignorance which is exploited by our enemies with great success. I say "by our enemies" and understand by that not those impoverished creatures who go peddling from one newspaper office to another, offering for sale their crude, absurd calumnies and dragging with them a few so-called patriots as *allumeurs:* these people can do no harm in the long run; they are too stupid and will at last bring it so far that the French will begin to doubt whether we Germans really invented gunpowder. No, our truly dangerous enemies are those familiars of the European aristocracy who sneak after us in all kinds of disguises, even in women's garments, to assassinate our good reputations in the darkness. The men of freedom who have managed to escape at home the dungeon, the secret execution, or those little arrest warrants[12] that make travelling so uncertain and uncomfortable, will find no peace here in France, and those who cannot be corporally mistreated will at least see their names disgraced and crucified daily.

II

. . . For these two neighboring nations nothing is more important than getting to know each other. Misconceptions here could have the bloodiest consequences. Ten years ago this insight moved me to come out against the book *De l'Allemagne* by Madame de Staël in a work with the same title. Since that time I have not printed anything here in France about German affairs. This silence has made my friends very suspicious of me. They have called me reprehensibly indifferent because I did not utter a single word when our dearest interests were defamed in the French daily press. By taking up the pen today, I am following more the wishes of others than my own inclinations. The present letter, which I have the honor of addressing to you, may serve as a cheerful prelude, and

12. Heine may be referring here to the warrants issued against certain German radicals in Paris, among them Karl Marx.

I shall limit myself in it to a few rectifications occasioned by your last article in the *Revue des Deux Mondes*.

This article, entitled "Études sur l'Allemagne," follows directly on the heels of two other articles by you, which I read in *La Presse* under the title "Georg Herwegh."[13] In them you portray with laudable partiality the poetic achievements of that young poet, achievements from which I do not in the least want to detract. You celebrate not only the author, but also the man. You assure us that he dresses well. You praise his beautiful eyes and remark then that in conversation he has the habit of staring modestly at the ground. I do not know what you told him so that he stared at the ground, but it is certainly possible that he did it. Everyone has his own method; I, for example, tend to hold my nose, as you no doubt must have noticed that last time I had the honor of seeing you. You also included the unfortunate letter (*la lettre malencontreuse*) that Mr. Herwegh wrote to the King of Prussia; I reproach at most its style: the great poet cannot write. Of course the King of Prussia answered in an even worse *gendarmerie*-style. However, that you, dear Sir, group the entire movement in Germany around Mr. Georg Herwegh—the younger school of Hegelians, Strauss, Bruno Bauer, Feuerbach, Marx, Ruge, the *Halle Yearbooks,* and all the Storm-and-Stress men of the present—that you make him the very center of the struggle and counter-struggle is more than absurd. Mr. Herwegh's letter, which you depict as a world-historical event and with which you associate the entire governmental reaction in Prussia, was only an amusing interlude in which both parties made fools of themselves.

But what should I say about the passages in which you on this occasion speak about Young Germany.[14] This goes beyond the bounds of all reason, and I can hardly believe my eyes when I read the words: . . .[15]

With all due respect allow me to remark that you know neither Young Germany nor the Hegelian school. When someone wants to write about the latest phases in German intellectual movements, one should at least not betray childlike innocence. Later I shall jot

13. German radical poet who attracted some attention by writing to Friedrich Wilhelm IV and receiving an audience with him.
14. Group of liberal German writers in the early 1830s. See pp. 100–101.
15. This quotation is missing in the manuscript.

down for you a few observations on both; particularly with respect to Young Germany I can unfortunately credit myself with the utmost competence. For, alas! I myself am Young Germany. Our illustrious German parliament deigned to bestow that title on me in that famous decree in which it placed me at the head of five other writers and accused me of the crime of wanting to overthrow the entire German social order, religion, morality, and the power of the nobility; in short, everything a human being holds sacred. Just as sometimes revolutionaries who have never seen each other and harbor opposing views are accused and condemned before the same tribunal of a criminal conspiracy, so my name was arbitrarily linked and literarily proscribed with four others who did not really belong together and who held heterogeneous principles. That is this notorious Young Germany against which they polemicize so much in the official and servile press. Its noble-minded enemies had an easy and safe time of it since they were fighting against a name which nobody claimed to represent and with which nobody bothered to declare solidarity. Among these polemicists the renowned Francophobe Wolfgang Menzel[16] distinguished himself above all others; they call him the devourer of Frenchmen because he eats up a dozen of them every day; afterwards he usually eats a Jew to please his palate (*pour avoir la bonne bouche*). In those days during his monkish harangues against Young Germany he went so far as to entreat all the flames of heaven to descend upon our wicked heads, and in the absence of these, the thunderbolts of the police in the various German states. He claimed that we were all Jews, although not a single member of Young Germany practiced the religion of Moses and none, with the exception of your humble servant, even had a drop of that glorious blood in him from which our Lord and Saviour sprang. For my part I limited myself to writing a submissive petition to the parliament as a protest against its decree; with it I endeavored to obtain permission to travel with impunity to Frankfurt in order to defend my incriminated writings in person before the bar of that illustrious assembly; this seemed necessary to me because here and there in Germany there still existed a few minor warrants for my arrest, and these could have made my trip more troublesome. Although I signed my supplicatory

16. See p. 26, note 66.

petition with *doctor juris* and cited the precedent once granted to Doctor Martin Luther for his defense, nevertheless I received no reply, and my writings were prohibited and confiscated in all German states; in Prussia they even banned everything that I would write in the future. I considered this measure to be a violation of my property rights, which should not be denied to anyone without a legal judgment; I sought in vain to make my complaint known. —In the muzzled press my complaint was not heard, and the censor in Prussia deleted not only what was written on my behalf, but what was written against me as well, and my name was barred from appearing in print. With time things became more liberal; however, during the past few months the entire severity of the Prussian censor has reappeared in all its infamous pettiness.

Since I am now giving you precise information about Young Germany anyway, I should mention an association of poor workers which later formed under this name in Switzerland. A few of these good fellows who were expelled from Switzerland and fled to Paris came to me as their legitimate superior, presented me with their papers, and demanded assistance as members of Young Germany. I protested in vain that I did not know this Young Germany and had nothing to do with it; but they responded with loyal naivete: "You need not pretend; we know very well that you are the head of Young Germany; for the German parliament has acknowledged it."

Preface to the French Edition of *Lutetia*

This book contains a series of letters and reports which I wrote
during the years 1840–1843 for the *Augsburg General Newspaper*. For important reasons I published them in Germany some
months ago as a separate work with Hoffmann and Campe under
the title *Lutetia*,[1] and I am induced by motives not less important
to publish the collection in French. Namely, since these letters
appeared in the aforementioned newspaper in complete anonymity
and underwent considerable alterations, I was afraid that they
would be published after my death in this dubious form, or even
be amalgamated perhaps with contributions by others under my
name. In order to avoid any such posthumous mishap I have
preferred myself to prepare an authentic edition of these letters.

But in thus vindicating at least the reputation of my style during
my lifetime, I have unfortunately furnished a weapon for malevo-
lence to cast suspicion on the character of my thought: the total
ignorance of the German language on the part of even many of
the most educated Frenchmen was exploited so deceitfully by
several of my compatriots of both the male and female sex that
the latter were able to make the former believe that my book
Lutetia defamed even my best friends and that in it every person
and object that the French cherish was debased with malicious
jokes. It was therefore a matter of personal exigency for me to
complete a French version of my book as quickly as possible, and

---

1. Latin name for Paris.

beloved Lutetia can now judge for herself whether in this book that bears her name she is treated amiably or hostilely. If I have here and there aroused her dissatisfaction with a crude expression or a tactless observation, then she should not ascribe it to a deficiency of sympathy, but merely to a deficient education. Don't forget, my love, my nationality: although I am one of the most spiffy German bears, I still cannot deny my nature entirely; my caresses can occasionally inflict injury, and I have perhaps thrown many a cobblestone on your head to protect you from flies! What is more, since I am extremely ill at the moment, I am not able to devote the time and cheerfulness to polishing my style; therefore the French version is greatly inferior to the German in this respect; in the latter the style generally mitigated the acerbity of the material. It is embarrassing, very embarrassing, that one has to pay homage to the elegant Lutetia on the Seine in such a miserable suit of clothes, when the most beautiful coats and many a splendid embroidered vest are lying at home in the German commode.

No, Lutetia, I never wanted to slander you, and if evil tongues insinuate the opposite, do not doubt the sincerity of the love which I harbor for you. In no case have base motives affected my . . .[2]

I just mentioned that the letters contained in the book *Lutetia* appeared anonymously in the *Augsburg General Newspaper*. Of course they were identified by a cipher; but this is by no means conclusive evidence that I was the author. In a footnote to the German edition of my book I explained these circumstances in detail, and I shall include here the central passage:

The editorial staff of the *Augsburg Newspaper* used to mark my articles as well as those of other anonymous contributors with a cipher to meet certain administrative exegencies, for example, to facilitate accounting; but in no way did they want to perform an easily deciphered charade and to identify for the venerable public, *sub rosa,* the name of the author. Since only my editorial board and not the actual author assumes responsibility for each anonymous article; since the editorial staff is forced to represent the journal before both the many minds of its readership as well as before many a mindless bureaucrat; and since they have to struggle

2. I have used the fragmentary German draft for the basis of this translation. Hence this essay, like the preceding "Letters," is not entirely complete.

daily with myriad hindrances of both a material and a moral nature; so they must be permitted to adapt each article that they accept to the demands of the day, to make it printable, as they see fit, through deletions, selections, additions, and alterations—even if the good intentions and the superior style of the author are shriveled up considerably in the process. A writer who is political in every respect has to make many compromises with brute necessity for the sake of his cause. There are enough obscure local papers in which we could pour out our heart with all its fire and fury—but these have only a meager and uninfluential readership, and one could just as well shoot off one's mouth in the beer hall or in the coffee house in front of the respective customers, as other great patriots do. We are much wiser when we temper our ardor, and, with sober phrases—perhaps even in a guise—avail ourselves of a newspaper which is justifiably considered to be of international repute and which informs several hundred thousand readers all over the world. Even with these pitiful distortions the word can thrive here; the most paltry hint sometimes brings forth a bountiful harvest in unfamiliar soil. Had I not been inspired by this thought, I would have never inflicted upon myself the tortures of writing for the *General Newspaper*. Since I was at that time unconditionally convinced of the fidelity and integrity of my dear life-long friend and comrade-in-arms, who headed the editorial staff, I was able to endure much of the horrible ravages of revising and bowdlerizing in my articles; for I always saw the honest eyes of my friend who seemed to say to the injured party: "Do you think I am lying in a bed of roses?"

In publishing now under my own name the letters that appeared anonymously some time ago, I am certainly entitled to claim, in view of my acknowledgment of authorship, the so-called *beneficium inventarii*,[3] just as in any case of questionable inheritance. I count on the reader's sense of fairness in considering the difficulties of time and place with which I had to struggle when I first published these letters. I accept complete responsibility for the truth of what I said, but not for the manner in which I said these things. Anyone who sticks to the mere word will find it easy to pick out a number

---

3. In cases of inheritance, a stipulation that the heir is responsible for the inherited debts only to the extent that they do not exceed the value of the inheritance.

of contradictions and frivolities and even a lack of honest intention in my reports. But anyone who comprehends the spirit of my communications will see everywhere the strictest unity of opinions, an unwavering love for the cause of humanity, and a perseverence in my democratic principles. The difficulties of place which I just mentioned were caused by censorship; the censorship exercised by the editorial board of the *Gen. News* was even more restrictive than that of the Bavarian authorities. I often had to decorate the ship of my thoughts with flags whose emblems were not exactly the true expression of my convictions. But the journalistic pirate could have little concern for the color of the rags hanging from the mast of his vessel, the rags with which the winds played their airy games. I only thought of the precious cargo that I had on board and wanted to smuggle into the harbor of public opinion. I succeeded often, and I shouldn't be rebuked for the means which I sometimes employed to reach a pious end. Knowing the traditions of the *Gen. News,* I know, for example, that it always set itself the task not only of bringing all facts of the time in the most expedient fashion to the attention of the public, but also of making a complete record of them as in a world archive. I therefore had to take care to clothe everything that I wanted to insinuate, the event as well as my opinion of it, everything I felt and thought, in the form of a fact; and I did this sometimes by placing my private views in the mouths of others or by proceeding parabolically. My letters thus contain many little stories and arabesques whose symbolism is incomprehensible and which the crude gaper could take as petty anecdotes or even as *commerage*. In the endeavor to let the form of the fact prevail, the tone was also an important means that enabled me to report on the most dangerous things. The most proven tone, however, was one of indifference. Many useful things were also made public indirectly, and the republicans who complain about my dereliction overlook that, in the cases where it was necessary, I portrayed them seriously enough as well as exposing relentlessly in its most repulsive nakedness the wretchedness of the ruling bourgeoisie. They are so slow to understand, these republicans—about whom, by the way, I earlier held a much higher opinion. I used to believe that their obtuseness was pretense; the republic played the role of Junius Brutus[4] in order to make the

4. In 510 B.C. Junius Brutus is supposed to have overthrown the Kingdom of

monarch carefree by the appearance of imbecility, and thus they could destroy him in the future with all the more certainty—but after the February Revolution I realized my error; I saw that the republicans were really honest people who could not deceive anyone and who were really what they appeared to be.

If the republicans proved to be a delicate theme for the correspondent of the *Gen. News,* this was true to an even greater degree for the socialists, or, to give the horror its correct name, the communists. And still I succeeded in treating this topic in the *Gen. News.* Many letters were suppressed by the editorial staff out of the well-intended fear that one shouldn't talk about the devil if one doesn't want him to appear. But they could not suppress everything, and, as I said, I succeeded in putting that fearful topic into print at a time when no one else had even an inkling of its real significance. I conjured up the devil, or, as a witty friend put it, I made a devilish advertisement for him. The communists, who were scattered in isolation in all countries and lacked a specific consciousness of their intentions, learned that they really existed through the *Gen. News;* they learned on such an occasion their true name, which had hitherto remained unknown to these poor foundlings of the old society. Through the *Gen. News* the dispersed communities of communists received authentic news concerning the daily progress of their cause; they learned to their astonishment that they were by no means a weak little group, but the strongest of all parties, that their day had not yet come, but that calmly waiting meant no loss of time for people to whom the future belongs. This confession, that the future belongs to the communists, was made by me in a tone of the greatest anxiety and apprehension, and alas!, this tone was in no way feigned! Indeed, I think of the time when these dark iconoclasts will rise to power with horror and dread: with their crude hands they will then utterly shatter all the marble statues of my beloved world of art; they will smash all those fantastic knick-knacks that were so dear to the poet's heart; they will dig up my forest of laurels and plant potatoes instead; the lilies that neither spun nor worked, and yet were as beautifully dressed as King Solomon, will be uprooted from the soil of society if they should refuse to take up the spindel; the roses, indolent

---

Rome and to have established a republic. He avoided persecution by the last king, Tarquinius Superbus, by feigning insanity.

brides of the nightingales, will not fare any better; the nightingales, these useless singers, will be chased away; and, alas!, the grocer will use my *Book of Songs*[5] as little paper bags in which to pour coffee or snuff for the little old ladies of the future—Alas! I can foresee it all, and an unspeakable grief seizes me when I think of the demise with which communism threatens my poems and the entire order of the old world.—But nonetheless, I confess it freely, it exercises a fascination on my mind that I cannot resist; in my bosom two voices speak on its behalf; they will not let themselves be silenced and are perhaps only diabolic enticements—but I am completely possessed by them and no exorcising power can subdue them. For the first of these voices is logic—"the devil is a logician," Dante said—a terrible syllogism bewitches me, and I cannot contradict its premise: "that all humans have the right to eat"; and so I must submit to the consequences—I could go mad because of it; all demons of truth dance triumphantly around me and finally a desparate magnanimity seizes me and I cry out: "Blessed be the grocer who will some day make little paper bags from my poems and pour coffee and snuff in them for the poor little old mothers, who in our present world of injustice perhaps have to do without such comforts—*fiat justitia, pereat mundus!*"[6]

And the second of these two compelling voices about which I am speaking is even more powerful than the first; for it is the voice of hatred, of a hatred that I harbor for that common enemy which constitutes the exact opposite of communism and which stood against the angry giant already at its first appearance—I am speaking about the party of the so-called representatives of nationalism in Germany, about those false patriots whose love of the fatherland consists only in a stupid hatred for foreign countries and neighboring nations and who daily vent their spleen, particularly against France.—Yes, the remnants or descendants of the Teutomaniacs from 1815 have merely changed their fool's costumes and had their ears shortened somewhat; I hated and struggled against them all my life, and now when the sword slips from my dying hand, I am comforted by the conviction that communism will surely finish them off, not with a club, but with the heel of its boot; just as one

5. Heine's popular collection of lyric poetry from the 1820s.
6. "Let there be justice, even if the world should perish."

crushes a toad underfoot, so this giant will trample them. My hatred of the nationalists could almost make me love the communists. At least they are not hypocrites who merely pay lip service to religion and Christianity; the communists, it is true, embrace no religion (everyone is entitled to one fault); they are even atheists (which is surely a cardinal sin); but in their most basic tenets they espouse a cosmopolitanism, a general love of nations, a world citizenry of all humankind that is entirely consonant with the chief dogma of Christianity, and are thus in their truest essence more Christian than our German pseudo-Christians, who practice the opposite of what they preach.

I am speaking too much, at least more than the sore throat that I have now as well as prudence will allow. Therefore only a few words in conclusion. I think I have indicated sufficiently the adverse circumstances under which the letters of *Lutetia* were written. Besides the difficulties of place I also had, as I said above, difficulties of time. The intelligent reader will readily understand what these entailed; he only needs to look at the dates of these letters and recall that at that time the nationalist or so-called patriotic party about which I spoke held great sway in Germany and that the author of these pages had a very difficult position, like that of an abandoned sentry surrounded by the enemy. The July Revolution pushed that party somewhat into the background of political life, but the fanfare of the French press in 1840 offered the gallophobic party the best occasion to assert itself again; they sang their Rhine song. At the time of the February Revolution they were drowned out by more rationalistic tones; but these soon faded when the great reaction set in; today these saviours of the fatherland again set the tone in Germany, bellowing with permission from the highest powers. Go ahead and bellow! The day will come when the fatal boot-heel will crush you. I can go to my final rest without cares.

And now, dear reader, I have done as much as possible to enable you to judge the conscientiousness and unity of thought in this book. I greet you in friendship, and *sur ce, je prie Dieu qu'il t'ait en sa sainte et digne garde!*

Paris, March 30, 1855   HEINRICH HEINE

ACKNOWLEDGMENTS

Every reasonable effort has been made to locate the owners of rights to previously published translations printed here. We gratefully acknowledge permission to reprint the following material:

The Romantic School and *Concerning the History of Religion and Philosophy in Germany* are from *Heinrich Heine: Selected Works,* edited by Helen M. Mustard. Copyright © 1973 by Random House, Inc. Reprinted by permission of the publisher.

The Introduction to *Khaldorf Concerning the Nobility,* "Various Conceptions of History," and the Second Book of *Ludwig Börne: A Memorial* are from *The Poetry and Prose of Heinrich Heine,* edited by Frederic Ewen. Copyright © 1969 by Citadel Press, Inc. Published by arrangement with Lyle Stuart, Inc.

THE GERMAN LIBRARY
in 100 Volumes

German Medieval Tales
Edited by Francis G. Gentry
Foreword by Thomas Berger

German Humanism and Reformation
Edited by Reinhard P. Becker
Foreword by Roland Bainton

Frederich Schiller
Plays: Intrigue and Love and Don Carlos
Edited by Walter Hinderer
Foreword by Gordon Craig

German Romantic Criticism
Edited by A. Leslie Willson
Foreword by Ernst Behler

Heinrich von Kleist
Plays
Edited by Walter Hinderer
Foreword by E. L. Doctorow

E.T.A. Hoffman
Tales
Edited by Victor Lange

German Literary Fairy Tales
Edited by Frank G. Ryder and Robert M. Browning
Introduction by Gordon Birrell
Foreword by John Gardiner

Heinrich Heine
Poetry and Prose
Edited by Jost Hermand and Robert C. Holub
Foreword by Alfred Kazin

Heinrich von Kleist and Jean Paul
German Romantic Novellas
Edited by Frank G. Ryder and Robert M. Browning
Foreword by John Simon

German Poetry from 1750 to 1900
Edited by Robert M. Browning
Foreword by Michael Hamburger

Gottfried Keller
Stories
Edited by Frank G. Ryder
Foreword by Max Frisch

William Raabe
Novels
Edited by Volkmar Sander
Foreword by Joel Agee

Theodore Fontane
Short Novels and Other Writings
Edited by Peter Demetz
Foreword by Peter Gay

Wilhelm Busch and Others
German Satirical Writings
Edited by Deiter P. Lotze and Volkmar Sander
Foreword by John Simon

Writings of German Composers
Edited by Jost Hermand and James Steakley

Arthur Schnitzler
Plays and Stories
Edited by Egon Schwarz
Foreword by Stanley Elkin

Rainer Maria Rilke
Prose and Poetry
Edited by Egon Schwarz
Foreword by Howard Nemerov

Essays on German Theater
Edited by Margaret Herzfeld-Sander
Foreword by Martin Esslin

Friedrich Dürrenmatt
Plays and Essays
Edited by Volkmar Sander
Foreword by Martin Esslin

Hans Magnus Enzensberger
Critical Essays
Edited by Reinhold Grimm and Bruce Armstrong
Foreword by John Simon